Christina Latham-Koenig
Clive Oxenden
Paul Seligson

GW00401062

ENGLISH FILE

Pre-intermediate   Student's Book B

Andrés Cevchiavo Molina.
318 612 0458.

OXFORD
UNIVERSITY PRESS

Paul Seligson and Clive Oxenden are the original co-authors of
English File 1 and *English File 2*

Contents

G uses of the infinitive with *to*
V verbs + infinitive: *try to, forget to,* etc.
P weak form of *to,* linking

What do I need to do?

It's important not to be late.

7A How to...

1 READING & LISTENING

a Look at the poster of a well-known film. Do you know what it's about? Have you seen it?

Robert **De Niro**
Ben **Stiller**

He finally met the girl of his dreams.
Too bad her dad's a nightmare.

Meet the **Parents**

From the director of "Austin Powers"

b With a partner, think of two pieces of advice for somebody who is going to meet their partner's parents for the first time.

c Now read an article adapted from the website *wikiHow*. Is your advice there?

d Read the article again and complete the gaps with the verbs in the list.

---
to answer not to be ~~to do~~ (x2) to have to know
to make to say to show not to talk
---

e (3 23)) Listen to Nigel meeting his girlfriend's parents for the first time. Does the meeting start well or badly? How does it end?

f Listen again and answer the questions.
1 What does he do wrong?
2 What does he do right?

g Do you think the advice in the article would be good for people in your country? Why (not)? Do you think the advice would be the same for a girl meeting her boyfriend's parents for the first time?

How to... Survive Meeting Your Girlfriend's Parents for the First Time

It's stressful, but these top tips can help you to get it right…

Tips

1 **You need** to do **some 'homework'** before you go. Ask your girlfriend about her parents. Where does her mother work? Does her father like football? Do you have any common interests? If you do this, it will be easy _____ a conversation with them.

2 **Make sure you dress** _____ the right impression. Don't wear a suit, but don't just wear your old jeans and the Che Guevara T-shirt you bought in the market.

3 **Be punctual.** It's very important _____ late at a first meeting.

4 **When they greet you at the door** shake the father's hand firmly (no father likes a weak handshake!). Ask your girlfriend what kind of greeting her mum will prefer.

5 **Call her parents Mr and Mrs** (Smith) until they ask you to call them 'Dave' and 'Sharon'.

6 **Be ready** _____ questions about yourself! Her parents will want _____ everything about you and your ambitions. Make a good impression!

7 **If you are invited for a meal,** eat everything they give you and say something positive about the meal, like 'This is absolutely delicious!'. Offer _____ the washing-up after the meal (_____ them that you are a 'new man').

8 **Be yourself,** and don't be a 'yes' man. If they ask you for your opinion, be honest. However, try _____ about controversial subjects – this isn't the moment to give your views on religion and politics!

9 **If the conversation is dying** and you can't think what _____, ask them what your partner was like as a child. This is a brilliant tactic! All parents love talking about their children and it shows you have a deep interest in their daughter.

Adapted from wikiHow

2 GRAMMAR
uses of the infinitive with *to*

a Match sentences a–d from the article with rules 1–4.

a ☐ If you do this, it will be easy **to have** a conversation with them.

b ☐ Offer to do the washing-up after the meal (**to show** them that you are a 'new man').

c ☐ If the conversation is dying and you can't think what **to say**, ask them what your partner was like as a child.

d ☐ You need **to do** some 'homework' before you go.

Use the infinitive with *to*...
1 after some verbs, e.g. *need, want*, etc.
2 after adjectives
3 to give a reason for doing something
4 after a question word, e.g. *who, what, how*

b Look at the other infinitives you used to complete the article. Which rules are they?

c ➤ **p.138 Grammar Bank 7A.** Learn more about uses of the infinitive and practise them.

3 VOCABULARY verbs + infinitive

a Without looking back at the article try to remember the missing verbs.

1 You _____ to do some homework before you go.

2 Her parents will _____ to know everything about you and your ambitions.

3 _____ to do the washing-up after the meal...

4 However, _____ not to talk about controversial subjects...

b ➤ **p.158 Vocabulary Bank** *Verb forms.* Do part 1 (Verbs + infinitive).

4 PRONUNCIATION & SPEAKING
weak form of *to*, linking

a (3 26)⟫ Listen to two sentences. Is *to* stressed? How is it pronounced?

> I want to come.
> He decided to leave.

🔍 **Linking words with the same consonant sound**
When a word ends in a consonant sound and the next word begins with the same or a very similar sound, we often link the words together and only make the consonant sound once. This happens when a verb ends in /t/ or /d/ before *to*, so *want to* is pronounced /ˈwɒntə/ and *decided to* is pronounced /dɪˈsaɪdɪtə/.

b (3 27)⟫ Listen and write six sentences. Then practise saying them.

c Work in pairs. **A** ask **B** the first six questions. **B** give as much information as you can. Swap roles for the last six questions.

- Have you ever offered to look after somebody's dog (or other pet)?
- Do you think it is difficult to stay friends with an ex-boyfriend/girlfriend?
- Have you ever tried to learn something new and failed?
- Do you think it is important to learn to cook at school?
- How long do you usually spend deciding what to wear in the morning?
- Do you know how to change a wheel on a car?

- Do you think it's possible to learn a foreign language studying on your own at home?
- Are you planning to go anywhere next weekend?
- Would you like to work or study in another country?
- Have you ever pretended to be ill (when you weren't)?
- Have you ever forgotten to turn off your mobile phone during a class or concert?
- What do you think is the most interesting thing to do for a visitor to your town?

d ➤ **Communication** *How to...* **A** *p.103* **B** *p.107.* Read and re-tell two more *How to...* articles.

5 WRITING

With a partner, write a 'How to...' article. Choose one of the titles below, and try to think of at least four tips.

How to...
- make a good impression on your first day in your English class.
- make a good impression at a job interview.

G uses of the gerund (verb + -ing)
V verbs + gerund
P the letter i

What's your idea
of happiness?

Making soup.

7B Being happy

1 GRAMMAR uses of the gerund

a Talk to a partner. Is there a book, a film, or a song that makes you feel happy whenever you read, watch, or listen to it? What is it? Why does it make you feel happy?

b Read a magazine article where different people on the magazine's staff say what happiness is for them. Who do you think said what? Match the people to the paragraphs.

Erin, *fashion editor*

Harriet, *health editor*

Sebastian, *music editor*

Kate, *cinema editor*

Marco, *food editor*

Andrew, *travel editor*

c Read the article again. Is there anybody you really agree/don't agree with? Compare with a partner.

d Look at the highlighted phrases in the first paragraph. Find an example of a gerund (verb + -ing):

 1 after another verb _____
 2 after a preposition _____
 3 used as a noun _____

e ➤ p.138 Grammar Bank 7B. Learn more about the uses of the gerund and practise them.

f Write your own continuation for *Happiness is…*

g Work in groups of four. Read the other students' texts. Do you agree with their ideas of happiness?

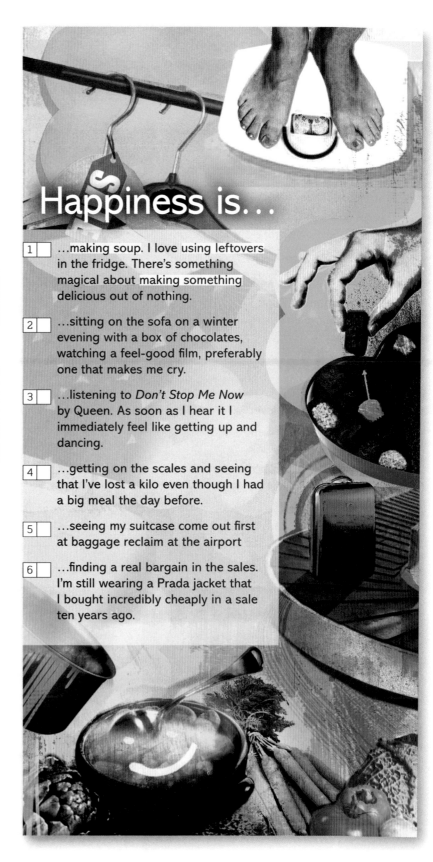

Happiness is…

1 ☐ …making soup. I love using leftovers in the fridge. There's something magical about making something delicious out of nothing.

2 ☐ …sitting on the sofa on a winter evening with a box of chocolates, watching a feel-good film, preferably one that makes me cry.

3 ☐ …listening to *Don't Stop Me Now* by Queen. As soon as I hear it I immediately feel like getting up and dancing.

4 ☐ …getting on the scales and seeing that I've lost a kilo even though I had a big meal the day before.

5 ☐ …seeing my suitcase come out first at baggage reclaim at the airport

6 ☐ …finding a real bargain in the sales. I'm still wearing a Prada jacket that I bought incredibly cheaply in a sale ten years ago.

2 VOCABULARY & SPEAKING
verbs + gerund

a ➤ p.158 **Vocabulary Bank** *Verb forms*.
Do part 2 (Verbs + gerund).

b Choose five things to talk about from the
list below.

> **Something…**
> • you **don't mind doing** in the house
> • you **like doing** with your family
> • you **love doing** in the summer
> • you **don't feel like doing** at weekends
> • you **spend too much time doing**
> • you **dream of doing**
> • you **hate doing** at work / school
> • you **don't like doing** alone
> • you are **thinking of doing** this weekend
> • you think you are **very good (or very bad)
>   at doing**

c Works in pairs. **A** tell **B** about the
five things. Say why. **B** ask for more
information. Then swap roles.

3 PRONUNCIATION the letter *i*

a Put the one-syllable words below into the
right column.

> find give high hire kind like
> mind miss night right skin slim
> thin time which win with

fish		bike	

b (3 30)) Listen and check. Then look at the
words in each column. What rules can you
see for the pronunciation of…

• *i* + consonant + *e* (but which word is an
  exception?)
• *ind* and *igh*
• *i* between other consonants

c (3 31)) Now listen to some two-syllable
words. Is the *i* pronounced /ɪ/ or /aɪ/?
Listen and check.

> arrive decide engine invite
> online practise promise
> revise service surprise

d What's the difference in the stress
between the verbs in **c** where *i* is
pronounced /ɪ/ and where *i* is
pronounced /aɪ/?

4 SPEAKING & LISTENING

a Ask and answer with a partner.
1 When you are happy do you sometimes feel like singing?
2 Do you ever sing…?
   • in the shower   • karaoke
   • in the car   • in a choir or band
   • while you're listening to music, e.g. on an iPod
3 Is there a particular singer whose songs you like singing? Do you
   have a favourite song?

b In pairs, say if you think sentences 1–7 are **T** (true) or **F** (false).
1 Singing is good for your health.
2 If you want to sing well, you need to learn to breathe correctly.
3 People who sing are usually fatter than people who don't.
4 Not everybody can learn to sing.
5 You need to know how to read music to be able to sing well.
6 If you make a surprised face, you can sing high notes better.
7 It takes years to learn to sing better.

c (3 32)) Now listen to an interview with the director of a singing
school and a student who did a course there. Were you right?

d Listen again. Choose the right answer.
1 When you are learning to sing you need to ____ correctly.
   a stand   b dress   c eat
2 Singing well is 95% ____ .
   a repeating   b listening   c breathing
3 Gemma's course lasted ____ .
   a one day   b one week   c one month
4 Gemma has always ____ .
   a been good at singing   b been in a choir   c liked singing
5 At first the students learnt to ____ .
   a breathe and sing   b listen and breathe   c listen and sing
6 At the end of the day they could sing ____ .
   a perfectly   b much better   c a bit better

e Would you like to learn to sing (better)? Are there
any tips from the listening that you could use?

5 (3 33)) SONG *Don't Stop Me Now* ♫

iTutor

G *have to, don't have to, must, mustn't*
V modifiers: *a bit, really,* etc.
P *must, mustn't*

> You have to come to all the classes.
> You don't have to do an exam.

7C Learn a language in a month!

1 GRAMMAR
have to, don't have to, must, mustn't

a Match the notices to the rules.

1 ☐ You have to pay before the end of the month.
2 ☐ You don't have to pay to see this.
3 ☐ You mustn't eat here.
4 ☐ You must turn off your phone before you come in.

A

B THE ENGLISH THEATRE COMPANY THURSDAY 8PM ENTRANCE FREE

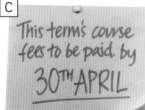
C This term's course fees to be paid by 30TH APRIL

D NO FOOD TO BE TAKEN INTO THE LIBRARY

b Look at the highlighted expressions and answer the questions.

1 Which two phrases mean…?
It is a ⊞ rule. There's an obligation to do this. _____ _____

2 Which phrase means…?
a It isn't permitted. It is against the rules.
_____

b It isn't obligatory or it isn't necessary.
_____

c ➤ p.138 Grammar Bank 7C. Learn more about *have to, don't have to, must,* and *mustn't,* and practise them.

d With a partner, complete four sentences about the school where you are learning English.

We have to…   We don't have to…
We must…   We mustn't…

e Compare your rules with another pair. Which rule do you think is the most important?

2 PRONUNCIATION *must, mustn't*

a ③36》 Listen to these sentences. Which letter is <u>not</u> pronounced in *mustn't*? Listen again and repeat.

You must use a dictionary.   You mustn't use a dictionary.

b ③37》 Listen and write five sentences.

3 READING & LISTENING

a Do you think people from your country are good at learning languages? Why (not)? Are British people good at learning your language?

b Read about Max, a British journalist who did an intensive Spanish course. Then cover the article and answer the questions.

1 What reputation do the British have?
2 What experiment did Max's newspaper want to do?
3 Why did Max choose to learn Spanish?
4 Where did he do the course? How long was it?
5 What did he find easy and difficult about Spanish?
6 What were the four tests? What were the rules?

c ③38》 Which test do you think was the easiest for Max? Which do you think was the most difficult? Listen to Max doing the tests in Madrid and check your answers.

d Listen again. Mark the sentences **T** (true) or **F** (false). Correct the false information.

1 The waiter didn't understand Max. (F)
2 The bill was six euros. (F)
3 The chemist's was the first street on the right. (F)
4 The driver understood the name of the stadium. (F)
5 Max made a grammar mistake when he left the voicemail message. ( )
6 Max's final mark was eight. (T)
7 Max says you can learn Spanish in a month. (F)

I will survive (in Spanish)... or will I?

The British have a reputation for being bad at learning languages, but is it really true? I work for a newspaper which was doing a series of articles about this. As an experiment, they asked me to try and learn a completely new language for one month. Then I had to go to the country and do some 'tests' to see if I could 'survive' in different situations. I decided to learn Spanish because I would like to visit Spain and Latin America in the future. If I go, I don't want to be the typical Brit who expects everyone else to speak English.

I did a one-month intensive course in Spanish at a language school in London. I was a complete beginner but I soon found that some Spanish words are very similar to English ones. For example, *hola* isn't very different from 'hello' and *inglés* is very similar to 'English'. But other things were more difficult, for example the verbs in Spanish change for each person and that means you have to learn a lot of different endings. My biggest problem was the pronunciation. I found it very difficult to pronounce some letters in Spanish, especially *r* and *j*. I downloaded sentences in Spanish onto my phone and I listened and repeated them again and again.

When my course finished I went to Madrid for the weekend to do my tests. A Spanish teacher called Paula came with me and gave me a mark out of 10 for each test and then a final mark for everything.

These were the tests and the rules:

TESTS
You have to...
1 order a drink and a sandwich in a bar, ask how much it is, and understand the price.
2 ask for directions in the street (and follow them).
3 get a taxi to a famous place in Madrid.
4 leave a message on somebody's voicemail.

RULES
– you mustn't use a dictionary or phrase book
– you mustn't speak English at any time
– you mustn't use your hands or mime or write anything down

4 VOCABULARY modifiers

My pronunciation of the stadium wasn't **very** good. I was feeling **a bit** nervous at this point.

a Complete the chart with the words in the box.

| a bit | incredibly | not very | quite | really | very |

Spanish is

_____

very

_____ difficult.

_____

not very

> 🔍 **a bit**
> We only use *a bit* before <u>negative</u> adjectives and adverbs, e.g. *a bit difficult, a bit slowly*.

b Complete the sentences with one of the words or phrases so that it makes a true sentence. Compare with a partner.
1 I'm _actually_ good at learning languages. ✓
2 I'm _incredibly_ motivated to improve my English.
3 English pronunciation is _quite_ difficult.
4 English grammar is _very_ complicated.
5 I'm _quite_ worried about the next English exam.
6 English is _very_ important for my work / studies.

5 SPEAKING

a How well do you think you could do Max's four tests in English? Why?

I think I could order a drink and a sandwich quite well...

b Talk to a partner.

> **HAVE YOU EVER...**
> • spoken to a tourist in English? When? Why?
> • had to speak in English on the phone? Who to? What about?
> • seen a film or video clip in English? Which? Did it have subtitles? How much did you understand?
> • read a book or magazine in English? Which one(s)?
> • asked for directions in English in a foreign city? Where? What happened?
> • used an app or website to improve your English? Which one?
> • learnt another foreign language? How well can you speak it?

6 WRITING

➤ p.115 Writing *A formal email*. Write an email asking for information.

1 ▢ RUNNING IN CENTRAL PARK

a ③ 39))) Watch or listen to Rob and Jenny. Are they enjoying their run?

b Watch or listen again and answer the questions.

1 How does Rob say he feels?
2 What does Jenny say about Central Park?
3 Is Rob happy he came to New York?
4 What is Rob tired of doing?
5 What does Jenny invite him to do?
6 How many more times are they going to run round the park?

2 VOCABULARY feeling ill

a Match the phrases and pictures.

What's the matter?

☐ I have a <u>hea</u>dache. /ˈhedeɪk/   ☐ I have a <u>tem</u>perature. /ˈtemprətʃə/
☐ I have a cough. /kɒf/   ☐ I have a bad <u>sto</u>mach. /ˈstʌmək/
☐ I have flu. /fluː/   ☐ I have a cold.

b ③ 40))) Listen and check. Cover the phrases and practise with a partner.

What's the matter?   *I have a headache.*

3 ▢ GOING TO A PHARMACY

a ③ 41))) Cover the dialogue and watch or listen. Circle the correct answer.

1 Rob thinks he has *a cold | flu*.
2 The pharmacist gives Rob *ibuprofen | penicillin*.
3 He has to take the medicine every *four hours | eight hours*.
4 They cost *$16.99 | $6.99*.

b Watch or listen again. Complete the **You Hear** phrases.

))) You Hear	You Say ◯
Good morning. Can I help you?	I'm not feeling very well. I think I have flu.
What are your symptoms?	I have a headache and a cough.
Do you have a _____?	No, I don't think so.
Are you allergic to any drugs?	I'm allergic to penicillin.
No _____. This is ibuprofen. It'll make you feel _____.	How many do I have to take?
_____ every four hours.	Sorry? How often?
_____ every four hours. If you don't feel better in _____ hours, you should see a doctor.	OK, thanks. How much is that?
That's $6.99, please.	Thank you.
You're _____.	

> 🔍 **British and American English**
> *pharmacy* = American English (and sometimes British English)
> *chemist's* = British English
> *drugs* = *medicine* in American English
> *drugs* = *illegal substances* in British and American English

c (3 42)))) Watch or listen and repeat the **You Say** phrases. <u>Copy</u> the <u>rhythm</u>.

d Practise the dialogue with a partner.

e 👥 In pairs, roleplay the dialogue.

   A (book closed) You don't feel very well. Decide what symptoms you have. Are you allergic to anything?
   B (book open) You are the pharmacist. You begin *Can I help you?*

f Swap roles.

4 ▢ DINNER AT JENNY'S APARTMENT

a (3 43)))) Watch or listen to Rob and Jenny. Mark the sentences **T** (true) or **F** (false).

   1 Rob broke up with his girlfriend a year before he met Jenny.
   2 Jenny hasn't had much time for relationships.
   3 Jenny knew that Rob wasn't feeling well in the morning.
   4 Rob wants to go back to his hotel because he's tired.
   5 Jenny is going to call a taxi.

b Watch or listen again. Say why the **F** sentences are false.

c (3 44)))) Read the information box about *have got*. Listen and repeat the phrases.

> 🔍 **have got**
> We sometimes use *have got* instead of *have* to talk about possession.
> ***I've got** a busy day tomorrow.*
> ***Have you got** any children?*   **Yes, I have. I've got** *a girl and a boy.*
>   **No, I haven't. I haven't got** *children.*
>
> ➤ See **appendix** *p.165.*

d Ask and answer with a partner. Use *Have you got…? Yes, I have. | No, I haven't.* Give more information if you can.

   A any pets   a bike or motorbike   a garden
   B any brothers and sisters   a car   a laptop

   Have you got any pets? ⤵ ⤴ *Yes I have. I've got two dogs.*

e Look at the **Social English phrases**. Can you remember any of the missing words?

> **Social English phrases**
> **Rob** That was a lovely _____.   **Jenny** I'm _____ you're feeling better.
> **Rob** That isn't very _____ for you. **Rob** Thanks again for a _____ evening.
> **Rob** I'm _____ I'll be fine.   **Jenny** _____ time.
> **Rob** I think I _____ get back to the hotel now.

f (3 46)))) Watch or listen and complete the phrases.

g Watch or listen again and repeat the phrases. How do you say them in your language?

> 🧑 **Can you…?**
> ☐ describe symptoms when you feel ill
> ☐ get medicine at a pharmacy
> ☐ talk about possessions with *have got*

What should I do?

You should talk to her.

8A I don't know what to do!

1 READING

a Talk to a partner.

1 If you have a problem that you need to talk about, do you talk to a friend or to a member of your family? Why?

2 Do you think that men find it more difficult than women to talk about their problems? Why (not)?

b Read three problems from a weekly article in a British newspaper. Match two pieces of advice to each problem.

c Read the problems and advice again. Look at the highlighted verb phrases and guess their meaning.

d Talk to a partner. Which piece of advice do you agree with most for each problem? Do you have any other suggestions?

Too macho to talk?

Are you a man who finds it difficult to talk about feelings and problems with your friends and family?
Send us your problem and you will get advice from our readers.

Problem A
Three weeks ago I asked my girlfriend to marry me – we have been together for 18 months. It was an impulse, but now I am having second thoughts. I am deeply in love with her, but is this too soon? Please help.

Problem B
My wife is running her first marathon in London and she really wants me to go and watch her. However, there is a business conference in New York the same weekend and my boss would like me to attend. What should I do?

Problem C
My girlfriend wants us to spend two weeks in France in the summer with her family, but I find her sister really difficult to get on with. Should I go and risk having arguments all the time or should I suggest separate holidays this year?

Our readers' advice!

1 ☐ *This seems an easy one – go, but try to avoid her where possible, and if you can't avoid her, then just smile and don't get into a conversation.*

2 ☐ *In my opinion, I don't think it's worth making problems at work. Why don't you suggest that she asks a girlfriend or a family member to go with her instead?*

3 ☐ *You should tell your girlfriend how you feel. Be polite and, above all, be honest. You do not have to like her sister. If she really is difficult, everyone else will already know.*

4 ☐ *You felt it was right at the time, but for some reason now you are not sure. You clearly love this girl and I think you should go for it. I got married after four months of dating, and we celebrated 30 years this year.*

5 ☐ *You should be there. Maybe this is a once in a lifetime moment for her. You can always keep in touch with colleagues on your phone.*

6 ☐ *You shouldn't do anything in a hurry. Fix a date 18 months from now which will give you time to be sure you're doing the right thing. And don't plan too much. If you start booking restaurants and getting clothes for the big day, it will make things worse if you then change your mind.*

Adapted from a British newspaper

2 GRAMMAR *should*

a Find and <u>underline</u> seven examples of *should* / *shouldn't* in the problems and advice in **1**. Answer with a partner:

1 What do we use *should* for?
2 How do you make negatives and questions with *should*?

b ➤ p.140 Grammar Bank 8A. Learn more about *should* and practise it.

3 PRONUNCIATION
/ʊ/ and /uː/, sentence stress

a (3 48))) Listen and repeat the words and sounds. What's the difference between the two sounds?

| 🐂 bull | good put should would |
| 👢 boot | do soon true you |

b (3 49))) Are the pink letters in these words sound 1 (/ʊ/) or sound 2 (/uː/)? Listen and check. Which consonant <u>isn't</u> pronounced in *should*, *would*, and *could*?

book   could   flew   food   foot   look   school

c (3 50))) Listen and write six sentences.

d Listen again and repeat the sentences. <u>Copy</u> the <u>rhythm</u>.

e ➤ Communication *What should I do?*
A *p.103* B *p.107*. Listen to your partner's problems and give advice.

4 LISTENING & SPEAKING

a (3 51))) Listen to someone phoning a radio programme called *What's the Problem?* What is the problem about? Make notes in the chart.

	problem	expert's advice
caller 1	*Are us.Bost fred flct with his gilfnd*	*Talk to his Girlfriend. and ask what she feels*
caller 2	*Muvclu Brhigton Husbacd go*	

wife. she deays needs calls,

b Compare your notes with a partner. What do *you* think the man should do?

c (3 52))) Now listen to an expert giving advice and make notes in the chart. Is it the same as yours? Is it good advice? Why (not)?

d (3 53, 54))) Now repeat for caller 2.

5 VOCABULARY *get*

a Look at three sentences from the lesson. Match the examples of *get* with meanings a–c.

a buy / obtain   **b** receive   **c** become

1 ☐ Send us your problem and you will **get** advice…
2 ☐ If you start booking restaurants and **getting** clothes for the big day…
3 ☐ I'm **getting** really stressed about it.

b ➤ p.159 Vocabulary Bank *get*.

c In pairs, ask and answer the questions with *get*.

1 When was the last time you **got a present**? What was it? Who was it from?
2 Would you like to **get fitter**? What do you think you should do?
3 What website do you use if you want to **get tickets** a) to travel b) for the cinema / theatre / concerts?
4 Who do you **get on with** best in your family? Is there anybody you don't get on with?
5 How do you **get to work** / **school**? How long does it usually take you?
6 What's the first thing you do when you **get home** from work / school?
7 Do you have a good sense of direction, or do you often **get lost**?
8 How many **emails** or **text messages** do you **get** a day? Are they mostly from friends? Do you usually reply immediately?

6 WRITING

a Read two problems on a website. Write a response to one of them giving advice.

Goodadvice.com
Post your problems here and you'll get advice from all over the world.

My best friend wants to borrow some money to help her buy a car. I have the money, and she says she'll pay me back next year. But I'm worried that it's not a good idea to lend money to friends. What should I do?

My friend Anna has gone away on holiday for two weeks and I'm looking after her cat. Yesterday I couldn't find the cat anywhere. My friend is coming home in three days. I'm desperate. Should I phone her now and tell her? What should I do?

🔍 **Language for giving advice**
(I think / don't think) you should…   Why don't you…?
You shouldn't…   You could…

b In groups of four read your responses. Whose advice is the best?

7 (3 56))) SONG *Why Do I Feel So Sad?* 🎵

G *if* + present, *will* + infinitive (first conditional)
V confusing verbs
P linking

If we change queues, this one will move quicker.

Yes, that always happens!

8B If something can go wrong,...

1 READING

a If you are waiting to check in at the airport and you change queues, what will usually happen?

b Read the first two paragraphs of the article and check. Who was Murphy? What is his 'Law'?

c Now look at the eight examples of Murphy's Law in the article and match them with sentences A–H.

A your flight will be delayed.
B you will spill wine or coffee on it.
C you will find a parking space right in front of it.
D all the traffic lights will be red.
E will have a problem with their credit card.
F (they) will already have a partner.
G there will be a hyperactive five-year-old in the seat behind you.
H it will work when the shop assistant tries it.

d Do any of these things or things like this often happen to you?

2 GRAMMAR   *if* + present, *will* + infinitive

a In pairs, cover A–H and look at 1–8 in the text. How many of the Laws can you remember?

b Look at the sentences again. What tense is the verb after *if*? What form is the other verb?

c ➤ **p.140 Grammar Bank 8B.** Learn more about the first conditional and practise it.

d In pairs, complete these Murphy's Laws.

1 If you find something in a shop that you really like,...
2 If you stop waiting for a bus and start walking,...
3 If you call a telephone company helpline,...
4 If you leave your mobile phone at home,...
5 If you lose a glove and buy a new pair,...

e Compare your laws with other students. Do you have the same (or similar)?

IT ALWAYS HAPPENS!

If you are in a check-in queue and you change to another queue which is moving more quickly, what will happen? The queue you were in before will suddenly start moving faster. What will happen if you take your umbrella because you think it's going to rain later? It won't rain, of course. It will only rain if you forget to take your umbrella. These are examples of Murphy's Law, which says, 'If there is something that can go wrong, it will go wrong'.

Murphy's Law took its name from Captain Edward Murphy, an American aerospace engineer from the 1940s. He was trying to improve safety for pilots flying military planes. Not surprisingly, he got a reputation for always thinking of the worst thing that could happen in every situation. Here are some more examples of Murphy's Law.

AIR TRAVEL
1 [A] If you get to the airport early,...
2 [G] If you want to sleep on the plane,...

SHOPPING
3 [E] If you are in a hurry, the person in front of you...
4 [H] If you take something that doesn't work back to a shop,...

DRIVING
5 [D] If you're late for something important,...
6 [C] If you park a long way from a restaurant,...

SOCIAL LIFE
7 [F] If you are single and you meet somebody at a party who you really like,...
8 [B] If you wear a new white shirt or dress,...

The verb after if is in the Present Simple and the other verb is the future (will/won't + infinitive)

3 PRONUNCIATION linking

> 🔍 **Sound linking**
> Remember that if a word finishes with a consonant and the next word begins with a vowel, we usually link the words together, e.g. we'll eat in a pub

a **4 3**》 Listen and repeat the sentences. Try to link the marked words.

1 If I see her, I'll tell her.
2 We'll go if it doesn't rain.
3 If I get there early, I'll order the food.
4 They'll arrive at eight if their flight's on time.
5 If you aren't in a hurry, we can walk.

b **4 4**》 Listen and write five more sentences.

4 VOCABULARY & SPEAKING
confusing verbs

a What's the difference between *know* and *meet*, and *wear* and *carry*?

b ➤ **p.160 Vocabulary Bank** *Confusing verbs*.

c (Circle) the right verb. Then ask and answer with a partner.

1 Who do you *look | look like* in your family?
2 How many classes have you *missed | lost* this year?
3 What gadgets do you always *bring | take* with you when you go on holiday?
4 Do you think sports people *win | earn* too much money?
5 What is the best way to *know | meet* new friends?
6 Is it sometimes OK to *say | tell* a lie?

5 LISTENING

a With a partner, think of three things that could go wrong when you are on holiday.

b Match the words to their definitions.

1 [E] a mon<u>soon</u> /mɒnˈsuːn/   5 [ ] a <u>bli</u>zzard /ˈblɪzəd/
2 [ ] an <u>earth</u>quake /ˈɜːθkweɪk/   6 [ ] a flood /flʌd/
3 [ ] a tsu<u>na</u>mi /tsuːˈnɑːmi/   7 [ ] a <u>for</u>est fire
4 [ ] a <u>cy</u>clone /ˈsaɪkləʊn/   /ˈfɒrɪst faɪə/

A a very bad storm with snow and strong winds
B a very strong wind that moves in a circle
C a big fire that can destroy many trees and houses
D a very large wave in the sea
E when it rains very heavily for three months or more
F when there is too much water in a river and it comes onto the streets or fields
G when the ground suddenly shakes very strongly

The Svanström family

Holiday couple survive seven natural disasters!

c **4 6**》 Listen to what happened to Mr and Mrs Svanström. Mark their route on the map. What natural disaster happened in each place?

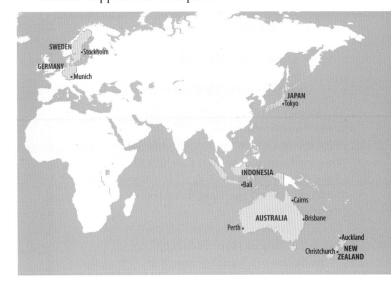

d Listen again and answer the questions.

1 How long did they have to wait at Munich airport?
2 What weather were they expecting in Bali?
3 Where were the streets full of smoke?
4 Where did they sleep in Cairns?
5 Why did they fly to Auckland and not to Christchurch in New Zealand?
6 What were they doing when the Japanese earthquake struck?
7 Where did they go for the last part of their holiday? Did anything happen to them there?

e Do you think they were lucky or unlucky? Why?

G possessive pronouns
V adverbs of manner
P sentence rhythm

You must be mine.

Yes. I'll be yours.

8C You must be mine

Girl

BY O. HENRY

PART 1

"I've found where she lives," said the detective quietly. "Here is the address."

Hartley took the piece of paper. On it were the words "Vivienne Arlington, No. 341 East 49th Street."

5 "She moved there a week ago," said the detective. "I can follow her if you want. It will only cost you $7 a day and expenses…"

"No, thank you," interrupted Hartley. "I only wanted the address. How much is it?"

10 "One day's work," said the detective. "Ten dollars." Hartley paid the man. Then he left the office and took a tram to Broadway. After walking a short distance he arrived at the building that he was looking for. Hartley rang the bell. The door opened.

15 He went in and began to climb the stairs.

On the fourth floor he saw her standing in an open door. Vivienne was about twenty-one. Her hair was red gold, and her eyes were sea-blue. She was wearing a white top and a dark skirt.

20 "Vivienne," said Hartley, "you didn't answer my last letter. It took me a week to find your new address! Why didn't you answer me? You knew I was waiting to see you and hear from you."

1%

1 READING

a You are going to read and listen to a short story. First look at the picture and answer the questions.

1 What do the people look like? What are they wearing?
2 Where are they?
3 In what century do you think the story takes place?

b (4 7)) Read and listen to Part 1. Then answer the questions with a partner.

1 What did the detective give Hartley? What did he offer to do?
2 What did Hartley do when he got the address?
3 What did Vivienne look like?
4 Why was Hartley angry with her?
5 Why do you think she didn't answer his letter?

c Look at the following words and phrases in the story. With a partner, guess what they mean.

moved (line 5)   expenses (line 7)   tram (line 12)
rang the bell (line 14)   climb (line 15)

d (4 8)) Read and listen to Part 2. Then answer the questions with a partner.

1 Why wasn't Vivienne sure about accepting Hartley's offer?
2 How did Hartley try to persuade her?
3 Where did Hartley and Vivienne first meet?
4 What did Hartley think was the reason why Vivienne didn't say yes to his offer?
5 What do you think Hartley wanted Vivienne to do?
6 Who do you think Héloise is?

Adverbs of manner
We often use adverbs of manner in writing to show how the characters are feeling, behaving, or speaking.

e Look at the highlighted adverbs. With a partner, guess what they mean.

PART 2

The girl looked out the window dreamily. "Mr Hartley," she said slowly, "I don't know what to say to you. I understand all the advantages of your offer, and sometimes I feel sure that I could be happy with you. But, then sometimes I am less sure. I was born a city girl, and I am not sure that I would enjoy living a quiet life in the suburbs."

"My dear girl," said Hartley, "You will have everything that you want. You can come to the city for the theatre, for shopping, and to visit your friends as often as you want. You can trust me, can't you?"

"I can trust you completely," she said, smiling at him. "I know you are the kindest of men, and that the girl who you get will be very lucky. I heard all about you when I was at the Montgomerys'."

"Ah!" exclaimed Hartley, "I remember so well the evening I first saw you at the Montgomerys'. I will never forget that dinner. Come on, Vivienne, promise me. I want you. Nobody else will ever give you such a happy home."

Vivienne didn't answer. Suddenly Hartley was suspicious. "Tell me, Vivienne," he asked, "is there – is there someone else?"

"You shouldn't ask that, Mr. Hartley," she said. "But I will tell you. There is one other person – but I haven't promised him anything."

"Vivienne," said Hartley, masterfully. "You must be mine."

Vivienne looked him in the eye.

"Do you think for one moment," she said calmly, "that I could come to your home while Héloise is there?"

1%

Glossary
advantage *n* a positive thing
suburbs *n* an area where people live outside the centre of the city
trust *v* believe that somebody is good, honest, etc.
suspicious *adj* feeling that somebody has done something wrong

2 PRONUNCIATION sentence rhythm

a (4 9)⟩⟩ Listen to the last five lines of Part 2. What tells the speakers…?

   a where to pause

   b in what way to say the dialogue

> 🔍 **Reading aloud**
> Reading stories or poems aloud gives you the opportunity to focus on pronunciation, especially sentence rhythm.

b ➤ **Communication** *Reading dialogue p.103.* Practise reading the dialogue with a partner.

3 LISTENING

a (4 10)⟩⟩ Listen to Part 3 of the story. Answer the questions.

   1 What did Hartley say about Héloise? *will go*

   2 What did Vivienne promise to do? *she will yours*

   3 Who do you think the lady in the white dress is? *They Pliss. cout to reloise.*

b (4 11)⟩⟩ Listen to Part 4 of the story.

   1 Who was the lady?

   2 Who was Vivienne?

   3 Who was Héloise?

c Did the ending surprise you? Why (not)?

4 GRAMMAR possessive pronouns

a Look at some extracts from the story. Complete them with *my, mine, your,* or *yours.*

   1 'Vivienne, you didn't answer _my_ last letter.'

   2 'I understand all the advantages of _your_ offer.'

   3 'Vivienne … you must be _mine_.'

   4 'My answer is yes. I will be _yours_.'

b ➤ p.140 Grammar Bank 8C. Learn more about possessive pronouns and practise them.

c (4 13)⟩⟩ Listen. Say the sentences with a possessive pronoun.

   ⟩⟩ *It's my book.* ⟨ *It's mine.*

5 WRITING using adverbs

a Make adverbs from the following adjectives.

   angry lazy quiet sad serious slow

b (4 14)⟩⟩ Listen to some lines from stories. Add an adverb from **a** after 'said' to show how the person is speaking.

   1 'I'm sorry, but I don't love you,' he said _sadly_.

   2 'Give me back all my letters,' she said _angrily_

   3 'I think… I have an idea,' he said _slowly_

   4 'Don't make a noise. Everyone is asleep,' she said _quietly_

   5 'I don't feel like doing anything,' he said _lazily_

   6 'This is a very important matter,' she said _seriously_

c In pairs, write a short scene between Hartley's wife and Héloise, when she is telling the cook to leave. Include at least two adverbs of manner after *said*.

GRAMMAR

Circle a, b, or c.

1 I need _____ some emails.
   a to answer   b answer   c answering
2 The situation is difficult _____.
   a for explain   b explain   c to explain
3 I don't know what _____.
   a do   b to do   c that I do
4 I don't really mind _____ housework.
   a do   b to do   c doing
5 _____ is one of the best forms of exercise.
   a Swiming   b Swimming   c Swim
6 _____ bring our books tomorrow?
   a Do we have to
   b Have we to
   c Do we must
7 It's free. You _____ pay.
   a don't have to   b mustn't   c haven't to
8 You must _____ your grandmother.
   a to call   b calling   c call
9 You _____ drink so much coffee.
   a not should   b don't should   c shouldn't
10 I think you should _____ to her about it.
   a to talk   b talk   c talking
11 If she _____, she won't come back.
   a goes   b went   c 'll go
12 If they don't come soon, we _____ them.
   a don't see   b won't see   c aren't see
13 Call me if you _____ a taxi.
   a won't find   b don't find   c didn't find
14 A Whose book is that?   B It's _____.
   a my   b mine book   c mine
15 She forgot his birthday, but he didn't forget _____.
   a her   b she   c hers

VOCABULARY

a Circle the right verb.

1 When did you *know* / *meet* your husband?
2 Did you *tell* / *say* Mark about the party?
3 If we don't run, we'll *miss* / *lose* the train!
4 I really *wait* / *hope* she's passed the exam.
5 My mother always *carries* / *wears* a lot of jewellery.

b Complete with a verb from the list.

enjoy finish forget hate learn mind promise try

1 Don't _____ to turn off the light before you go.
2 I want to _____ to speak Italian.
3 Can you _____ to make less noise, please?
4 I _____ to pay you back next week.
5 I really _____ making cakes.
6 Do you _____ waiting here until I'm ready?
7 My parents are very punctual – they _____ being late.
8 When are you going to _____ using the computer? I need it!

c Complete the modifiers.

1 A How are you?   B V_____ well, thanks. And you?
2 I was in_____ lucky – I won £100.
3 She's a b_____ tired – she needs to rest.
4 You're driving r_____ fast – slow down!
5 My bag is q_____ heavy because I've got my laptop in it.

d Complete the *get* phrases.

1 We didn't have satnav in the car and we **got** _____ on the way home from Edinburgh.
2 I'm always really hungry when I **get** _____ from school.
3 She was very ill, but luckily she's **getting** _____.
4 We **got** two _____ for the theatre to see a show.
5 I **get** _____ very well with my brothers and sisters.
6 They were married for ten years, but six months ago they **got** _____.
7 I **got** a text _____ from Carol. She says she's going to be late.

PRONUNCIATION

a Circle the word with a different sound.

1	mine	find	right	give
2	win	fit	child	promise
3	choose	could	would	look
4	should	impression	dictionary	sandwich
5	earn	wear	learn	heard

b Underline the stressed syllable.

1 pre|tend   3 re|mem|ber   5 qui|et|ly
2 im|por|tant   4 sa|la|ry

CAN YOU UNDERSTAND THIS TEXT?

a Read the article once. What does Michael think is the main reason the British aren't good at speaking languages?

b Read the article again and tick the reasons why, according to the writer, the British are bad at languages.

1. ☐ British people rarely travel abroad.
2. ☐ English is an international language.
3. ☐ British people who live abroad often find the local language too difficult to learn.
4. ☐ British people who live abroad often don't socialize with the local people.
5. ☐ Language teachers in British schools are not very good.
6. ☐ Many British secondary school pupils don't study a foreign language.
7. ☐ British children don't know enough about their own grammar.
8. ☐ British people don't want to waste money learning languages.

c Look at the highlighted words or phrases in the text. Guess their meaning from the context. Check with your teacher or with a dictionary.

Why are the British so bad at learning languages?

Michael Reece has lived and worked in France for fifteen years.

The British are bad at speaking foreign languages. It's a fact. In any city around Europe you can find British tourists asking for the restaurant menu in English. At best they will try to say a couple of phrases they have learnt from a phrase book, but they will stop making an effort the moment they discover the waiter knows a little English.

I read a survey once which found that only 5% of British people could count to 20 in another language. So why is this? I think laziness is possibly the key factor. There is a general feeling among British people that 'everyone speaks English nowadays so it's not worth learning other languages'. In multinational companies English is often the official language of communication within the company. Also, British people who live abroad can always find other British expatriates to talk to, to watch British TV with, even to go to British pubs with – all reasons for never bothering to learn the local language.

The situation in British schools doesn't help. Ten years ago, about 80% of children at secondary school studied a foreign language. Today, that number has gone down to 48%. And even the few pupils who study foreign languages at school don't have as many hours of classes as pupils in other European countries. I think it is also a problem that British children don't study English grammar any more, which makes it more difficult for them to learn the grammar of another language.

CAN YOU UNDERSTAND THESE PEOPLE?

4 15))) **In the street** Watch or listen to five people and answer the questions.

Stacey   Heba   Ruth   Ben   Nick

1. Stacey thinks that happiness is having _____.
   a somewhere nice to live and a lot of friends
   b a lot of money and a close family
   c a reasonable amount of money and friends and family
2. Heba _____.
   a speaks a little Arabic and a little French
   b speaks Arabic and French very well
   c speaks Arabic well and a little French
3. If Ruth has relationship problems, she talks to _____.
   a her friends
   b her mother
   c her mother and her friends
4. Ben thinks people who have problems sleeping should _____.
   a drink less coffee and do more exercise
   b do physical work before going to bed
   c drink less coffee and try to relax more
5. Nick thinks that Americans are bad at learning languages because _____.
   a they don't want to learn languages
   b they find learning languages too difficult
   c they aren't interested in travelling abroad

CAN YOU SAY THIS IN ENGLISH?

Do the tasks with a partner. Tick (✓) the box if you can do them.

Can you...?

1. ☐ talk about something you would like to learn to do, and someone you think would be interesting to meet
2. ☐ talk about three things you like, love, and hate doing
3. ☐ talk about the rules in your (language) school using *must* and *have to*
4. ☐ give someone advice about learning English using *should* and *shouldn't*
5. ☐ remember three of Murphy's Laws in English
6. ☐ say two true sentences using *mine* and *yours*

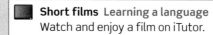

Short films Learning a language
Watch and enjoy a film on iTutor.

G *if* + past, *would* + infinitive (second conditional)
V animals
P word stress

9A What would you do?

What would you do if you saw a bear?

I'd run away.

1 READING & SPEAKING

a Read the quiz questions and answers. Complete each question with an animal from the list.

bee bull dog jellyfish shark snake

b Look at the highlighted verbs and verb phrases. With a partner, try to guess their meaning from the context.

c Read the quiz again and (circle) your answers, a, b, or c.

d ➤ **Communication** *Would you know what to do?* **A** *p.104* **B** *p.107* **C** *p.110.* Read the answers to one section and tell the others. Did you all choose the right answers?

e Have you ever been in any of these situations? What did you do?

2 GRAMMAR
if + past, *would* + infinitive

a Look at questions 1–6 again. Are they about a past situation or an imagined future situation? What tense is the verb after *if*?

b ➤ **p.142 Grammar Bank 9A.** Learn more about the second conditional and practise it.

c Complete the sentences so that they are true for you. Compare with a partner.

1 If I had five extra hours every week,…
2 I would be very happy if…
3 If I could live anywhere in the world,…
4 I would learn English more quickly if…
5 If I won a lot of money in the lottery,…

3 VOCABULARY animals

a ➤ **p.161 Vocabulary Bank** *Animals.*

b (**4 18**)) Listen. Which animals can you hear?

Would you know what to do?

We all love seeing animals on TV and in zoos. But some animals can be dangerous. If you met one in real life, would you know the right thing to do? Read about some common and some less common situations. Would you know what to do?

In the city

1 What would you do…
… if a large aggressive dog ran towards you?
a I would shout 'down' at it several times.
b I would put my hands in my pockets and walk slowly backwards.
c I would keep completely still and look at it in its eyes.

2 What would you do…
… if you were driving and a bee flew into the car?
a I would open all the windows and wait for it to fly out.
b I would try to kill it with a map or a newspaper.
c I would wave my hand to make it go out.

In the country

3 What would you do...

... if a poisonous _snake_ bit you on the leg, and you were more than 30 minutes from the nearest town?

a I would put something very cold on it, like a water bottle.

b I would suck the bite to get the poison out.

c I would tie something, e.g. a scarf on my leg above the bite.

4 What would you do...

... if you were in the middle of a field and a _bull_ started running towards you?

a I would run to the gate.

b I would throw something (e.g. a hat or a bag) in another direction.

c I would shout and wave my arms.

In the water

5 What would you do...

... if you were in the sea and a _jellyfish_ stung you?

a I would rub the sting with a towel to clean it.

b I would wash the sting with fresh water.

c I would wash the sting with vinegar or sea water.

6 What would you do...

... if you were in the sea quite near the shore and you saw a _shark_?

a I would swim to the shore as quickly and quietly as possible.

b I would float and pretend to be dead.

c I would shout for help.

4 PRONUNCIATION word stress

> 🔍 **Stress in words that are similar in other languages**
> Some words in English, e.g. for animals, are similar to the same words in other languages, but the stress is often in a different place.

a Look at the animal words below. Can you remember which syllable is stressed? Under<u>line</u> it.

ca|mel cro|co|dile dol|phin e|le|phant
gi|raffe kan|ga|roo li|on mo|squi|to

b (4 19)) Listen and check. Are any of these words similar in your language? Is the stress in the same place?

c In pairs, ask and answer the questions.

1 What's the most dangerous animal in your country?

2 If you went on a safari, what animal would you most like to see?

3 What's your favourite film about an animal?

4 What's your favourite cartoon animal?

5 Are there any animals or insects you are really afraid of?

6 Do you (or did you) have a pet? What?

7 Are you allergic to any animals or insects?

8 If you could be an animal, which animal would you like to be?

5 SPEAKING

Work in groups of three. Take turns to choose a question and ask the others in the group. Then answer it yourself.

> ## What would you do...
>
> ... if you saw a mouse in your kitchen?
>
> ... if you saw somebody being attacked by a dog?
>
> ... if a bird or a bat flew into your bedroom?
>
> ... if you saw a large spider in the bath?
>
> ... if it was a very hot day and you were on a beach that was famous for shark attacks?
>
> ... if someone offered to buy you a fur coat?
>
> ... if your neighbour's dog barked all night?
>
> ... if a friend asked you to look after their cat or dog for the weekend?
>
> ... if you went to somebody's house for dinner and they gave you...?
>
> a horse meat   b goat   c kangaroo

> 🔍 **Talking about imaginary situations**
> I think I'd (probably)...
> I (definitely) wouldn't...
> I don't think I'd...

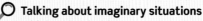

G present perfect + *for* and *since*
V phobias and words related to fear
P sentence stress

Do you have any phobias?

Yes, I've been afraid of spiders since I was a child.

9B I've been afraid of it for years

1 VOCABULARY
phobias and words related to fear

a Look at the picture. How many things can you see that some people have a phobia of?

b Look at the names of five phobias. Match them to explanations A–E.

1 acrophobia 3 glossophobia 5 arachnophobia
2 agoraphobia 4 claustrophobia

A [5] People with this phobia are terrified of spiders. Rupert Grint, the actor who played Ron Weasley in the Harry Potter films, has this phobia, and so does his character Ron.

B [2] This phobia can have a severe effect on sufferers' lives. These people are frightened of being in open and public spaces like shops and busy streets. They often feel panic when they go out and only feel safe at home.

C [4] People with this phobia are afraid of being in closed spaces like lifts, or travelling on the underground. This phobia can make life very difficult for people who live and work in cities.

D [1] People who suffer from this phobia are scared of heights, and they get very nervous if they have to go up high, for example on a ski lift or if they are on a balcony on the 20th floor.

E [3] People with this phobia suffer from a fear of public speaking. They get very nervous if they have to speak in front of other people, for example at work or in class or at a conference. The actor Harrison Ford has been afraid of public speaking all his life. He even gets nervous when a character in a film he is making has to make a speech.

c Read the explanations again. Find in the texts…

1 the noun made from the adjective *afraid* fear.
2 one adjective which means *very afraid* terrified.
3 two synonyms for *afraid* scared, fear. frightened

2 LISTENING & SPEAKING

a (4 20)) Listen to three people talking about their phobias. Answer question 1 for each person.

	1	2	3
1 What is he / she afraid of?	Rats.	claustrophob	clowns.
2 When did it start?	14, 4 yrs old. since 12 year ago.	10 years ago.	long time since she was child 7 years old
3 How does it affect his / her life?	Nervous, in the dark. tennis Racket.	scared in the underground flying	to because she don see clowns very often

b Listen again and answer questions 2 and 3 for each person. Which person do you think is most affected by their phobia?

c Ask and answer with a partner.

1 Which of the phobias in this lesson do you think is the most irrational?
2 Which do you think makes the sufferers' lives most complicated?
3 Do you or anyone you know have a phobia? When and how did it start? How does it affect your or their lives?

My brother is really afraid of flying. He gets very nervous before he flies somewhere. It started about ten years ago when…

3 GRAMMAR present perfect + *for* and *since*

a Look at this extract from the first interview in **2**. Answer the questions.

> 'How long have you had this phobia?'
> 'I've had it for about 40 years. Since I was 12 years old.'

1 When did she begin to be afraid of bats?
2 Is she afraid of bats now?
3 What tense do we use to talk about something that started in the past and is still true now?
4 Complete the rule with *for* or *since*.
Use _____ with a period of time.
Use _____ with a point in time.

b ➤ **p.142 Grammar Bank 9B.** Learn more about the present perfect + *for* and *since*, and practise it.

c (4 22)) Listen and say the phrase with *for* or *since*.

)) 1984 (since 1984

4 PRONUNCIATION sentence stress

a (4 23)) Listen and repeat. Copy the rhythm.

1 for ten years → worked here for ten years
→ I've worked here for ten years.
2 since 2002 → lived here since 2002
→ We've lived here since 2002.
3 known him → have you known him
→ How long have you known him?

b (4 24)) Listen and write five sentences.

5 SPEAKING

a Look at the questions below. What two tenses are they? What are the missing words?

		Name
have	/ a pet? How long / it?	
	/ a bike ? How long / it?	
live	/ in a modern flat ? How long / there?	
	/ near this school ? How long / there?	
know	/ anybody from another country? How long / him (her)?	
be	/ a fan of a football team? How long / a fan?	
	/ a member of a club or organization? How long / a member?	
	/ married? How long / married?	

b Move around the class and ask other students. If they answer *Yes, I do* or *Yes, I am* to the first question, ask the second question. Try to find a different person for each question.

6 READING

a Do you know of any kinds of treatment for people who have phobias? No, I don't.

b Read the text and mark the sentences **T** (true) or **F** (false).

1 30% of people have some kind of phobia. F
2 Doctors have created a new drug to cure phobias. F
3 In exposure therapy people learn to relax when they are exposed to something they are afraid of. T
4 Exposure therapy is always successful. F
5 The drug affects the way people learn and remember things. T
6 The study showed that the drug helped people to lose their fear. T

Scared of spiders?
Take this pill.

There are many different kinds of phobias and they affect at least a quarter of the population. But doctors believe that they may soon have a cure. They have discovered that a drug, which is given to patients suffering from tuberculosis, can also help people to overcome their phobias.

The normal treatment for people with strong phobias is some kind of exposure therapy. The most commonly used exposure therapy involves gradually exposing people to the object or situation that produces the fear. For example, if you have a dentist phobia, you might first sit in the waiting room of a dentist, then talk to the dentist, and then sit in the dentist's chair. These exposures are combined with relaxation techniques.

However, exposure therapy does not work for everybody, and doctors think that the new drug, which causes changes to a part of the brain which is used in learning and memory, could be used in the future to make this therapy more effective. Michael Davis at Emory University School of Medicine in Atlanta, Georgia did a study with 30 acrophobics – people who are scared of heights – and put them in a glass lift that appeared to go up and down. The people who were given the pill felt much less afraid then those who took a placebo.

Adapted from a British newspaper

c With a partner, guess the meaning of the highlighted words and phrases.

d What stages of exposure therapy do you think could be used for a someone with
a) arachnophobia b) claustrophobia?

G present perfect or past simple? (2)
V biographies
P word stress, /ɔː/

9C Born to sing

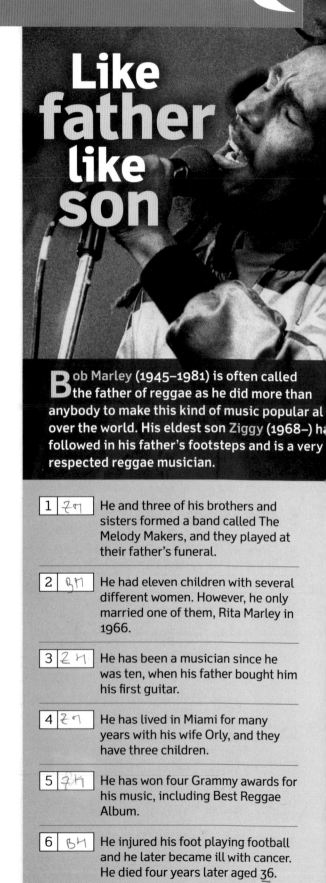

He was born in Jamaica.

How many Grammy's has he won?

Like father like son

Bob Marley (1945–1981) is often called the father of reggae as he did more than anybody to make this kind of music popular al over the world. His eldest son Ziggy (1968–) ha followed in his father's footsteps and is a very respected reggae musician.

1	ZM	He and three of his brothers and sisters formed a band called The Melody Makers, and they played at their father's funeral.
2	BM	He had eleven children with several different women. However, he only married one of them, Rita Marley in 1966.
3	ZM	He has been a musician since he was ten, when his father bought him his first guitar.
4	ZM	He has lived in Miami for many years with his wife Orly, and they have three children.
5	ZM	He has won four Grammy awards for his music, including Best Reggae Album.
6	BM	He injured his foot playing football and he later became ill with cancer. He died four years later aged 36.

1 VOCABULARY & PRONUNCIATION

biographies, word stress, /ɔː/

a (4 25)) Look at the highlighted words in the list below. Which syllable is stressed? Listen and check.

Events in your life

1	be born	5	go to university	11	get divorced
8	marry sb / get married	4	leave school	12	retire
2	go to primary school	10	separate	7	fall in love
9	have children	6	get a job	13	die
3	go to secondary school				

b Number the expressions in what you think is the most logical order. Compare with a partner. Do you agree?

c (4 26)) Listen and repeat the words and sound.

/ɔː/ horse	born divorced fall

d Practise saying these words. Circle the ones with the /ɔː/ sound.

more   work   world   small   walk   worse
talk   ball   form   bought   four   word

e (4 27)) Listen and check. What rule can you see for words with *wor* + consonant?

2 READING

a Look at the photos of Bob and Ziggy Marley and read the introduction. Have you heard their music? Do you like it?

b Read ten facts about the lives of the two men. In pairs, decide which five are about Bob Marley (**BM**) and which five are about Ziggy Marley (**ZM**).

c Work in pairs. **A** re-read the facts about Bob Marley and **B** about Ziggy Marley. Close your books and tell your partner what you can remember.

3 GRAMMAR present perfect or past simple? (2)

a Answer the questions.

1 Look at the five facts about Bob Marley. What tense are all the verbs? Why?

2 Look at the five facts about Ziggy Marley. What three tenses are there? Why?

b ➤ p.142 Grammar Bank 9C. Learn more about the difference between the present perfect and the past simple, and practise it.

Bob Marley

Ziggy Marley

7	BM	He was born in a small village in Jamaica. His father was a captain in the British army.
8	ZM	He was born in Kingston, Jamaica in 1968 and he was 13 years old when his father died. His father's last words to him were 'Money can't buy you life.'
9	BM	His music was very influenced by social problems in his homeland, Jamaica.
10	BM	With his band, The Wailers, he made eleven albums. His most famous songs included *No Woman, No Cry, Three Little Birds*, and *I Shot the Sheriff*.

4 LISTENING

a Look at the photos of another famous father and son, Julio and Enrique, who are both singers. What's their surname? Who do you think is more famous?

Julio

Enrique

1 Madrid 1975
2 Miami
3 Enrique Martinez
4 'Enrique Iglesias' 1995
5 'Escape' 2001
6 Anna Kournikova
7 100 million

b You are going to listen to a radio programme about Enrique. Look at the information. Before you listen, guess what the connection is to him.

I think he was born in Madrid in 1975.

c **4 29)))** Now listen and make notes. Compare with a partner.

d Do you think Ziggy and Enrique have been successful because of their surnames, or because they are genuinely talented? Do you think it's common for children to want to do the same job as their parents?

5 SPEAKING & WRITING

a Think about an older person, a friend or a member of your family, who is alive and who you know well. Prepare to answer the questions below about their life and to tell your partner any other interesting information about them.

The past
• When / born?
• Where / born?
• What / do after (he / she) leave school? (e.g. get a job, go to university, get married, have children, etc.)

The present
• Where / live now?
• How long / live there?
• What / do? (job) How long...?
• What / do in (his / her) free time?

• Do you think (he / she) has had a good life? Why (not)?

b Interview your partner about his / her person. Ask for more information. Do your two people have anything in common?

I'm going to tell you about my grandmother. *When was she born?*

c **➤ p.116 Writing** *A biography*. Write a biography of a person you know, or a famous person.

6 **4 30)))** SONG *You're My #1* ♫

1 ■ HOLLY AND ROB IN BROOKLYN

a **4 31))** Watch or listen to Rob and Holly. Mark the sentences **T** (true) or **F** (false).

1 Rob has just done an interview.
2 He is in a hurry.
3 He has another interview in Manhattan.
4 He has another coffee.
5 Barbara phones Rob.
6 The restaurant is booked for 7 o'clock.

> **British and American English**
> *rest room* = American English; *toilet* = British English
> *the subway* = American English; *the underground* = British English

b Watch or listen again. Say why the **F** sentences are false.

2 VOCABULARY directions

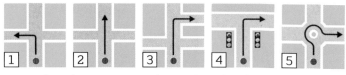

a Look at the pictures and complete the phrases.

1 Turn _____.
2 Go _____ on.
3 Take the _____ turning on the right.
4 Turn right at the _____ lights.
5 Go round the _____ and take the third exit.

b **4 32))** Listen and check.

3 ■ ASKING HOW TO GET THERE

a **4 33))** Cover the dialogue and watch or listen. Mark Rob's route on the map.

b Watch or listen again. Complete the **You Hear** phrases.

You Say 💬	))) You Hear
How do I get to Greenwich Village on the subway?	Go to the subway station at Prospect Park. _____ the B train to West 4th Street.
How many stops is that?	Six or seven.
OK. And then?	From West 4th Street take the A train, and get _____ at 14th Street.
Could you say that again?	OK. From Prospect Park take the B train to West 4th Street, and then take the A train to 14th Street. That's only one _____.
Where's the restaurant?	Come out of the subway on Eighth Avenue, go _____ on for about 50 yards and take the _____ left. That's Greenwich Avenue. The restaurant's on the _____. It's called The Tea Set.
OK, thanks. See you later.	And don't get _____!

c (4 34))) Watch or listen and repeat the **You Say** phrases. <u>Copy</u> the <u>rhythm</u>.

d Practise the dialogue with a partner.

e 👥 In pairs, roleplay the dialogue.

A **B** is at Prospect Park. Choose a destination on the subway map. Give **B** directions. You start with *Go to the subway station at…*.

B Follow **A**'s directions, and tell **A** which subway stop you have arrived at. Were you right?

f Swap roles.

(*Take the A train to… Then…*

4 ▢ ROB IS LATE…AGAIN

a (4 35))) Watch or listen to Rob and Jenny. Is the date a success?

b Watch or listen again and answer the questions.

1 What excuse does Rob give for being late?
2 How long has Jenny waited for him?
3 What does Rob suggest they do?
4 What does Jenny say that Rob could do?
5 Who is Rob interested in: Holly or Jenny?

c Look at the **Social English phrases**. Can you remember any of the missing words?

Social English phrases
Rob I'm so _____.
Rob I _____ I'm sorry.
Jenny I don't want to _____ here any more.
Jenny I don't _____ like a walk.
Jenny It's been a _____ day.
Jenny I didn't _____ to say that.

d (4 36))) Watch or listen and complete the phrases.

e Watch or listen again and repeat the phrases. How do you say them in your language?

👤 **Can you…?**
☐ give and understand directions in the street
☐ give and understand directions for using public transport
☐ apologize

G passive
V verbs: *invent, discover*, etc.
P /ʃ/, *-ed*, sentence stress

I think it was invented by a woman.

Are you sure?

10A The mothers of invention

disposable nappies

a dishwasher

a zip

windscreen wipers

bullet-proof vest

POLICE

Tipp-Ex

a washing machine

a hairdryer

1 LISTENING

a Look at the photos. Five of these things were invented by women. In pairs, decide which five you think they are.

b (4 37)) Now listen to a radio programme about inventions. Were you right? Complete the sentences with the invention.

1 The _____ was invented by Josephine Cochrane in 1886.
2 _____ were invented by Mary Anderson in 1903.
3 _____ were invented by Marion Donovan in 1950.
4 _____ was invented by Bette Nesmith Graham in 1956.
5 The _____ was invented by Stephanie Kwolek in 1966.

c Listen again and answer the questions.

1 What happened after Josephine Cochrane's dinner parties?
2 What was the problem with cars in 1903 when it rained or snowed?
3 How many disposable nappies are used every day?
4 What was Bette Nesmith Graham's job?
5 What was special about the material Stephanie Kwolek invented?

d Which of the five inventions do you think was the best?

2 GRAMMAR passive

a Make five true sentences using the words in the chart.

The dishwasher	is called	Tipp-Ex today.
Disposable nappies	was invented	by Marion Donovan.
More than 55 million nappies	are protected	every day.
Mrs Graham's invention	were invented	by the bullet-proof vest.
Policemen all over the world	are used	by an American woman.

The dishwasher was invented by an American woman.

b Look at the two sentences below and answer the questions.

 a An American woman invented the dishwasher.
 b The dishwasher was invented by an American woman.

1 Do the sentences have the same meaning?
2 In which sentence is the focus more on the dishwasher?
3 In which sentence is the focus more on the woman?

c ➤ **p.144 Grammar Bank 10A.** Learn more about the passive and practise it.

3 READING & VOCABULARY

verbs: *invent*, *discover*, etc.

a Match the verbs to the dictionary definitions.

> base   design   discover   invent

1 _Discover_ verb to find or learn sth for the first time, e.g. *DNA was ~ in 1953.*

2 _based_ verb to make sth using sth else as a starting point, e.g. *This film is ~ on a true story.*

3 _design_ verb to draw a plan which shows how to make sth, e.g. *The building was ~ by a German architect.*

4 _invent_ verb to make or think of sth for the first time, e.g. *Who ~ the bicycle?*

b Complete the 'Did you know…?' text with the past participle of a verb from the list.

> base   call   design   discover   give
> invent   open   play   show   use

c Read the text again. One of the pieces of information is not true. Which one do you think it is?

4 PRONUNCIATION /ʃ/, -ed, sentence stress

a ④ 39)) Listen and repeat the words and sounds.

∫ shower	dishwasher invention
	special washing machine

b What four ways can you see for spelling the /ʃ/ sound? Which one do you think is not typical? Go to the **Sound Bank** *p.167* and check.

c How is -ed pronounced in these past participles? Put them in the right column.

> based   called   cre|a|ted   de|signed   di|rec|ted
> di|sco|vered   in|ven|ted   pain|ted   pro|duced   used

d dog	t tie	/ɪd/

d ④ 40)) Listen and check. <u>Underline</u> the stressed syllable in each multi-syllable verb.

e ④ 41)) Listen and write six sentences. Then listen again and repeat. Copy the <u>rhy</u>thm.

5 SPEAKING

➤ **Communication** *Passives quiz* **A** *p.105* **B** *p.109.* Make sentences for your partner to decide if they are true or false.

Did you know…?

One of the most famous logos in the world is the **Nike** logo. It was [1] _designed_ by an American student, Carolyn Davidson, in 1971. Ms Davidson was only paid $35 dollars for her design. However, she was later [2] _given_ a gold ring in the shape of the logo and Nike shares.

Tinned food was [3] _invented_ in 1810 in Britain by Peter Durand. Unfortunately, he did not also invent a tin opener, so tins were [4] _opened_ with difficulty using a knife and a hammer. It wasn't until nearly 50 years later that the American Ezra Warner invented the tin opener.

When people at toy company Parker Brothers were first [5] _shown_ the board game '**Monopoly**', they were not interested. They said it had 52 fundamental errors, including taking too long to play. However, a few days later the company president saw the game and took it home to try it. He stayed up until 1 a.m. to finish playing it, and the next day he wrote to the inventor, Charles Darrow, and offered to buy it!

The modern game of golf was invented in Scotland in the 18th century. It was originally only [6] _played_ by men, and was [7] _called_ 'golf' because of the rule **G**entlemen **O**nly **L**adies **F**orbidden. This is how the word *golf* entered into the English language.

Botox was first [8] _used_ in 1985 to correct strabismus (lazy eye) in children. The possibility of using it to make people's faces look younger was only [9] _discovered_ 20 years later.

The character Gregory House in the hit TV series **House M.D.** is [10] _____ on Conan Doyle's detective Sherlock Holmes. Like Holmes, House uses his intelligence and knowledge of psychology to solve cases. House's relationship with his friend Dr James Wilson is similar to that between Holmes and his friend, Dr John Watson, and the address on his driving licence is 221B Baker St, a direct reference to Holmes's address.

G *used to*
V school subjects
P *used to / didn't use to*

Did you use to like primary school?

Yes, I did. I used to have a great time.

10B Could do better

1 VOCABULARY school subjects

a Read the report and match the subjects and pictures.

Subject	Mark
art	65%
foreign languages (English, etc.)	72%
geography	86%
history	44%
IT (= information technology)	50%
literature	57%
maths	42%
PE (=physical education)	78%
science (physics, chemistry, and biology)	61%

Behaviour
Lazy and untidy. Talks a lot in class.

b (4 42)) Listen and check.

c Look at the report again. What do *marks* and *behaviour* mean?

d Did you have any other subjects at primary or secondary school? Which subjects were you…?

a good at   b OK at   c bad at

I was very bad at maths.

> **good at**
> We use **at** after *good* and *bad* to talk about our abilities, e.g. *I was very bad* **at** *maths.*
> *I'm very good* **at** *cooking.*

2 GRAMMAR *used to*

a When you were at school did you get a report at the end of every term or year? Were they usually good or bad? Did you always show them to your parents?

b Read some extracts from *Could do better*, a collection of famous British people's school reports. Are the comments positive or negative?

Could do Better

She must try to be less emotional … with others.

Princess Diana
mother of Princes William and Harry

Kenneth reads well and expresses himself well, and is good at arithmetic but everything he does is spoiled by his attitude and his bad behaviour.

Ken Follett
best-selling author of *The Pillars of the Earth*

Constantly late for school and always losing his books and papers.

Winston Churchill
politician, Prime Minister during the Second World War 1940–45

c Read the extracts again and match the people to sentences 1–5. Write **KF**, **JL**, **PD**, **WC**, or **HF**.

1 WC didn't use to get to school on time.
2 JL used to make the other children laugh.
3 KF was clever, but didn't use to behave well.
4 HF used to use very complicated vocabulary.
5 PD used to cry a lot at school.

d Look at sentences 1–5 again. Does *used to* refer to…?

1 a the present
  b the past
2 a things that happened once
  b things that happened repeatedly

e ➤ **p.144 Grammar Bank 10B.** Learn more about *used to* and practise it.

He is… a clown in class and wastes other pupils' time.

John Lennon
musician, member of the Beatles 1960–69

Subject: *English*

Helen must learn not to use such flowery language.

Helen Fielding
author of *Bridget Jones's Diary*

3 PRONUNCIATION *used to / didn't use to*

> 🔍 **Pronouncing *used to***
> When we say *used to* or (*didn't*) *use to* we link the two words together. They are both pronounced /ˈjuːstə/.

a (4 44)) Listen and <u>underline</u> the stressed words. Then listen and repeat.

1 He used to hate school.
2 I used to be good at French.
3 They didn't use to behave well.
4 She didn't use to wear glasses.
5 Did you use to walk to school?

b (4 45)) Now listen and write six more sentences.

4 LISTENING

a (4 46)) Listen to six people talking about their memories of school. Write ✓ if they liked it, ✗ if they didn't like it, and ✓✗ if they liked some things but not others.

1 ✗ 2 ✗ 3 ✓ 4 ✗ 5 ✓✗ 6 ✓

b Listen again and answer the questions.

Who…?	
4	didn't like being at a same-sex school
6	didn't use to study a lot, but got good marks
5	had a very good physics teacher
1	hated doing sport
2	liked one school, but not another
3	used to read a lot at school

c Do you identify with any of the speakers? Why?

5 SPEAKING

a Think about when you were at primary or secondary school. Prepare your answers to the questions below. Think of examples you could give.

Did you use to…?

- be disorganized or very organized
- be late for school or on time
- get a lot of homework or a little
- have a teacher you really liked
- be a good or a bad student
- wear a uniform
- have a teacher you hated
- have a nickname

b Work in groups of three. **A** tell **B** and **C** about how you used to be. **B** and **C** listen and ask for more information. Then swap roles. Did you have anything in common?

(I used to be very disorganized, for example
  I often left my books or my sports clothes at home.

6 (4 47)) SONG *ABC* ♫

Are you going to the party?

I might go, but I might not.

10C Mr Indecisive

Go to the party or stay in?

Car or taxi?

Get there early or get there late?

Come on! Make up your mind!

1 GRAMMAR *might*

a Do you know anybody who is very indecisive? What is he / she indecisive about?

b (4 48)) Cover the dialogue and listen. What does Adrian decide in the end?

c Listen again and complete the dialogue.

> **Tina** Hi, Adrian.
> **Adrian** Oh. Hi, Tina.
> **T** It's Alice's party tonight. You are going, aren't you?
> **A** I don't know. I'm not sure. I might _go_, but I might not. I can't decide.
> **T** Oh, come on. It'll be good. Lots of Alice's friends are going to be there. You might _meet someone_.
> **A** Yes, that's true... OK. I'll go then.
> **T** Great. Shall we get a taxi there?
> **A** No, I'll take my car... No, wait. It might _be difficult_ to park. Let's get a taxi.
> **T** Fine. What time shall I get the taxi for? 9.30?
> **A** Yes... No... Listen. I'll take my car. I'll pick you up at 9.00.
> **T** Are you sure about that?
> **A** Yes, I'm sure... I think.

d (4 49)) Adrian phones Tina later. What happens?

e Underline the verb phrases in the dialogue with *might*. Do we use them for...?

   1 an obligation   OR   2 a possibility

f ▶ p.144 Grammar Bank 10C. Learn more about *might* and practise it.

g Take turns to ask and answer the questions below. Use *I'm not sure. I might...* and give two possibilities each time.

> What are you going to do after class?
>
> I'm not sure. I might go home or I might go shopping. What about you?

   1 What are you going to do after class?
   2 What are you going to have for dinner tonight?
   3 What are you going to do on Saturday night?
   4 Where are you going to have lunch on Sunday?
   5 Where are you going to go for your next holiday?

2 PRONUNCIATION diphthongs

a (4 51)) Listen and repeat the picture words and sounds.

b Look at the other words. Which one has a different sound?

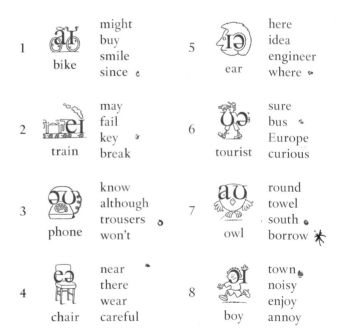

1 bike	might buy smile since		5 ear	here idea engineer where	
2 train	may fail key break		6 tourist	sure bus Europe curious	
3 phone	know although trousers won't		7 owl	round towel south borrow	
4 chair	near there wear careful		8 boy	town noisy enjoy annoy	

c (4 52)) Listen and check.

3 SPEAKING & READING

a Interview your partner with the questionnaire. Ask for more information. Which of you is more indecisive?

ARE **YOU** INDECISIVE?

Do you have problems deciding...?
- what to buy when you go shopping
- what to wear when you go out
- what to eat in a restaurant
- what to do in your free time
- where to go on holiday

Do you often change your mind about things? What kind of things?

Do you think you are indecisive?

☐ Yes ☐ No ☐ I'm not sure

b Read the article carefully. Complete it with sentences A–E.

A And it isn't just in the coffee bar.

B But if all this choice is bad for us, what can we do about it?

C Buying a cup of coffee isn't as easy as it used to be.

D People often think that being able to choose from a lot of options is a good thing.

E Research shows that we feel happier when we have less choice.

c Do you agree that there is too much choice in the following? Why (not)?

a in supermarkets	d in coffee shops
b on TV	e in restaurants
c in clothes shops	

4 VOCABULARY

word building: noun formation

> **Noun formation**
> With many verbs you can make a noun by adding *-ion*, *-sion*, or *-ation*, e.g.
> decide → decision   imagine → imagination
> Other verbs change when you form a noun, e.g.
> see (verb) → sight (noun)

a With a partner try to complete the chart.

Verb	Noun (+ *-ion*, *-sion*, or *-ation*)
opt	*option*
decide	*decision*
imagine	*imagination*
inform	information
elect	election
invite	invitation
organize	organization
educate	education
confuse	confusion

Verb	Noun (new word)
choose	choice
live	life
die	death
succeed	success

b **4 53))** Listen and check. Underline the stressed syllable in the verbs and nouns.

Is **too much** choice making us unhappy?

1 [C]. Years ago there were only two kinds of coffee – black or white. But nowadays when you go into a coffee shop in the UK you are given about twenty different options. Do you want a Cappuccino, a Latte, a Caramel Macchiato, an Americano, or a White Mocha?

2 [A]. In big supermarkets we have to choose between thousands of products – my local supermarket has 35 different kinds of milk! When we are buying clothes or electrical gadgets, looking for a hotel on a travel website, or just deciding which TV channel to watch, we are constantly forced to choose from hundreds of possibilities.

3 [D]. However, university researchers have discovered that too much choice is making us feel unhappy and dissatisfied. The problem is that we have so many options that we get stressed every time we have to make a decision, because

we are worried about making the wrong one. Then when we choose one thing we feel bad because we think we are missing other opportunities, and this makes us dissatisfied with what we have chosen.

4 [E]. Professor Mark Lepper at Stanford University in America found that people who tried six kinds of jam felt happier with their choice than those who were offered 24 jams to taste.

5 [B]. Professor Lepper suggests that we should try to relax when we have to choose something to buy. 'Don't take these choices too seriously or it will become stressful,' he says. 'If you pick a sofa from IKEA in 30 seconds, you'll feel better than if you spend hours researching sofas – because you won't know what you're missing.'

Adapted from a British newspaper

GRAMMAR

Circle a, b, or c.

1 If I _____ a snake, I'd be terrified.
   a see   b saw   c seen

2 What _____ if a large dog attacked you?
   a you would do
   b will you do
   c would you do

3 I _____ that bike if I were you.
   a wouldn't buy   b didn't buy   c won't buy

4 I _____ in this house since I was 12.
   a live   b lived   c have lived

5 We haven't seen my uncle _____ a long time.
   a since   b during   c for

6 _____ have you had this car?
   a How long   b How much   c How long time

7 I ___ ___ married for 15 years. I got divorced in 2010.
   a have been   b am   c was

8 When _____ Queen Victoria die?
   a did   b has   c was

9 The dishwasher _____ in 1886.
   a were invented   b was invented   c is invented

10 The first book in the series was _____ ten years ago.
   a write   b wrote   c written

11 The *Mona Lisa* was painted _____ da Vinci.
   a for   b by   c to

12 When I was a child I _____ have very long hair.
   a use to   b used to   c used

13 Jack _____ like sport when he was at school.
   a don't use to
   b didn't used to
   c didn't use to

14 I might _____ Sophie a ring for her birthday.
   a buy   b to buy   c buying

15 Sue _____ come tonight. She has to work late.
   a might no   b not might   c might not

VOCABULARY

a Make nouns from the verbs.

   1 elect _____
   2 decide _____
   3 choose _____
   4 organize _____
   5 die _____
   6 succeed _____
   7 imagine _____

b Circle the word that is different.

   1 butterfly   goat   fly   mosquito
   2 pig   sheep   cow   lion
   3 spider   shark   jellyfish   whale
   4 scared   afraid   frightened   fear
   5 maths   marks   history   biology

c Complete with a verb from the list in the right form.

   base   design   discover   fall   retire

   1 In Britain most people _____ when they are 65.
   2 I _____ in love for the first time when I was 15.
   3 Penicillin was _____ by Alexander Fleming in 1928.
   4 The *Lord of the Rings* films were _____ on the books written by Tolkien.
   5 The first Apple computer was _____ by Steve Wozniak.

d Write the words for the definitions.

   1 **k**_____ a wild animal that lives in Australia
   2 **b**_____ an insect that makes honey
   3 **cr**_____ a reptile that lives in rivers in Africa and Australia
   4 **b**_____ a male cow
   5 **t**_____ very afraid
   6 **s**_____ a couple usually do this before they get divorced
   7 **s**_____ a school subject that includes physics, chemistry, and biology
   8 **r**_____ information you get from your school at the end of each term which says how you have done

PRONUNCIATION

a Circle the word with a different sound.

   1 🔟 fear   near   idea   bear
   2 📞 phobia   cow   show   homework
   3 🚲 primary   children   spider   might
   4 🪑 scared   there   nervous   wear
   5 /ju/ subject   student   used   confusion

b Underline the stressed syllable.

   1 gi|raffe   2 e|le|phant   3 se|con|dary   4 re|tire   5 de|sign

CAN YOU UNDERSTAND THIS TEXT?

a Read the article once. How did the dolphins protect the swimmers from the shark?

b Read the article again and mark the sentences **T** (true) or **F** (false).

1 The swimmers were swimming very near the beach.

2 The dolphins were doing strange things.

3 Mr Howes and Helen were separated from the other two swimmers.

4 One of the dolphins jumped out of the water.

5 Mr Howes saw a big fish swimming around the other two girls.

6 Mr Howes understood that the dolphins were trying to help them.

7 The dolphins stopped the shark from attacking them.

8 In the end the swimmers were rescued by lifeguards.

9 An expert said that dolphins very often behave in this way.

c Look at the highlighted words or phrases in the text. Guess their meaning from the context. Check with your teacher or with a dictionary.

DOLPHINS SAVE SWIMMERS FROM A SHARK ATTACK

Lifeguard Rob Howes, his daughter Niccy, 15, Karina Cooper, 15, and Helen Slade, 16, were swimming 100m out to sea at Ocean Beach in New Zealand when suddenly seven dolphins swam towards them.

'They were behaving really weirdly,' Mr Howes said, 'swimming in circles around us, and hitting the water with their tails.' One dolphin swam towards Mr Howes and Helen, who were about 20m away from the other two, and was trying to push them towards the other two girls.

'Then suddenly I saw another huge fish swimming around me and Helen,' said Mr Howes. It was in fact a three metre-long great white shark.

'It was only about two metres away from us,' he said. At that point, he realised that the dolphins 'were trying to herd the four of us together to protect us'.

The shark then went towards the other two girls. Mr Howes was terrified, especially because one of the swimmers was his daughter.

But the dolphins pushed the four swimmers back together and circled around them for another 40 minutes. Mr Howes decided not to tell the three girls a shark was sharing the water with them.

Fortunately, the shark finally swam away, and the swimmers all reached the beach safely.

'I swim with dolphins perhaps three or four times a year and I have never seen them behave like that,' said Mr Howes. However, dolphin expert Ingrid Visser said that there have been other reports from around the world about dolphins protecting swimmers. She said that, in this case, the dolphins probably sensed the humans were in danger and took action to protect them.

Adapted from a British newspaper

CAN YOU UNDERSTAND THESE PEOPLE?

4 54)) In the street Watch or listen to five people and answer the questions.

David   Joanna   Polly   Sarah Jane   Justin

1 David has had _____ since he was a child.
   a arachnophobia
   b agoraphobia
   c claustrophobia

2 Joanna would like to see leopards in the wild because _____.
   a they have always been her favourite animals
   b she saw them before on a safari and loved them
   c they are one of the wild animals she hasn't seen yet

3 When Polly was at school _____.
   a she didn't have many friends
   b she liked most subjects
   c she didn't like French or maths

4 Sarah Jane has been a teacher _____.
   a since 2006   b for 6 years   c for 16 years

5 Justin loves the Empire State Building because _____.
   a he thinks it's in exactly the right place
   b he loves its height, and the view from the top
   c it's one of the oldest skyscrapers in New York

CAN YOU SAY THIS IN ENGLISH?

Do the tasks with a partner. Tick (✓) the box if you can do them.

Can you…?

1 ☐ say what you would do if…
   a a dog attacked you
   b you won the lottery
   c you had more free time

2 ☐ talk about how long you have…
   a lived where you are now
   b had your laptop or computer
   c been at this school

3 ☐ describe your life story

4 ☐ talk about when three things were invented or built

5 ☐ talk about three things you used to do when you were a child

6 ☐ say three things you might do next week

Short films Marwell Wildlife
Watch and enjoy a film on iTutor.

G expressing movement
V sports, expressing movement
P sports

11A Bad losers

Where did the ball go?

It went over the bar.

1 PRONUNCIATION & SPEAKING sports

a What sports can you see in the photos?

b (4 55)) Look at the sports in the list. How do you pronounce them in English? Listen and check, and underline the stressed syllable. Do you know the names of any other sports in English?

ath|le|tics base|ball ba|sket|ball box|ing cy|cling
foot|ball golf hand|ball ho|ckey mo|tor ra|cing
rug|by ski|ing te|nnis vo|lley|ball wind|sur|fing

> **Verbs with sports**
> 1 We use **play** for sports with a ball, e.g. *I play hockey at school.*
> 2 With sports ending in -ing (cycling, skiing, windsurfing, etc.) we normally use the verb, e.g. *I cycle at weekends*, or **go + sport**, e.g. *I go cycling at weekends.*
> 3 We use **do** for sport and exercise in general, e.g. *I do sport at weekends*, and for martial arts, athletics, yoga, Pilates, etc., e.g. *I do yoga twice a week.*

c Ask and answer with a partner. Give and ask for as much information as you can.

SPORT — YOU LOVE IT OR YOU HATE IT.

- Do you do any sport or exercise?
  ☐ Yes. What? Do you enjoy it?   ☐ No. Why not?
- Did you use to do any other sports or exercise? Why did you stop?
- Which sports do you think are the most exciting to watch?
- Which sports do think are the most boring?
- Are you (or is anyone in your family) a fan of a sports team? Which one?
- Do you (or they) watch their matches?
- What is the most exciting sporting event you have ever seen?

2 VOCABULARY

sports, expressing movement

a Put these words in the correct column. Do you know any other words connected to these sports?

(bunker) corner hole lap match point
penalty serve track

athletics	football	golf	tennis
track lap	Penalty corner	hole bunker	match point serve

b (4 56)) Listen to the sports commentaries. What are the four sports?

c Listen again and complete the sentences with one word. Then match sentences 1–4 with pictures a–d.

1 [b] The ball has gone ~~into~~ the lake.
2 [c] The ball has gone over the bar.
3 [a] Now they have to run ~~around~~ the track one more time.
4 [d] That's a very hard return, but the ball has gone ~~away~~! out

d ▶ p.162 Vocabulary Bank *Expressing movement.*

3 GRAMMAR expressing movement

a Complete the sentences with a verb from the list.

> hit   kick   run   throw

1 In basketball you have to ~~throw~~ the ball **through** a ring with a basket.
2 In football you have to ~~kick~~ the ball **into** a goal.
3 In tennis you have to ~~hit~~ the ball **over** a net.
4 In the 800 metres you have to ~~run~~ twice **round** the track.

b Look at the sentence below. Try to think of three different verbs you could put in the gap, e.g. *walked*.

The man _____ **along** the street until he got to the corner.

c ➤ p.146 Grammar Bank 11A. Learn more about expressing movement and practise it.

d Look at the photos in **1**. Say what the people are doing.

> He's hitting the ball over the net.

4 READING & SPEAKING

a When you play a sport or a game with family or friends, how do you react if you lose? Are you a good or bad loser? Are any of your family or friends bad losers?

b Read the text and answer with a name. Which of the bad losers…?

1 insulted the match official   *John McEnroe*
2 did not want to do his job after the match   *Australian Prime minister*
3 became very emotional when he couldn't take part   *Jon Drummond*
4 tried to hit somebody   *Nelson Piquet*
5 said sorry after the event   *Luciano Gaucci*

c Read the text again and complete the gaps with the prepositions in the list.

> down   in   out   out of (x2)   past

d Look at the highlighted words in the text which are all related to sport. With a partner guess their meaning.

e In pairs answer the questions.

1 Who do you think was the worst loser?
2 Whose behaviour do you think was understandable?
3 Do you know any famous sportspeople who are bad losers?

5 WRITING

a Talk to a partner. Do you think there is too much football on TV? Why (not)?

b ➤ p.117 Writing *An opinion essay*. Read a model essay about football on TV, and then write one.

6 (4 59)) SONG *The Final Countdown* ♫

Bad losers?

The hardest lesson to learn in sport is how to lose with dignity, without blaming your defeat on the referees or refusing to shake hands with your opponent. Here are some famous moments when losing was just too hard…

In 1981 at Wimbledon a young John McEnroe was serving. The umpire said that his serve was ¹ ~~out~~, but McEnroe thought it was ² ~~in~~. He became furious and shouted 'You CANNOT be serious!' at the umpire. He also called the umpire 'an incompetent fool!'

In the 2003 Athletics World Championship the 100 metres runner, Jon Drummond, was disqualified for a false start. Drummond lay ³ ~~down~~ on the track and began to cry. Two hours later his coach told journalists: 'He's still crying. We're making him drink water because he's becoming dehydrated.'

In the 1982 German Grand Prix Nelson Piquet was winning the race. He was trying to pass Eliseo Salazar (who was last in the race), but Salazar didn't let him go ⁴ ~~past~~ him and Piquet crashed into Salazar. Piquet jumped ⁵ ~~out of~~ his car and started trying to hit and kick Salazar (without much success!).

South Korean footballer Ahn Jung-Hwan scored the goal that sent Italy ⁶ ~~out of~~ the 2002 World Cup when they beat them 2–1. But Jung-Hwan also played for the Italian football club Perugia. After the match the president of the club, Luciano Gaucci, announced that the player's contract would not be renewed. 'That gentleman will never set foot in Perugia again,' Gaucci said. 'I have no intention of paying a salary to somebody who has ruined Italian football.' Gaucci later apologized, but Ahn Jung-Hwan left the club and never went back to an Italian club.

When England won the Rugby World Cup in 2003 by beating Australia in the last minute of the match, the Australian Prime minister, John Howard, was so angry that in the medals ceremony he almost threw the medals at the English players. His behaviour was described by a journalist as being 'like an unhappy five-year-old at a birthday party who starts throwing toys around.'

Adapted from a British newspaper

G word order of phrasal verbs
V phrasal verbs
P linking

11B Are you a morning person?

What's the first thing you do when you wake up?

I turn on the radio.

1 SPEAKING & READING

a Answer the questions with a partner.

1 What time do you wake up during the week?
2 Do you use an alarm clock to wake up? If not, what makes you wake up?
3 Do you get up immediately after you wake up?
4 When you first get up do you feel...?
   a awful
   b quite sleepy
   c awake and energetic

b Read an interview with Sara Mohr-Pietsch. Match the questions and answers.

A Do you choose what you wear the night before?
B Do you have anything to eat before you go to work?
C Do you use an alarm clock to wake up?
D How do you feel when you wake up?
E How do you get to work?
F How does this affect your social life?
G ~~What time do you get up when you're doing the Breakfast show?~~
H What time do you go to bed when you're working the next day?
I Would you like to change your working hours?

c Cover the answers and look at the questions. With a partner remember her answers.

d Answer the questions with a partner.

1 Would you like to work the same hours as the radio presenter?
2 In general are you a morning or evening person?

Early bird!

Sara Mohr-Pietsch tells us what it's like to be an early morning presenter on the Breakfast programme on BBC Radio 3.

[1] *What time do you get up when you're doing the Breakfast show?*
I get up at 4.45 a.m. and leave the house at 5.20.

[2]

Yes. I usually set my radio alarm to come on at 4.30 so that I can wake up slowly as I listen to the world news. I set my phone alarm for 4.45 and leave it on the other side of the room so I have to get up to turn it off!

[3]

It depends – some mornings I feel rested and awake, but other mornings it's quite hard to get out of bed. It depends on the season. I find I need much more sleep in the winter.

[4]

If I'm slow to get up, then I wait until I'm in the studio before having breakfast, but most mornings I have a bowl of cereal before I leave the house.

[5]

That depends on the season too. In the summer I usually wait until the morning to decide. But in the winter I often leave clothes out the night before so that I can stay in bed until the last minute!

[6]

A car picks me up at 5.20.

[7]

In the winter, any time between 8.30 and 9.30 p.m. In the summer, usually more like 9.00 to 10.00 p.m.

[8]

What social life? I certainly can't go out for a wild night during the week, but I'm lucky because a lot of my closest friends live near me, so I can see them in the evenings and still go to bed quite early.

[9]

Sometimes I think I would like to have more normal working hours, but I love my job so much that I'd never want to give it up. The buzz of being 'live' on the radio early in the morning as people start their days is really wonderful.

PURE   Siesta mi   0430

2 VOCABULARY phrasal verbs

a Look at some sentences from the interview. With a partner say what the highlighted phrases mean.

> 'I leave it on the other side of the room so I have to get up to turn it off!'
>
> 'A car picks me up at 5.20.'
>
> 'I love my job so much that I'd never want to give it up.'

🔍 **Phrasal verbs**
Wake up, get up, turn on / off, give up, etc. are common phrasal verbs (verbs with a preposition or adverb).
Sometimes the meaning of the two separate words can help you guess the meaning of the phrasal verb, e.g. *turn off*. Sometimes the meaning of the two words does not help you, e.g. *give up*.

b Read the information box. Can you think of a phrasal verb which means…?

1 to try to find something you have lost
2 to put on clothes in a shop to see if they are the right size
3 to have a friendly relationship (with somebody)

c ▶ **p.163 Vocabulary Bank** *Phrasal verbs.*

3 GRAMMAR word order of phrasal verbs

a Look at the picture and underline the **object** of the phrasal verb in each sentence.

1 Turn off the alarm clock!
2 **Turn the alarm clock off!**
3 **Turn it off!**

b Complete the rules about separable phrasal verbs with *noun* or *pronoun*.

1 If the object of a phrasal verb is a _____, you can put it **after** the verb + *up, on*, etc. **OR between** the verb and *up, on*, etc.
2 If the object of a phrasal verb is a _____, you <u>must</u> put it **between** the verb and *up, on*, etc.

c ▶ **p.146 Grammar Bank 11B.** Learn more about the word order of phrasal verbs and practise it.

4 PRONUNCIATION linking

a **5 4))** Listen and write the missing words.

1 There's a wet towel on the floor. Please ____ ____ ____.
2 I can't concentrate with that music on. Please ____ ____ ____.
3 If you don't know what the word means, ____ ____ ____.
4 Why have you taken your coat off? ____ ____ ____!
5 This book was very expensive. Please ____ ____ ____.
6 Why are you wearing your coat in here? ____ ____ ____!

b Practise saying the sentences. Try to link the phrasal verbs and pronouns, e.g. pick‿it‿up.

5 SPEAKING

a Read the questions in the questionnaire and think about your answers.

b Work in pairs. Interview your partner with the questions.

PHRASAL VERB QUESTIONNAIRE

- Have you ever forgotten to **turn** your mobile phone **off** in a concert or the cinema?
- Do you **throw away** old clothes or do you give them to other people?
- Do you enjoy **trying on** clothes when you go shopping?
- Do you often **go away** at the weekend? Where to?
- Before you go shopping do you usually **write down** what you have to buy? Do you only buy what's on the list?
- Do you enjoy **looking after** small children? Why (not)?
- Have you ever asked your neighbours to **turn** the TV or the music **down**? What happened?
- What's the first thing you **turn on** after you **wake up** in the morning?

G *so, neither* + auxiliaries
V similarities
P sentence stress, /ð/ and /θ/

I have a son called James.

So do I.

11C What a coincidence!

'I'm Jim.'

'So am I.'

In the USA, identical twin brothers were adopted soon after they were born. One brother was adopted by a couple named Lewis in Lima, Ohio, and his brother was adopted by a couple named Springer in Dayton, Ohio. By coincidence, both boys were called 'Jim' by their new parents. When Jim Lewis was six years old, he discovered that he had an identical twin brother. When he was thirty-nine, he decided to find and contact his brother. Six weeks later, he met Jim Springer in a café in Dayton, and they probably had a conversation something like this...

1 GRAMMAR *so, neither* + auxiliaries

a Look at the photos and describe the two men.

b Read about the two men and answer the questions.
1 Who are Jim Springer and Jim Lewis? *Identical twin broth*
2 Why didn't they know each other? *Because they were adopted by different*
3 What did Jim Lewis decide to do when he was 39? *to find his brother*
4 How long did it take him? *six weeks*

c (5 5)) Cover the dialogue. Listen once. Try to remember three things they have in common.

d Listen again and complete the gaps.

> **A** Hi! I'm Jim.
> **B** So *am* I. Great to meet you. Sit down. Are you married, Jim? *Positive*
> **A** Yes... well, I've been married twice. *the "have" is auxiliary*
> B Yeah? So ² *have* I. Do you have any children?
> **A** I have one son.
> **B** So ³ *do* I. What's his name? *Present tense do → auxiliary for present tense here*
> **A** James Allen.
> **B** That's amazing! My son's name is James Allen too!
> **A** Did you go to college, Jim?
> **B** No, I didn't. *Past tense*
> **A** Neither ⁴ *did* I. I was a terrible student.
> **B** So ⁵ *was* I. Hey, this is my dog Toy. *Negative*
> **A** I don't believe it! My dog's called Toy too!
> **B** He wants to go outside. My wife usually takes him. I don't do any exercise at all.
> **A** Don't worry. Neither ⁶ *do* I. I drive everywhere.
> **B** What car do you have?
> **A** A Chevrolet.
> **B** So ⁷ *do I* I!
> **A+B** Let's have a beer, Jim.
> **A** What beer do you drink?
> **B** Miller Lite.
> **A** So ⁸ *do I* I!

e Which coincidence do you think is the most surprising?

f Look at the dialogue again. Answer the questions with a partner.
1 Find two phrases that the twins use...
   when they have something ⊞ in common.
   when they have something ⊟ in common.
2 Why do you think the auxiliary verb changes?

g ➤ p.146 Grammar Bank 11C. Learn more about *so*, *neither*, etc. and practise them.

2 PRONUNCIATION sentence stress, /ð/ and /θ/

a (5 7)) Listen and repeat the words and sounds.

🧑	mother	brother neither they
👍	thumb	both thirty throw

b (5 8)) Add four words to each row. Listen and check.

although maths other there thing thirsty through without

c (5 9)) Listen and repeat the dialogues. <u>Underline</u> the stressed words.

1 **A** I like <u>tea</u>. **B** So do I. 3 **A** I don't smoke. **B** Neither do I.
2 **A** I'm <u>tired</u>. **B** So am I. 4 **A** I'm not hungry. **B** Neither am I.

d (5 10)) Listen and respond. Say you're the same.

)) *I catch the bus to work.* *So do I.*

3 SPEAKING

a Complete the sentences so they are true for you.

Me	Who else in the class?
I love Vallect . (a kind of music)	
I don't like Cachate . (a drink)	
I'm very Sociable . (adjective of personality)	Johanna
I'm not very good at Volleyball . (sport or activity)	Patty
I'm going to best after class. (an activity)	Sandra
I have to work every day. (an obligation)	Johanna
I don't eat cabby . (a kind of food)	Monica

b Move around the class saying your sentences. For each sentence try to find someone like you, and write down their name. Respond to other people's sentences. Say *So do | am I,* or *Neither do | am I* if you have something in common.

A *I love heavy metal.* **B** *Really? I hate it!* **C** *So do I.*

4 VOCABULARY similarities

a Read about some more similarities between the two Jims. Complete the text with a word from the list.

<del>as</del> both identical like <del>neither</del> <del>similar</del> <del>so</del>

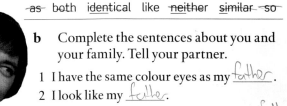

b Complete the sentences about you and your family. Tell your partner.

1 I have the same colour eyes as my father .
2 I look like my father .
3 My personality is quite similar to my father 's.
4 My cousin and I both like Reel Madid .
5 I like Paskall and so does my brother . nephew
6 I don't like cabby and neither does my

5 LISTENING

Facebook coincidence brings couple together

a (5 11)) Look at the photo of a couple and listen to a news story about them. What is the coincidence?

b Listen again and answer the questions.

1 Why did Kelly Hildebrandt put her name into Facebook? she was bored
2 What did she discover? A man have her same name
3 What did she do next? write him
4 What other things do they have in common? both working
5 Why were they worried? have the same
6 What do they call each other? called boy, willie
7 What problem did they once have? booking flight
8 What are they definitely *not* going to do? Cable Call son.

c Have you ever put your name into Google or Facebook? Did you discover anything interesting?

Same → els
look → like
Similar → to
→ both

apparience
aparência física

some need
"en" proposition

s schoolboys, the two Jims looked exactly
¹ alike each other. They ² both liked
maths and carpentry – but hated spelling.
After school they had ³ similar jobs: Lewis was
a security guard and Springer was a deputy
sheriff. Jim Lewis first married a woman
called Linda, and then a woman called
Betty, (exactly the same names ⁴ as
Jim Springer's first and second wives.
Even their tastes in sport are ⁵ identical –
Jim Springer likes baseball and ⁶ so
does Jim Lewis. Jim Lewis doesn't like basketball
and ⁷ neither does Jim Springer.

1 ◼ ROB AND JENNY TALK ABOUT THE FUTURE

a (5 12)) Watch or listen to Rob and Jenny. Mark the sentences **T** (true) or **F** (false).

F 1 Rob is going home today.

F 2 He says it will be difficult to stay in touch.

T 3 Jenny suggests that she could go to London.

F 4 Rob thinks it's a good idea.

T 5 They're going to a restaurant tonight.

F 6 Barbara wants to talk to Jenny.

> 🔍 **British and American English**
> *You just missed him* = American English;
> *You've just missed him* = British English
> *cell (phone)* = American English;
> *mobile (phone)* = British English

b Watch or listen again. Say why the **F** sentences are false.

2 ◼ ON THE PHONE

a (5 13)) Cover the dialogue and watch or listen. Answer the questions.

Barbara

1 Who does Rob want to speak to?

2 How many times does he have to call?

90

b Watch or listen again. Complete the **You Hear** phrases.

))) You Hear	You Say 💬	
Hello. *Broadway Grill*.	Oh, sorry. I have the wrong number.	①
NewYork24seven. <u>How</u> can I help you?	Hello. Can I speak to Barbara Keaton, please?	②
Just a second. I'll put you <u>thuyl</u>. ... Hello.	Hi, is that Barbara?	
No, I'm sorry. She's not at her <u>desk</u> right now.	Can I leave a message, please?	
Sure.	Can you tell her Rob Walker called? I'll call back later.	
I'll give her the <u>message</u>. You could try her cell phone.	Yes, I'll do that. Thank you.	
I'm sorry, I can't take your <u>call</u> at the moment. Please <u>leave</u> a message after the beep.	Hello, Barbara. This is Rob returning your call.	⑧
NewYork24seven. How can I help you?	Hello. It's Rob again. Can I speak to Barbara, please?	④
Just a second. I'm sorry, the line's <u>busy</u>. Do you want to hold?	OK, I'll hold.	
Hello.	Hi, Barbara. It's me, Rob.	
Rob, hi! I tried to call you earlier.	What did you want to talk about?	

c (5 14))) Watch or listen and repeat the **You Say** phrases. <u>Copy</u> the <u>rhy</u>thm.

d Practise the dialogues with a partner.

e 👥 In pairs, roleplay the dialogue.

   A (book open) You are the Broadway Grill, the receptionist, etc. You start *Hello. Broadway Grill.*
   B (book closed) You want to speak to Barbara.

f Swap roles.

3 ◼ IN CENTRAL PARK AGAIN

a (5 15))) Watch or listen to Rob and Jenny. Is it a happy ending or a sad ending?

b Watch or listen again and answer the questions.
   1 Who has some news? both
   2 What did Barbara offer Rob? A job
   3 What did Jenny do this morning? Design
   4 What does Jenny ask Barbara to do? Delete her e-...

c Look at the **Social English** phrases. Can you remember any of the missing words?

> **Social English phrases**
> **Rob** You <u>go</u> first.
> **Jenny** That's great <u>news</u>.
> **Jenny** I'll <u>call</u> her.
> **Jenny** I'll explain <u>later</u>.
> **Barbara** Is everything <u>alright</u>?
> **Jenny** <u>Now</u> better.

d (5 16))) Watch or listen and complete the phrases.

e Watch or listen again and repeat the phrases. How do you say them in your language?

> 👤 Can you...?
> ☐ phone somebody and say who you are / who you want to talk to
> ☐ leave a message for somebody
> ☐ respond to news

G past perfect
V verb phrases
P contractions: *had / hadn't*

Why did the people shout? Because a shark had come into the pool.

12A Strange but true!

NEWS ROUND THE WORLD   NEWS ROUND THE WORLD   NE

Here is our selection of last week's true stories

AUSTRALIA

In Sydney, early in the morning, some swimmers were having a swim in an outdoor swimming pool which was very close to the sea. The swimmers were very surprised when suddenly the pool assistants started shouting 'Get out of the water! Quickly!' The swimmers immediately got out. Then they realized that there was a shark at the other end! _____ Fortunately none of the swimmers were hurt and the shark was caught in a net and put back into the sea.

ENGLAND

Security guards at Stansted airport were amazed when they saw a dog getting off a train and walking on its own towards the airport terminal. They caught the dog and took it to the police. Thanks to a microchip in its neck, they discovered that its name was Diesel and that it belonged to a woman called Sarah Chapman, who lived in London, 50 kilometres away. Sarah had gone on holiday for a few days and had left Diesel with some friends. _____ It had then got on a train and had travelled 50 kilometres to Stansted airport, changing trains on the way. Sarah said: 'I'm sure Diesel went to the airport to look for me!'

1 READING & SPEAKING

a Read the stories and look at the pictures. Complete the gaps with one of the sentences below.

AUSTRALIA
1 The shark had already attacked three people.
2 A large wave had carried the shark into the pool during the night.

ENGLAND
3 Unfortunately, the dog had bitten one of her friends.
4 The dog had run away and had gone to the local railway station.

ITALY
5 He had decided that he couldn't live with his mother and father for another day.
6 He had robbed a bank the night before.

SWEDEN
7 The woman had got confused at the check-in desk.
8 The woman had left her passport at home.

b Match verbs 1–10 with phrases A–J.

1 [H] get into / out of   A on the belt
2 [B] get on / off   B a swim
3 [E] free somebody   C holiday
4 [J] realize   D in prison
5 [A] put the luggage   E from prison
6 [F] go on   F a train
7 [C] have   G a woman
8 [I] leave the dog   H the swimming pool
9 [D] be   I with friends
10 [G] belong to   J that there was a shark in the pool

92

ITALY

An Italian man who was in prison for stealing was freed early from prison on the condition that he promised to live with his parents at their house. But after a week he arrived at his local police station and said 'Please arrest me again!'

Guido Beneventi, 30, told the police: 'My parents spent all their time telling me to do housework. It was like being a child again!'

SWEDEN

Airport workers in the luggage area at Arlanda airport in Sweden were surprised to see an old lady sitting on the luggage belt next to her suitcase.   She had put her luggage on the belt and then had sat down on the belt herself. A spokesman at Stockholm's Arlanda airport said 'Unfortunately, she did not understand when she was given check-in instructions. She got on the belt together with her bag. Luckily, it wasn't a long ride – only a few metres.'

2 GRAMMAR past perfect

a   Look at these highlighted verbs from the Australia story. Answer the questions.

> **A**   Then they realized that there was a shark at the other end!
>
> **B**   A large wave had carried the shark into the pool during the night.

1   Which action happened first, **A** or **B**?
2   What are the two parts of the verb in sentence **B**?

b   Look at the other three stories again (including the missing sentences) and underline examples of *had* + past participle. Did these actions happen before or after the main part of the story?

c   ➤ **p.148 Grammar Bank 12A.** Learn more about the past perfect and practise it.

d   Complete the following sentences in your own words. Use the past perfect.

1   When I got to the check-in desk I suddenly realized that…
2   When we arrived back from our holiday we found that…
3   When the film started I realized immediately that…
4   I couldn't answer any of the exam questions because I…
5   We spent 20 minutes in the car park looking for the car because we couldn't remember…

e   Compare with a partner. Are your sentences the same or different?

f   Work with a partner. **A** re-read the story about Australia, **B** re-read the story about Italy. Underline the key words and events. Then **A** (books closed) re-tell the story in your own words. **B** (books open) help **A** when necessary. Then swap.

3 PRONUNCIATION
contractions: *had / hadn't*

> 🔍 **Contractions: past perfect**
> In conversation we often contract *had* in the past perfect after a subject pronoun (*I, you,* etc.), e.g.
>
> *When I got to the airport I realized that **I'd** forgotten my passport.*
>
> *I suddenly remembered that we **hadn't** told Sue about the party.*

a   **5 18**)) Listen and write six past perfect sentences. Then practise saying the sentences.

b   ➤ **Communication** *What had happened?* **A** *p.104* **B** *p.109.* Try to guess your partner's sentences.

4 LISTENING

a   **5 19**)) Listen to another news story. Then number the events in order.

☐ Joey attacked her.
☐ Joey sat on her plate.
☐ Joey went to sleep.
☐ Katie came home from work.
☐ Katie met her neighbour.

b   With a partner, try to guess what you think had happened.

c   **5 20**)) Now listen and find out what had happened. Had anybody guessed right?

G reported speech
V *say* or *tell*?
P double consonants

She told him she was leaving.

He said that he would write.

12B Gossip is good for you

1 SPEAKING & LISTENING

a Read the dictionary definition and then answer the questions with a partner.

> gossip /ˈɡɒsɪp/ *(v and n)* to talk about other people, especially their private life

1 What kind of people gossip more?
  a people in cities or people in small towns
  b young people or old people
  c men or women

2 Who do people most often gossip about?
  a their neighbours
  b people at work or school
  c celebrities

3 Do you have any friends who gossip a lot?

4 How do you feel when people gossip about *you*?

b (5 21))) Listen to a conversation between Rosemary and Iris. What has happened to Jack and Emma? Listen again and answer the questions.

1 Jack and Emma are the woman's…
  a neighbours. b friends. c children.
2 Rosemary thinks she heard them having…
  a a conversation.
  b a party.
  c an argument.
3 According to Rosemary, Emma said she was…
  a seeing another man.
  b looking for a new job. (T)
  c going to stay with her mother.
4 She said she had…
  a left the dog with a neighbour.
  b left the children with her sister. (T)
  c left the dinner in the microwave.
5 Iris is going to…
  a tell her husband.
  b tell her family.
  c tell another neighbour.

c (5 22))) Now listen to what Jack and Emma *really* said last night. Was Rosemary right about everything?

2 GRAMMAR reported speech

a Look at some extracts from the conversations. Compare what Emma said (direct speech) with what Rosemary says that she said (reported speech). Underline the words which are different in the highlighted reported speech.

1 **What Emma said**
  I'm going to stay with my mum.
  I won't come back…
  I've taken the children to my sister…

2 **What Rosemary and Iris said**
  She said that she was going to stay with her mum! She told him that she wouldn't come back.
  Ooh, how awful. What about the children?
  She said she'd taken them to her sister.

b ➤ p.148 Grammar Bank 12B. Learn more about reported speech and practise it.

c (5 24))) Listen to some sentences in direct speech. Say them in reported speech. Begin *He said…* or *She said…*

))) I'm in a hurry. (She said that she was in a hurry.

))) I'll write. (He said that he would write.

3 VOCABULARY say or tell?

Complete the sentences with the right form of *say* or *tell*.

1 'I have a problem,' Annie _said_
2 Annie _told_ us that she had a problem.
3 Lisa _said_ that she was leaving her husband.
4 He _told_ the teacher that he had left his homework at home.
5 His teacher _said_ that he didn't believe him.
6 Can you _tell_ Mark that I can't meet him tonight?
7 What did you _say_ to her?
8 When I was a child my mother used to _tell_ us not to _say_ hello to people we didn't know.

4 SPEAKING

a Work in pairs. **A** tell your partner the following. **B** Listen and take notes. Then swap roles.

- something about your parents or grandparents
- a place you have been to
- something that you're planning to do in the summer
- something that you did last weekend

The information can be true or invented, but it must be interesting!

b Change partners. Tell partner 2 what partner 1 said. Decide together whether you think your previous partners were telling the truth or had invented the information.

He told me (that)...   *He said (that)...*

5 PRONUNCIATION double consonants

a Look at five groups of words. Match each group to a vowel sound.

1 ☐   2 ☐   3 ☐   4 ☐   5 ☐

a	gossip	offer	sorry	bottle	robber
b	hurry	rubbish	runner	summer	butterfly
c	written	miss	bitten	different	middle
d	happy	married	nappies	rabbit	baggage
e	letter	better	message	umbrella	tennis

b **5 25))** Listen and check.

> 🔍 **Double consonants**
> The vowel sound before a double consonant is normally short when it is the stressed syllable, e.g. *gossip* /ɒ/, *hurry* /ʌ/, *written* /ɪ/, *happy* /æ/, and *letter* /e/.
> Double consonants are pronounced the same as single consonants.

c How do you think you pronounce the words below? Check the pronunciation and meaning with your dictionary.

kettle   nanny   pottery   slippers   supper

6 READING

HERE'S A SECRET:
Gossip might be good for you

We all enjoy gossiping about people we know, although sometimes we might feel guilty about it afterwards. However, new research shows that gossiping might be good for us.

Professor McAndrew, a professor of psychology, believes that gossiping is in our genes and we feel pleasure when we share interesting information. McAndrew says that gossiping is a social skill, and we need to learn to do it well. According to the professor, gossip can be a positive thing when people use it to build connections with other people in their social group. But it can be a negative thing when somebody gossips about another person only to make themselves feel more important in the group.

Professor McAndrew's research also showed that people were happy to pass on good news but only if it was about a friend. They also enjoyed passing on negative information about other people when it was about somebody they disliked.

Another thing that the new study showed was that men and women gossip differently. In general, the men in the study shared gossip with their wives or girlfriends, but not with their male friends. Women however, gossiped with both partners and friends.

Adapted from a British newspaper

a Read the article and mark the sentences **T** (true) or **F** (false).

1 We sometimes feel bad after we gossip. T
2 Professor McAndrew says that we are programmed to gossip. T
3 Gossiping can be good or bad – it depends on why we do it. T
4 People enjoy sharing bad news about people they like. F
5 Men gossip with their friends more than with their family. F

b Look at the highlighted words and phrases. With a partner, guess their meaning.

c Do you agree with what the article says about the way men and women gossip?
Yes.

7 **5 26))** SONG

I Heard It Through the Grapevine ♫

Who painted that picture?

I can't remember.

12C The *English File* quiz

1 GRAMMAR questions without auxiliaries

a With a partner, see how many of the quiz questions you can answer from memory.

b Now try to find the answers you couldn't remember in Files 1–11.

c Look at 1 and 2 in the quiz. Answer these questions.

1 How is question 1 different from question 2?
2 What is the subject of the verb in question 1?
3 What is the subject of the verb in question 2?
4 Which other questions in the quiz are similar grammatically to question 1?

d ➤ p.148 Grammar Bank 12C. Learn more about questions without auxiliaries and practise them.

The
ENGLISH FILE QUIZ

1 Who painted *Mr and Mrs Clark and Percy*?
2 How did Caroline de Bendern lose a fortune?
3 Which airport in Asia has a pet hotel?
4 What does *toy boy* mean?
5 Whose wedding dress did Lindka Cierach design?
6 What vitamin does sunlight produce?
7 Who plays Dr House in the series *House M.D.*?
8 What did Captain Edward Murphy give his name to?
9 How many natural disasters did Mr and Mrs Svanström experience on their round-the-world trip?
10 Who wrote the short story *Girl*?
11 Which singer made reggae popular all over the world?
12 Who invented the dishwasher, a man or a woman?
13 Who never arrived at school on time when he was a child?
14 Who shouted 'You CANNOT be serious!' at a tennis umpire at Wimbledon?
15 What is Kelly Hildebrandt's husband called?

2 WRITING & SPEAKING

a ➤ **Communication** *General knowledge quiz* **A** *p.105* **B** *p.110*. First write the questions. Then ask them to your partner.

b With a partner, make your own quiz. Write two questions with or without auxiliaries for each category. Make sure you know the answers!

c Ask your questions to another pair.

HISTORY

MUSIC

SCIENCE

ART

CINEMA

GRAMMAR

Circle a, b, or c.

1 The golf ball _____ the hole, and everybody cheered.
   a went on   b went   c went into

2 The door opened and two men _____.
   a came out   b came out of   c out

3 Your towel's on the floor. _____!
   a Pick up it   b Pick up   c Pick it up

4 I've lost my keys. Can you help me _____?
   a look them for
   b look for them
   c look after them

5 A I love travelling.   B _____.
   a So do I   b Neither do I   c So am I

6 A I can't do this exercise.   B _____.
   a So can I
   b Neither can't I
   c Neither can I

7 A I went to the cinema last night.
   B _____. What did you see?
   a So went I   b So I did   c So did I

8 I was too late and when I got to the station _____.
   a the train has left
   b the train had left
   c the train left

9 When we got to the airport we remembered that we _____ all the windows in our house.
   a hadn't closed
   b didn't close
   c haven't closed

10 Lisa told me that she _____ to marry Nigel.
   a wants   b want   c wanted

11 Kevin said he _____ back in ten minutes.
   a would be   b was   c will be

12 My grandfather _____ that he had worked in a factory when he was young.
   a said us   b told   c told us

13 Who _____ in the house next door?
   a lives   b live   c does live

14 Where _____ that dress?
   a you bought   b bought you   c did you buy

15 How many people _____ to go on the excursion?
   a do want   b does want   c want

VOCABULARY

a   Complete with a word from the list.

along   down   into   off   out   back   past   towards   through   up

1 We drove _____ a lot of tunnels on our way to St Moritz.
2 When it started to rain we went _____ a café to wait until it stopped.
3 She walked _____ the street, looking in all the shop windows.
4 When the dog started running _____ me I was terrified.
5 Go _____ the petrol station, and it's the next turning on the right.
6 You have to take _____ your shoes before going into the temple.
7 If you don't know the meaning of a word, look it _____ in the online dictionary.
8 Can you turn _____ the heating? It's very hot in here.
9 If you don't like the jacket, take it _____ to the shop.
10 Can you find _____ what time the film finishes?

b   Complete the missing words.

1 Julia and Jane are i_____ twins.
2 I live in the same street a_____ my sister.
3 Her new novel is quite s_____ to her last one.
4 Dave isn't very tall and n_____ is his son.
5 My parents b_____ love classical music.

c   Complete the phrases with a verb from the list.

do   get   give   go   have   leave   look   put   tell   turn

1 _____ skiing   6 _____ up the music
2 _____ on your coat   7 _____ a swim
3 _____ me a story   8 _____ off the train
4 _____ forward to sth   9 _____ up smoking
5 _____ your dog with friends   10 _____ karate

PRONUNCIATION

a   Circle the word with a different sound.

1 [↑] hurry   rugby   summer   put
2 [🐟] find   written   middle   fill
3 [aʊ] around   down   through   out
4 [θ] neither   throw   nothing   both
5 [ð?] gossip   together   message   negative

b   Underline the stressed syllable.

1 ath|le|tics 2 to|wards 3 for|ward 4 si|mi|lar 5 di|fferent

CAN YOU UNDERSTAND THIS TEXT?

a Read the article once. What was the amazing coincidence?

b Read the article again and number the events in the order they happened

- [ ] Their daughter was born.
- [ ] They both had a heart operation in the same hospital.
- [ ] Alistair had another heart operation.
- [ ] They got married.
- [ ] They discovered that they had been in the same hospital twenty years earlier.
- [ ] They discovered they had the same heart problem.
- [ ] They met at a swimming pool.
- [ ] Alistair asked Alison to marry him.

c Look at the highlighted words or phrases in the text. Guess their meaning from the context. Check with your teacher or with a dictionary.

Heart couple's amazing coincidence

When Suzanne met Alistair Cotton at a swimming pool in the UK in 1995, they were amazed to discover that they both suffered from the same extremely rare heart condition. They started going out together and fell in love, but several months later they discovered an even bigger coincidence.

Almost twenty years earlier when they were children (Suzanne was seven and Alistair was fourteen) they had both had a life-saving heart operation in the same hospital, on the same day performed by the same heart surgeon. After their operations, they had spent several days recovering in the same hospital ward (although they have no memories of seeing or speaking to each other.) They certainly had no idea that twenty years later they would meet and fall in love with the child in the next bed. Suzanne, now 43, said, 'We were very shocked by the coincidence. We were obviously destined to be together.'

After Alistair and Suzanne moved in together Alistair continued to have difficulties with his heart and he had to have another major heart operation. As soon as he woke up after the operation, he proposed to Suzanne and the couple got married in 2002.

The following year, Suzanne became pregnant and baby Hannah was born in 2004 and is now a happy, healthy child who shows no signs of having inherited any heart problems from her parents. Suzanne said, 'Many heart patients can't have children or their children are born with heart problems themselves, so for our amazing story to have such a happy ending is just wonderful.'

Adapted from a British newspaper

CAN YOU UNDERSTAND THESE PEOPLE?

5 28)) **In the street** Watch or listen to five people and answer the questions.

Nick   Ruth   Hew   Andy   Alison

1 The twins that Nick knows __a__.
  a have very similar personalities
  b are very similar in appearance
  c have the same appearance and personality

2 Ruth doesn't mind losing when __a__.
  a the person who wins is better than she is
  b she has really enjoyed the game
  c she thinks she hasn't played very well

3 The sport Hew doesn't mention is __c__.
  a cycling   b hockey   c rugby

4 Andy __a__.
  a was an evening person in the past
  b was a morning person in the past (*present*)
  c has never been good in the morning

5 Alison thinks that __c__.
  a women gossip more than men
  b men gossip more than women
  c men and women both gossip

CAN YOU SAY THIS IN ENGLISH?

Do the tasks with a partner. Tick (✔) the box if you can do them.

Can you...?

1 [ ] describe three things that you have to do in certain sports using a verb and a preposition of movement

2 [ ] make true sentences with *take off*, *turn down*, and *look after*

3 [ ] say true things about you – your partner responds with *so (am I*, etc.) and *neither (do I*, etc.)

4 [ ] continue these sentences with the past perfect:
  a I got to the station, but…
  b When I saw him I was surprised because…

5 [ ] report two things that somebody said to you yesterday using *said* or *told me*

6 [ ] ask your partner three questions without an auxiliary verb beginning with *Who*, *How many*, and *Which*

> **Short films** Sports in New Zealand
> Watch and enjoy a film on iTutor.

This page was intentionally left blank.

Communication

7A HOW TO... Student A

a Read the article **How to survive at a party**. Then without looking at the text tell **B** the five tips. When you finish decide with **B** which is the most important tip.

How to ... Survive at a Party
(when you don't know anybody)

1 Don't stand in the corner. You need to be positive. Find somebody you think you would like to talk to and introduce yourself.

2 Try to ask impersonal questions like 'I love your bag. Where did you get it?' This will help to start a conversation.

3 Don't dominate the conversation. When you are nervous it's very easy to talk about yourself all the time. Nobody wants to listen to your life story when they have just met you for the first time.

4 Smile! Use your body language to give a positive, friendly impression.

5 If you need to escape from a really boring person, say that you are going to the bar to get a drink or that you need to go to the bathroom. Don't come back!

b **B** will tell you five tips for **How to survive a first date**. Listen and when he or she finishes decide together which is the most important tip.

8A WHAT SHOULD I DO? Student A

a Read problem 1 to **B**. He / she will give you some advice.

Problems
1 I don't know what to get my boyfriend / girlfriend for his / her birthday. It's tomorrow!
2 I have problems going to sleep at night.
3 My children want a dog, but my husband / wife is allergic to animals.
4 My neighbour's dog barks all the time and it's driving me crazy!
5 My laptop isn't working well – it's very slow.

b Thank **B** and say:

That's a good idea.
OR Thanks, but that's not a very good idea because…

c Now listen to **B**'s problem 1. Give him / her advice. Begin with one of the phrases below.

I think you should…   You shouldn't…   I don't think you should…

d Continue with problems 2–5.

8C READING DIALOGUE
Students A+B

a Work with a partner. First practise saying the names.

Hartley /ˈhɑːtli/
the Montgomerys /mɒnˈɡʌmeriːz/
Vivienne /ˈvɪvien/
Héloise /eluːˈiːz/

b Act out the dialogue. Use the adverbs in brackets to help you, and remember to pause at the commas.

H (anxiously) Vivienne, you didn't answer my last letter. It took me a week to find your new address! Why didn't you answer me? You knew I was waiting to see you and hear from you.

V (slowly) Mr. Hartley, I don't know what to say to you. I understand all the advantages of your offer, and sometimes I feel sure that I could be happy with you. But then sometimes I am less sure. I was born a city girl, and I am not sure that I would enjoy living a quiet life in the suburbs.

H My dear girl, you will have everything that you want. You can come to the city for the theatre, for shopping, and to visit your friends as often as you want. You can trust me, can't you?

V (seriously) I trust you completely. I know you are the kindest of men, and that the girl who you get will be very lucky. I heard all about you when I was at the Montgomerys'.

H Ah! I remember so well the evening I first saw you at the Montgomerys'. I will never forget that dinner. Come on, Vivienne, promise me. I want you. Nobody else will ever give you such a happy home.
(suspiciously) Tell me, Vivienne, is there – is there someone else?

V (defensively) You shouldn't ask that, Mr. Hartley. But I will tell you. There is one other person – but I haven't promised him anything.

H (masterfully) Vivienne, you must be mine.

V (calmly) Do you think for one moment that I could come to your home while Héloise is there?

c Change roles.

Communication

9A WOULD YOU KNOW WHAT TO DO? Student A

a   Read the answers to **In the city**.

b   Tell **B** and **C** the right answers, and why the other ones are wrong.

c   Listen to **B** and **C** tell you about the other sections (**In the country** and **In the water**). Check your answers.

> ### In the city
>
> 1   The answer is b. Dogs like to attack any part of you that is moving, usually hands or arms. It is also dangerous to turn your back on the dog. You shouldn't look the dog in its eyes because this will make him angry. Shouting 'down' or 'go away' at the dog will not work because dogs usually only react to their master's voice.
>
> 2   The answer is a. Bees will usually fly out of an open window, but don't wave your hands around as bees follow movement and might try to sting you. And you mustn't hit the bee as this will make the bee very angry. Of course, as soon as you can you should stop the car and open the doors.

12A WHAT HAD HAPPENED? Student A

a   Look at the odd numbered sentences (1, 3, 5, 7, 9, and 11) and think of the missing verb (⊞ = positive verb, ⊟ = negative verb). Don't write anything yet!

1   Diana was very angry because her husband _____ the dinner. ⊟

2   We went back to see the house where we **had lived** when we were children.

3   He couldn't catch the plane because he _____ his passport. ⊞

4   The flat was very dirty because nobody **had cleaned** it for a long time.

5   We went back to the hotel where we _____ on our honeymoon. ⊞

6   The crocodile was hungry because it **hadn't eaten** anything for two days.

7   After I left the shop I suddenly remembered that I _____ for the jacket. ⊟

8   I ran to the station, but the last train **had gone.**

9   Miriam was surprised to hear that she _____ the exam. ⊞

10   I didn't want to lend Jane the book because I **hadn't read** it.

11   Jack was angry because I _____ him to my party. ⊟

12   They got to the cinema late and the film **had started**.

b   Read sentence 1 to **B**. If it's not right, try again until **B** tells you 'That's right'. Then write in the verb.

c   Listen to **B** say sentence 2. If it's the same as 2 above, say 'That's right'. If not, say 'Try again' until **B** gets it right.

d   Take it in turns with sentences 3–12.

10A PASSIVES QUIZ Student A

a Complete your sentences with the verb in the passive and the right answer.

1 Until 1664 New York _____ (call)…
   a New Amsterdam
   b New Hampshire
   c New Liberty
2 The *Star Wars* films _____ (direct) by…
   a George Lucas
   b Steven Spielberg
   c Stanley Kubrick
3 The noun which _____ (use) most frequently in conversation is…
   a money   b time   c work
4 Penguins _____ (find)…
   a at the South Pole
   b at the North Pole
   c in Alaska
5 The Italian flag _____ (design) by…
   a Garibaldi   b Mussolini   c Napoleon
6 The first mobile phones _____ (sell) in…
   a 1963   b 1973   c 1983
7 The politician Winston Churchill _____ (born)…
   a on a train   b in a toilet   c under a bridge
8 The electric chair _____ (invent) by…
   a a teacher   b a dentist   c a politician

b Read your sentences to **B**. **B** will tell you if you are right.

c Now listen to **B**'s sentences. Say if he / she is right.

B's answers
1 The Smartphone was invented by IBM.
2 The *Lord of the Rings* films were directed by Peter Jackson.
3 The book which is stolen most often from libraries is *The Guinness Book of Records*.
4 In the world, 16,000 babies are born every hour.
5 Chess was invented by the Chinese.
6 The first Levi jeans were worn by miners.
7 Football was first played by the British.
8 In 1962 the original London Bridge was bought by a rich American.

12C GENERAL KNOWLEDGE QUIZ Student A

a Complete your questions with the verb in brackets in the past simple.

1 Who _____ the battle of Waterloo in 1815? (lose)
   a Duke of Wellington
   b Bismarck
   c **Napoleon**
2 Which Spanish actress _____ an Oscar in 2006? (win)
   a **Penelope Cruz**
   b Salma Hayek
   c Cameron Diaz
3 Who _____ the film *Avatar*? (direct)
   a Steven Spielberg
   b **James Cameron**
   c Ridley Scott
4 Which Formula 1 driver _____ in 2007, but returned to racing in 2010? (retire)
   a Fernando Alonso
   b **Michael Schumacher**
   c Sebastian Vettel
5 Which Roman Emperor _____ 'I came I saw I conquered'? (say)
   a Augustus   b Nero   c **Julius Caesar**
6 Who _____ the world record for the 100 and 200 metres race at the Beijing Olympics? (break)
   a **Usain Bolt**
   b Carl Lewis
   c Michael Johnson
7 Which painter _____ off part of his ear? (cut)
   a Picasso   b **Van Gogh**   c Matisse
8 Who _____ penicillin? (discover)
   a **Alexander Fleming**
   b James Watson
   c Thomas Edison

b Ask **B** your questions. Give your partner one mark for each correct answer.

c Answer **B**'s questions. Who got the most right answers?

Communication

7A HOW TO... Student B

a Read the article **How to survive a first date**.

b **A** will tell you five tips for **How to survive at a party**. Listen and when he or she finishes decide together which is the most important tip.

c Look again quickly at **How to survive a first date**. Then without looking at the text tell **A** the five tips. When you finish decide with **A** which is the most important tip.

> ### How to ... Survive a First Date (and make a success of it)
>
> **1** Think carefully about what to wear for the date. If you are a man, try to dress smartly but casually (no suits!). If you are a woman, it's important not to dress too sexily. Don't wear too much perfume or aftershave!
>
> **2** Choose a place that isn't too expensive (you don't know who is going to pay). Try to go somewhere that isn't very noisy.
>
> **3** Don't be too romantic on a first date. For example, arriving with a red rose on a first date isn't a good idea!
>
> **4** Remember to listen more than you talk but don't let the conversation die. Silence is a killer on a first date! Be natural. Don't pretend to be somebody you aren't.
>
> **5** If you are a man, be a gentleman and pay the bill at the end of the evening. If you are a woman, offer to pay your half of the bill (but don't insist!).

8A WHAT SHOULD I DO? Student B

a Listen to **A**'s problem 1. Give him / her advice. Begin with one of the phrases below.

I think you should…   You shouldn't…   I don't think you should…

b Read your problem 1 to **A**. He / she will give you some advice.

Problems
1 I share a flat with a friend but he / she never does the washing-up!
2 I want to take my boyfriend / girlfriend somewhere really special on Saturday night.
3 I need some new clothes for a wedding, but I don't know what to buy.
4 I think I'm getting a cold – I have a headache and a cough.
5 My sister always borrows my clothes, and when I want to wear them they're dirty.

c Thank **A** and say:

That's a good idea,
OR Thanks, but that's not a very good idea because…

d Continue with problems 2–5.

9A WOULD YOU KNOW WHAT TO DO? Student B

a Read the answers to **In the country**.

> ### In the country
>
> 3 **The answer is c.** If you tie a bandage or a piece of material above the bite, this will stop the poison from getting to your heart too quickly. However, be careful not to tie it too tightly. You shouldn't put ice or anything cold on the bite, as this will make it more difficult to get the poison out later, and never try to suck out the poison. If it gets into your mouth, it might go into your blood.
>
> 4 **The answer is b.** If you are lucky, the bull will change direction to follow the hat or bag and give you time to escape. It doesn't matter what colour the shirt is, bulls don't see colour, they only see movement. Don't try to run away, as bulls can run incredibly fast, and you mustn't shout or wave your arms because this will attract the bull's attention even more.

b Listen to **A** tell you about **In the city**. Check your answers.

c Tell **A** and **C** the right answers for **In the country**, and why the other ones are wrong.

d Listen to **C** tell you about **In the water**. Check your answers.

10A PASSIVES QUIZ Student B

a Complete your sentences with the verb in the passive and the right answer.

1 The Smartphone _____ *was invented.* (invent) by…
  (a) Apple b Nokia c IBM *was*
2 The *Lord of the Rings* films _____ (direct) by… *directed.*
  a Steven Spielberg
  b James Cameron
  (c) Peter Jackson
3 The book which _____ (steal) most often from *is stolen* libraries is…
  a The Bible
  (b) *The Guinness Book of Records*
  c *The Lord of the Rings*
4 In the world, 16,000 babies _____ (born)… *are born*
  (a) every second b every hour c every day *was invented*
5 Chess _____ (invent) by…
  a the Egyptians (b) the Indians c the Chinese
6 The first Levi jeans _____ (wear) by… *were worn*
  (a) miners b farmers c cowboys
7 Football *was* first *played* (play) by…
  (a) the British b the Romans c the Greeks
8 In 1962 the original London Bridge _____ (buy) by… *was bought*
  a a rich American
  b a museum
  (c) the Royal family

b Listen to **A**'s sentences. Say if he / she is right.

A's answers

1 Until 1664 New York was called New Amsterdam.
2 The *Star Wars* films were directed by George Lucas.
3 The noun which is used most frequently in conversation is *time*.
4 Penguins are found at the South Pole.
5 The Italian flag was designed by Napoleon.
6 The first mobile phones were sold in 1983.
7 The politician Winston Churchill was born in a toilet.
8 The electric chair was invented by a dentist.

c Read your sentences to **A**. **A** will tell you if you are right.

12A WHAT HAD HAPPENED?
Student B

a Look at the even numbered sentences (2, 4, 6, 8, 10, and 12) and think of the missing verb (+ = positive verb, − = negative verb). Don't write anything yet!

1 Diana was very angry because her husband **hadn't cooked** the dinner.
2 We went back to see the house where we _____ when we were children. +
3 He couldn't catch the plane because he **had forgotten** his passport.
4 The flat was very dirty because nobody _____ it for a long time. +
5 We went back to the hotel where we **had stayed** on our honeymoon.
6 The crocodile was hungry because it _____ anything for two days. −
7 After I left the shop I suddenly remembered that I **hadn't paid** for the jacket.
8 I ran to the station, but the last train _____. +
9 Miriam was surprised to hear that she **had passed** the exam.
10 I didn't want to lend Jane the book because I _____ it. −
11 Jack was angry because I **hadn't invited** him to my party.
12 They got to the cinema late and the film _____. +

b Listen to **A** say sentence 1. If it's the same as 1 above, say 'That's right'. If not, say 'Try again' until **A** gets it right.

c Read sentence 2 to **A**. If it's not right, try again until **A** tells you 'That's right'. Then write in the verb.

d Take it in turns with sentences 3–12.

Communication

12C GENERAL KNOWLEDGE QUIZ
Student B

a Complete your questions with the verb in brackets in the past simple.

1 Who _____ President of the USA eight years after his father had been the US president? (become)
   a Bill Clinton
   b John F Kennedy
   c **George Bush**

2 Who _____ the part of the mother in the film *Mamma Mia*? (play)
   a **Meryl Streep**
   b Julia Roberts
   c Sandra Bullock

3 Which tennis player _____ Wimbledon five years in a row between 2003 and 2007? (win)
   a **Roger Federer**
   b Rafael Nadal
   c Novak Djokovic

4 Who _____ the Sistine Chapel? (paint)
   a Leonardo da Vinci
   b **Michelangelo**
   c Raphael

5 Which film _____ eleven Oscars in 2003? (win)
   a *The King's Speech*
   b *The Queen*
   c ***The Return of the King***

6 Who _____ a wooden horse to enter the city of Troy? (use)
   a **the Greeks**
   b The Romans
   c The Persians

7 Which famous boxer _____ to fight in the Vietnam war in 1967? (refuse)
   a **Muhammad Ali**
   b Joe Frazier
   c Sugar Ray Robinson

8 Who _____ the telephone? (invent)
   a Marconi   b **Bell**   c Stephens

b Answer **A**'s questions.

c Ask **A** your questions. Give your partner one mark for each correct answer. Who got the most right answers?

9A WOULD YOU KNOW WHAT TO DO?
Student C

a Read the answers to **In the water**.

In the water

5 The answer is c. If a jellyfish stings you, you should clean the sting with vinegar as this stops the poison. If you don't have any vinegar, then use sea water. But don't use fresh water, for example water from a tap or mineral water, as this will make the sting hurt more. And you shouldn't rub the sting as this will make it worse too. After you have washed the sting, you should clean off any bits of tentacles that are on your skin. And take a pain killer!

6 The answer is a. If you are near the shore and the shark is not too close, you can probably swim to the shore without attracting its attention. For this reason it is important to swim smoothly and not splash or make sudden movements. Keeping still is dangerous because if the shark swims in your direction it will see you and it will attack you. Don't shout because shouting will provoke the shark and it will attack you.

b Listen to **A** and **B** tell you the answers in the other sections (**In the city** and **In the country**). Check your answers.

c Tell **A** and **B** the right answers for **In the water**, and why the other ones are wrong.

Writing

5 A FORMAL EMAIL

From: Antonio Ricci [antonior@tiscali.net]
To: The Priory Language School [enquiries@prioryedinburgh]
Subject: Information about courses

Dear Sir / Madam,

I am writing to ask for information about your language courses. I am especially interested in an intensive course of two or three weeks. I am 31 and I work in the library at Milan University. I can read English quite well, but I need to improve my listening and speaking. The book I am currently studying is 'pre-intermediate' (Common European Framework level A2).

I have looked at your website, but there is no information about intensive courses next summer. Could you please send me information about dates and prices? I would also like some information about accommodation. If possible I would like to stay with a family. My wife is going to visit me for a weekend when I am at the school. Could she stay with me in the same family?

I look forward to hearing from you.

Yours faithfully,

Antonio Ricci

a Read the email to a language school. Tick (✓) the questions that Antonio wants the school to answer.

- ☐ How much do the courses cost?
- ☐ When do the courses start and finish?
- ☐ How many students are there in a class?
- ☐ Are there Business English classes?
- ☐ Where can I stay?
- ☐ Where are the teachers from?

b Look at the highlighted expressions. How would they be different in an informal email (or letter)?

Formal	Informal
Dear Sir / Madam,	
I am writing	
I would like	
I look forward to hearing from you.	
Yours faithfully,	

Painting courses in Tuscany

Learn to paint in Tuscany, Italy.

- One-week courses, from April to October
- Your accommodation in Tuscany is included
- Beginners welcome

Email us for more information at **painttuscany@blueelephant.com**

Golf lessons in Florida

- One- or two-week courses in different parts of the state
- Professional golf coaches
- All levels, beginners to advanced
- Small groups or private lessons

For more information email us at info@golfinflorida.com

c Read the advertisements and choose a course. Think of two or three questions you would like to ask.

d Write a formal email asking for information. Write two paragraphs.

Paragraph 1	Explain why you are writing and give some personal information.
Paragraph 2	Ask your questions, and ask them to send you information.

e Check your email for mistakes (grammar, punctuation, and spelling).

◀ p.57

Writing

6 A BIOGRAPHY

a Read the biography of Norah Jones. Then cover the text and try to remember three things about her.

b Put the verbs in brackets in the past simple or present perfect.

> 🔍 **Writing a biography – use of tenses**
>
> If you write a biography of a person who is dead, the verbs will all be in the **past simple**.
>
> If the person is alive, all finished actions will be in the **past simple** (such as the person's early life, *e.g. was born, went to university,* etc. or specific actions in their life, *e.g. got married, moved to another town,* etc.).
>
> However, you must use the **present perfect** for unfinished actions which started in the past and are still true now (and which might change), *e.g. She has won nine Grammy awards. She has appeared in several films.*
>
> Use the **present simple** (or **present continuous**) to talk about the present day, *e.g. She lives in New York. She's working on a new album.*

c Write a biography of someone you know, or of a famous person, who is still alive. Write three paragraphs. Make notes before you begin.

Paragraph 1	where and when they were born, their early life (past simple)
Paragraph 2	their life as a young adult (mostly past simple)
Paragraph 3	their later life and their life now (past simple, present perfect, present simple / present continuous)

d Check your biography for mistakes (grammar, punctuation, and spelling). Show your biography to other students in the class. Which of your classmates' biographies is the most interesting?

◄ *p.73*

Norah Jones

Norah Jones is an American singer-songwriter and actress. She ¹*was born* (**be born**) in 1979 in New York. Her father is Ravi Shankar, a famous Indian sitar player, and her mother is the concert producer Sue Jones. In 1986 her parents ²sep̲a̲r̲a̲t̲e̲d̲ (**separate**) and later got divorced, and Norah went to live in Texas with her mother.

Norah ³h̲a̲s̲ ̲b̲e̲e̲n̲ (**be**) interested in music all her life. When she was young she played the saxophone and she was in two different choirs. She ⁴w̲e̲n̲t̲ (**go**) to the University of North Texas to study jazz piano, and while she was there she ⁵m̲e̲t̲ (**meet**) Jesse Harris. She started a band with him a year later, and since then they ⁶h̲a̲v̲e̲ ̲w̲o̲r̲k̲e̲d̲ (**work**) together on many different projects.

In 1999 she ⁷m̲o̲v̲e̲d̲ (**move**) to New York, and in 2001 she signed a contract with Blue Note records. Since then she h̲a̲s̲⁸ m̲a̲d̲e̲ (**make**) five albums, and they have all been very successful. She ⁹h̲a̲s̲ ̲w̲o̲n̲ (**win**) nine Grammy awards and has sold over 37 million albums worldwide. She has also appeared in several films, including *My Blueberry Nights*.

She has been in only one relationship, with Lee Alexander, but they ¹⁰b̲r̲o̲k̲e̲ ̲u̲p̲ (**break up**) in 2007. She still lives in New York. At the moment she is working on a new album.

7 AN OPINION ESSAY

a Read the article once. Do you agree with what it says?

'THERE IS TOO MUCH FOOTBALL ON TV.' DO YOU AGREE?

Every time I turn on the television, I'm sure to find a football match on one of the channels. If I change channels, there will probably be football on other channels too, especially at the weekend. ¹*In my opinion* there is definitely too much football on TV for the following reasons.

²_____, if you compare football with other sports, football completely dominates. The only place where you can watch other sports is on special sports channels, which you usually have to pay for. This is not fair for people who like other sports, ³_____ tennis, basketball, or athletics.

Secondly, the football matches on TV are not only the important matches. Every week they show boring matches from the second or third divisions.

⁴_____, I also believe that, at weekends, most people want to relax in front of the television. Many people, including me, don't like football and prefer to see good films or funny series.

⁵_____, I think that even on news programmes there is too much football. It is very annoying when they talk about football for hours every day, especially when there are more important things happening in the world.

⁶_____, I think TV should show fewer football matches and programmes about football, especially at the weekend. ⁷_____ it should show other sports too, and more films. On news programmes they should talk about important things that are happening in the world, not about football.

b Read the article again and complete the gaps with a word or phrase from the list. Use capital letters where necessary.

> finally   firstly   for example   thirdly
> ~~in my opinion~~   instead   to conclude

c You are going to write an article called **'There are too many reality shows on TV'. Do you agree?** With a partner decide if you agree or not, and think of three of four reasons.

d Write the article. Write four or five paragraphs.

Paragraph 1	Write an introduction. You can adapt the introduction in the model article. Say if you agree or not.
Middle paragraphs	Give your reasons. Begin the paragraphs with *Firstly, Secondly,* (*Thirdly,*) and *Finally*.
Last paragraph	Write a conclusion (this should be a summary of what you write in the middle paragraphs).

e Check your article for mistakes (grammar, punctuation, and spelling). Show your article to other students in the class. How many of your classmates agree with you? How many disagree?

◀ *p.85*

Listening

Nigel Hi Suze. Sorry I'm a bit late. I was watching the match.
Suzy Come on in then. Mum, this is Nigel. Nigel this is my mum.
Nigel Oh... hello.
Mum Nice to meet you, Nigel.
Suzy And this is my Dad.
Dad Hello, Nigel.
Nigel Hello.
Dad Come on into the living room.

Dad Would you like a drink, Nigel? Orange juice, beer?
Nigel Oh thanks, John. I'll have a beer, please.

Mum You're a vegetarian, aren't you, Nigel?
Nigel Yes, I am. Personally I think eating animals is totally wrong.
Mum Ahem, well, this is vegetable lasagne. I hope you like it. Suzy's Dad made it.

Dad Any more lasagne, Nigel?
Nigel Oh, er, no thanks. I'm not very hungry.
Girl The lasagne is delicious, Dad.
Mum Yes, it is.
Dad Thank you.

Suzy I'll do the washing up, Mum.
Dad No, I'll do it.
Nigel Er, where's the bathroom?

Nigel Did you watch the match this evening, John? Chelsea and Arsenal. It was fantastic!
Dad No, I didn't watch it. I don't like football at all. In fact I hate it.
Nigel Oh.

Mum So...what are you going to do when you finish university, Nigel?
Nigel Er, I don't know.
Dad What are you studying at university?
Nigel Sociology.
Dad Why did you choose sociology?
Nigel Because I thought it was easy.
Mum Is it interesting?
Nigel It's OK. Er ... What was Suzy like as a little girl, Marion? Do you have any photos of her?
Mum Photos of Suzy? Yes, we have thousands of photos. She was a lovely little girl, wasn't she John?
Dad Yes, she was. A beautiful little girl.
Nigel Can I see some?
Suzy Oh no, please.
Mum John, can you bring the photo albums?

Mum Look, and this is one when she was three years old.
Dad And this is when we went to Disneyland. That's Suzy with Mickey and Minnie Mouse.
Nigel Ah! She was so sweet.
Dad Would you like another beer, Nigel?
Nigel Yes, please, John.

Interviewer Good morning and welcome. In today's programme we're going to talk about singing. In the studio we have Martin, the director of a singing school in London, and Gemma, a student at Martin's school. Good morning to both of you.
Martin / Gemma Good morning.

Interviewer First, Martin, can you tell us, why is it a good idea for people to learn to sing?
Martin First, because singing makes you feel good. And secondly, because singing is very good for your health.
Interviewer Really? In what way?
Martin Well, when you learn to sing you need to learn to breathe correctly. That's very important. And you also learn to stand and sit correctly. As a result, people who sing are often fitter and healthier than people who don't.
Interviewer Are your courses only for professional singers?
Martin No, not at all. They're for everybody. You don't need to have any experience of singing. And you don't need to be able to read music.
Interviewer So how do your students learn to sing?
Martin They learn by listening and repeating. Singing well is really 95% listening.
Interviewer OK. Gemma, tell us about the course. How long did it last?
Gemma Only one day. From ten in the morning to six in the evening.
Martin Could you already sing well before you started?
Gemma No, not well. I've always liked singing. But I can't read music and I never thought I sang very well.
Interviewer So what happened on the course?
Gemma Well, first we did a lot of listening and breathing exercises, and we learnt some other interesting techniques.
Interviewer What sort of things?
Gemma Well, for example we learnt that it's easier to sing high notes if you sing with a surprised look on your face!
Interviewer Oh really? Could you show us?
Gemma Well, I'll try.
Interviewer For those of you at home, I can promise you that Gemma looked very surprised. Were you happy with your progress?
Gemma Absolutely. At the end of the day we were singing in almost perfect harmony. It was amazing. In just one day we really were much better.
Interviewer Could you two give us a little demonstration?
Martin / Gemma Oh, OK...

Journalist I arrived at Madrid airport where I met Paula. *Hola Soy Max.*
Paula *Encantada. Soy Paula.*
Journalist Paula took me to my hotel and that evening we went to the centre of Madrid and it was time for my first test. I had to order a sandwich and a drink in a bar then ask for the bill. I sat down at the bar and I tried to order a beer and a ham sandwich. *Por favor, una cerveza y un bocadillo de jamón.*
Waiter *En seguida.*
Journalist Fantastic! The waiter understood me first time. My pronunciation wasn't perfect but I got my beer and my sandwich. I really enjoyed it. But then the more difficult bit. Asking for the bill... *¿Cuánto es?*
Waiter *Seis noventa.*
Journalist *¿Cómo?*
Waiter *Seis noventa.*
Journalist Six ninety. I understood! Paula gave me eight points for the test. I was very happy with that. Next we went out into the street. Test

number two was asking for directions and (very important!) understanding them. We were in a narrow street and I had to stop someone and ask them for the nearest chemist, *Una farmacia.* I stopped a woman. At first I didn't understand anything she said!
Passer-by *Siga todo recto y tome la segunda por la derecha. Hay una farmacia en esa calle.*
Journalist I asked the woman to speak more slowly.
Passer-by *Todo recto y tome la segunda calle por la derecha DERECHA.*
Journalist I got it this time, I think. The second street on the right. I followed the directions and guess what? There was a chemist there! Seven points from Paula.
Test number three. I wasn't looking forward to this one. I had to get a taxi to a famous place in Madrid. Paula wrote down the name of the place on a piece of paper. It was the name of the football stadium where Real Madrid play. We stopped a taxi.
Journalist *El Bernabéu, por favor.*
Taxi driver *¿Qué? ¿Adónde?*
Journalist He didn't understand me. I tried again but he still didn't understand. I was desperate so I said *Real Madrid, Stadium, football.*
Taxi driver *¡Ah! El Santiago Bernabéu.*
Journalist Finally! Paula only gave me five because I ended up using English. Still, at least I made the taxi driver understand where I wanted to go. And so to the final test. I had to leave a message in Spanish on somebody's voicemail. I had to give my name, spell it, and ask the person to call me back. Paula gave me the number (it was one of her friends called Lola) and I dialled. I was feeling a bit nervous at this point, because speaking on the phone in a foreign language is never easy.
Lola *Deje su mensaje después de la señal.*
Journalist *Eh. Buenas noches. Soy Max. Max. M-A-X. Eh... Por favour... llamarme esta noche... Oh yes... a las 8.30, eh Gracias.* Well, my grammar wasn't right, but I left the message. Half an hour later, at half past eight Lola phoned me. Success! Paula gave me eight points. That was the end of my four tests. Paula was pleased with me. My final score was seven. I was quite happy with that. So how much can you learn in a month? Well, of course you can't learn Spanish in a month, but you can learn enough to survive if you are on holiday or on a trip. Now I want to go back to England and try and learn some more. *¡Adiós!*

Jenny Are you okay?
Rob Me? Never better.
Jenny It's beautiful here, isn't it? I think this is my favourite place in New York.
Rob Yeah, it's great.
Jenny So how's it all going? Are you happy you came?
Rob To Central Park? At seven fifteen in the morning?
Jenny To New York, Rob.
Rob Yeah. Of course I'm happy. It's fantastic.
Jenny Really? You aren't just saying that.
Rob No, I mean it.
Jenny You need to get in shape, Rob.
Rob I know. I am a bit tired of eating out all the time. It isn't good for my figure.
Jenny It's the restaurants you go to! Why don't you come over to my place after work? I could make you something a little healthier.

Rob I'd really like that. Thanks.

Jenny So, how do you feel now? Are you ready to go again?

Rob Oh yes! I'm ready for anything.

Jenny Are you sure you're okay?

Rob Absolutely.

Jenny Okay. We'll only go around two more times.

Rob Two? Excellent!

🎧 3 43))

Rob That was a lovely meal. Thanks, Jenny.

Jenny That's OK.

Rob It's been great being in New York. You know, your offer to work here came at a very good time for me.

Jenny Really?

Rob Yeah, I was looking for something new. Something different. You see, I broke up with my girlfriend a few months before I met you.

Jenny Oh… right.

Rob What about you?

Jenny What about me?

Rob You know… relationships?

Jenny Oh, I've been too busy recently to think about relationships. Getting this job at the magazine was a really big thing for me. I guess that's taken up all my time and energy.

Rob But that isn't very good for you. Only thinking about work, I mean.

Jenny Why didn't you tell me you weren't feeling well this morning? We didn't have to go for a run.

Rob I wanted to go. It was nice.

Jenny Well, I'm glad you're feeling better. Would you like another coffee?

Rob No, thanks. I think I should get back to the hotel now, I've got a really busy day tomorrow. Do you have a telephone number for a taxi?

Jenny Yeah…but it's much easier to get a cab on the street.

Rob Oh, OK, then.

Jenny I'll see you in the morning, if you're feeling OK.

Rob Oh, I'm sure I'll be fine. Thanks again for a great evening.

Jenny Any time.

Rob Goodnight.

Jenny Night, Rob.

🎧 3 51))

Presenter Welcome to this morning's edition of *What's the problem?* Today we're talking about friends, so if you have a problem with one of your friends, and you'd like our psychologist Catherine to give you some advice, just phone us on 800 700 550. Our first caller today is Kevin from Birmingham. Hello, Kevin.

Kevin Hi.

Presenter What's the problem?

Kevin Yes. My problem is with my best friend, Alan. Well, the thing is, he's always flirting with my girlfriend.

Presenter Your best friend flirts with your girlfriend?

Kevin Yes, when the three of us are together he always says things to my girlfriend like, 'Wow! You look fantastic today' or 'I love your dress, Suzanna', things like that. And when we're at a party he often asks her to dance.

Presenter Do you think he's in love with your girlfriend?

Kevin I don't know, but I'm getting really stressed about it. What can I do?

🎧 3 52))

Presenter Well, let's see if our expert can help. Catherine?

Catherine Hello, Kevin. Have you talked to your girlfriend about this?

Kevin No, I haven't. I don't want Suzanna to think I'm jealous.

Catherine Well, first I think you should talk to her, ask her how she feels and what she thinks of Alan's behaviour. Perhaps she thinks it's fine, and they are just good friends. That it's just his

personality. If that's what she thinks, then I think you should accept it and relax.

Kevin What should I do if she also finds it er, difficult, er, uncomfortable?

Catherine Then I think you should talk to Alan. Tell him that he's a good friend, but that you and Suzanna have problems with the way he behaves. I'm sure he'll stop doing it. He's probably never thought it was a problem.

Kevin Thanks very much for that. I'll talk to Suzanna tonight.

🎧 3 53))

Presenter And our next caller is Miranda from Brighton. Hi Miranda.

Miranda Hi.

Presenter And what's your problem?

Miranda My problem is with my husband's ex wife. They divorced five years ago, before I met him. But she still phones him at least once a week to chat, and if she has a problem in her flat or with her car, she always calls him and asks him to come and help her.

Presenter Does your husband have children with his ex-wife?

Miranda No, they don't have any children. That's why I think she should stay out of our lives.

Presenter Catherine, over to you. What do you think Miranda should do?

🎧 3 54))

Catherine Hi Miranda. Well, the first thing is have you spoken to your husband about this?

Miranda Yes, I have. He thinks I'm being difficult. He feels sorry for his ex – she's on her own, she doesn't have a partner.

Catherine OK. Miranda, do you have any male friends, men who are just good friends?

Miranda Yes, I have a friend called Bill. We've been friends since I was a teenager.

Catherine That's perfect. My advice is this: when your husband's ex-wife phones and asks him to go and see her, phone Bill and arrange to meet and have a drink or go to the cinema. Every time your husband meets his ex or has a long phone call, then you meet Bill or have a long phone call. He'll soon see what's happening, and he'll stop seeing his ex.

Miranda I think that's a great idea. Thank you, Catherine.

Presenter And the next caller is…

🎧 4 6))

Presenter And to finish our programme today, the incredible story of a Swedish couple who went on holiday and survived no fewer than seven natural disasters!

Stefan and Erika Svanström started their four-month trip last December. They were travelling with their young baby daughter. First they flew from Stockholm to Munich. But when they arrived in Munich they couldn't get their connecting flight to Thailand because there was a terrible blizzard in South Germany – the worst snowstorm for a hundred years! They had to wait at the airport for 24 hours. Mrs Svanström said:

Mrs Svanström 'We just thought things will get better.'

Presenter When they finally got to Thailand, they had a relaxing few weeks. But that was the last time they could really relax. From Thailand they flew to the island of Bali in Indonesia, a popular holiday destination. When they arrived in Bali they were expecting blue skies and sun, but what they got were terrible monsoon rains – the worst monsoons for many years. Mrs Svanström said:

Mrs Svanström 'Now we were thinking, what will happen next?'

Presenter They decided not to stay in Bali, but to go to Australia. They flew to Perth in Western Australia, but hours after they arrived Perth suffered terrible forest fires, and the streets were full of smoke. They travelled north to Cairns, and

arrived just in time for Cyclone Yasi – one of the worst cyclones ever to hit the city. They had to leave their hotel and spend 24 hours in a shopping centre with 2,500 other people.

Could things get any worse? Yes, they could. The Svanström family left Cairns and travelled south to Brisbane to visit friends, but the city was suffering from the worst floods in its history. So they left Brisbane and booked to fly to Christchurch in New Zealand. But just before their plane left Brisbane some friends phoned them to say that Christchurch had been hit by an earthquake and a large part of the city was destroyed. Their plane landed in another city, Auckland. They travelled around New Zealand for a while, and then they flew to Japan. On March 11th they were having lunch in a restaurant in Tokyo when suddenly everything began to shake. It was an earthquake: nine on the Richter scale and one of the worst that ever hit Japan. And after the earthquake came a devastating tsunami. Fortunately, Mr and Mrs Svanström and their child were not hurt. They travelled from Japan to China for the last part of their holiday. Luckily, they didn't have any more natural disasters, and they arrived safely home in Stockholm on 29th March. Mr Svanström said:

Mr Svanström 'We have learnt that in life you should always expect the worst, but hope for the best. Also, you need to be prepared for anything.'

🎧 4 10))

Part 3

Hartley "Héloise will go,"

Reader said Hartley angrily.

Hartley "I haven't had one day without problems since I met her. You are right, Vivienne. Héloise must go before I can take you home. But she will go. I have decided…"

Vivienne "Then,"

Reader said Vivienne,

Vivienne "my answer is yes. I will be yours."

Reader She looked into his eyes and Hartley could hardly believe his luck.

Hartley "Promise me,"

Reader he said.

Vivienne "I promise,"

Reader repeated Vivienne, softly. At the door he turned and looked at her happily,

Hartley "I will come for you tomorrow,"

Reader he said.

Vivienne "Tomorrow,"

Reader she repeated with a smile. An hour and forty minutes later Hartley stepped off the train when it stopped in the suburbs, and walked to his house. As he walked towards the door a woman ran to him. She had black hair and was wearing a long white dress. They kissed, and walked into the house.

🎧 4 11))

Part 4

Hartley's wife "My mother is here,"

Reader the woman said.

Hartley's wife "But she's leaving in half an hour. She came to have dinner, but there's nothing to eat."

Hartley "I have something to tell you,"

Reader said Hartley. He whispered something in her ear. His wife screamed. Her mother came running into the hall. The woman screamed again, but it was a happy scream – the sound of a woman whose husband loved her.

Hartley's wife "Oh, mother!"

Reader she cried,

Hartley's wife "What do you think? Vivienne is coming to be our cook! She is the cook that was with the Montgomery's. She's going to be ours! And now, dear,"

Reader she told her husband,

Hartley's wife "you must go to the kitchen and tell Héloise to leave. She has been drunk again all day."

1 **Interviewer** Do you have any phobias?
  A Yes, I'm terrified of bats.
  Interviewer Really? How long have you had the phobia?
  A I've had it for about forty years! Since I was 12 years old. At my school we had a swimming pool, and the changing rooms were in an old building near the pool. On the first day at school our teacher told us that there were bats in there and that we shouldn't move around too much as they might start flying around and get into our hair. She also said we mustn't turn the lights on because this would wake up the bats. We had to change as quickly and quietly as possible.
  Interviewer Did a bat every fly into your hair?
  A No, nothing ever happened, but I was terrified just at the thought of it.
  Interviewer Does it affect your life at all?
  A Yes, I often feel very nervous or start to panic if I'm outside when it's beginning to get dark, which is when bats appear. If I'm sitting in my garden in the evening, I always have a tennis racket, so if a bat flies near me, I can protect myself. And I can't watch a TV documentary about bats, or even look at them in photos.

2 **Interviewer** Do you have any phobias?
  B Yes, I get very bad claustrophobia.
  Interviewer How long have you had the phobia?
  B It just started one morning about ten years ago. I was going to work on the train and it was very crowded. I started thinking that if there were an accident, I'd never get out. I had a panic attack and I sort of felt my heart beating very quickly. I had to get off the train.
  Interviewer How does your phobia affect your life?
  B Well, I can't travel on crowded trains. I never ever travel on the underground because my worst nightmare would be if the train stopped in the tunnel. I also try to avoid lifts. What else? Oh yes, if I'm flying, I must have an aisle seat. I can't sit by the window.

3 **Interviewer** Do you have any phobias?
  C Yes, I have a pretty unusual phobia. I'm scared of clowns.
  Interviewer Clowns, really? How long have you had it?
  C I've had it for a long time. Since I was a child.
  Interviewer How did it start?
  C Well, I remember I went on a school trip to the circus when I was six or seven years old and there were clowns. I thought they were sort of stupid but I wasn't really afraid of them. Then I went to a birthday party and there were clowns and they were showing us how to paint our faces, and I found I didn't like being near them. At first I just didn't like them, but over the years my feelings have changed to fear.
  Interviewer Does your phobia affect your life at all?
  C Not really because luckily I don't see clowns very often!

Good evening and welcome to *Top Sounds*, our weekly music programme, and tonight the focus is on the Latin music star Enrique Iglesias. As I'm sure you all know, Enrique Iglesias is the son of the Spanish singer Julio Iglesias, who is one of the most successful singing artists of all time.

Enrique was born in Madrid, Spain in 1975. His mother is Isabel Preysler, a journalist and TV host from the Philippines. When he was three years old his parents got divorced and later he moved to Miami to live with his father. He started studying Business at Miami University, but he left after a year because he wanted to become a musician. He didn't want his father to know about his music career and he didn't want to use his famous surname to be successful. So when he sent some of his songs to several record companies he used the name Enrique Martinez and he eventually got a contract with a Mexican record company.

He made his first album, called *Enrique Iglesias* in 1995, which won him a Grammy. He then made two more albums and he had many hits in the Latin music charts. At first Enrique sang mainly in Spanish but later he began to sing more and more in English too.

His fourth album, *Escape* in 2001, was his biggest commercial success and included the singles *Escape* and *Hero*, sung in English, which became hits all over the world and made Enrique an international star. Since then he has made five other albums and has also had a few acting parts in films and TV programmes. Also in 2001, he began dating the Russian tennis player, Ana Kournikova, but they kept their relationship very private. Today Enrique Iglesias is recognized as one of the most popular artists in Latin America. He has sold 100 million albums, which makes him one of the best selling artists of all time.

Holly That was a good day's work, Rob. You did a great interview.
Rob You took some great photos, too. They're really nice.
Holly Thanks. Hey, let's have another coffee.
Rob I don't know. I have to get to Manhattan.
Holly You don't have to go right now.
Rob I'm not sure. I don't want to be late.
Holly Why do you have to go to Manhattan?
Rob I've got a... erm…
Holly A date? You have a date?
Rob Mm hm.
Holly Is it with anybody I know?
Rob No, it isn't. Anyway, excuse me a minute. I need to go to 'the rest room'.
Holly That's very American. I'll order more coffees.
Rob OK.
Jenny Rob?
Holly Is that you, Jennifer?
Jenny Oh, hi Holly. Erm… is Rob there?
Holly Yeah, one second. Rob! Not anybody I know, huh?
Rob Hi, Jenny.
Jenny Rob? Are you still in Brooklyn?
Rob Yeah.
Jenny You know the reservation at the restaurant's for eight, right?
Rob Don't worry. I'll be there! Oh, how do I get to Greenwich Village on the subway?

Rob Jenny! I'm here.
Jenny Hi.
Rob I'm so sorry. There was a problem on the underground.
Jenny We call it the subway here.
Rob Right. Anyway, the train stopped for about twenty minutes. I tried to call but there was no signal.
Jenny I've been here since seven forty-five.
Rob I know. I ran from the underground... subway station… I'm so sorry.
Jenny You're always late. It's funny, isn't it?
Rob I said I'm sorry. Look, why don't we go back inside the restaurant?
Jenny I waited for an hour for you. I don't want to stay here anymore.
Rob Maybe we could... we could go for a walk. We could find another restaurant.
Jenny I don't feel like a walk. It's been a long day.
Rob OK.
Jenny But the night is still young. Maybe you have time to meet up with Holly again.
Rob Holly?
Jenny I'm sorry. I didn't mean to say that.
Rob I don't care about Holly.
Jenny Forget it, Rob. Now if you don't mind, I'd like to go home.

Rob Listen to me, Jenny. Holly is just a colleague.
Jenny I said forget it. It's OK.
Rob No, it isn't OK. Look. I know I'm always late. And I know the underground is the subway. But that's not the point! I'm not interested in Holly. I came to New York because of you. The only person I'm interested in is you!

Presenter Good afternoon, and welcome to another edition of *Science Today*. In today's programme we are going to hear about women inventors. When we think of famous inventors we usually think of men, people like Alexander Graham Bell, Guglielmo Marconi, Thomas Edison. But, as Sally will tell us, many of the things which make our lives easier today were invented by women.
Sally That's absolutely right. Let's take the dishwasher for example. This was invented by a woman called Josephine Cochrane in 1886. She was a rich American who gave a lot of dinner parties. But she was annoyed that her servants used to break plates and glasses when they were washing up after a party. So, Josephine decided to try and invent a machine which could wash a lot of plates and glasses safely. Apparently she said: 'If nobody else is going to invent a dishwasher, then I will!' She designed the machine and then she found a company to make it. At first only hotels and restaurants bought Josephine's new machine but today the dishwasher is used by millions of people all over the world.
The car was invented by a man, but it was a woman, Mary Anderson, who in 1903 solved one of the biggest problems of driving. Until her invention it was impossible for drivers to see where they were going when it was raining or snowing. They had to open their window. The name of Mary's invention? Windscreen wipers.
An invention that definitely improved the lives of millions of people was disposable nappies. They were invented by a woman called Marion Donovan. Her father and uncle were inventors, and when she had young children she sat down and invented a nappy that you could use and then throw away. Anybody who has a small baby will know what a big difference disposable nappies make to our lives. But although she invented it in 1950, it wasn't until 1961 that an American company bought Marion's idea. Today millions of disposable nappies are used every day and Marion's invention has been made more eco-friendly. Now you can buy biodegradable nappies!
And now to our next inventor. In 1956, Bette Nesmith Graham was working as a secretary. Like all secretaries at that time she used to get very frustrated and angry when she made typing mistakes. In those days if you made a mistake, you had to get a new sheet of paper and start again from the beginning. Then she had a brilliant idea, which was to use a white liquid to paint over mistakes. Her invention is called Tipp-Ex today. Mrs Graham was a divorced mother and her invention made her a very rich woman. Her son, Mike Nesmith, became a famous pop star – he was a member of the American group, The Monkees.
And finally… policemen, soldiers, and politicians all over the world are protected by something which was invented by a woman. In 1966 Stephanie Kwolek invented kevlar, a special material which was very light but incredibly strong, much stronger than metal. This material is used to make bullet-proof vests. Stephanie's invention has probably saved thousands of lives.
Presenter Thanks very much, Sally. So, if you thought that everything was invented by men, think again.

4 46)))

1 Presenter Did you like school?
A No, definitely not.
Presenter Why?
A I didn't like most of the lessons – I was always bored, and I hated exams. And the worst thing of all was PE. Where I went to school we used to play rugby. Ugh – it was torture.

2 Presenter Did you like school?
B I loved primary school, but I didn't really like secondary school.
Presenter Why not?
B Well the school was very big and it was sort of cold and impersonal. It took me a very long time before I felt at home there. And I'm not really very academic, but the school was. We used to get loads of homework which I hated.

3 Presenter Did you like school?
C Er, yes, I did.
Presenter Why?
C I was very curious about everything when I was little, so I liked school because I learned about new things. And of course I used to see my friends every day. The other thing I loved was the library – my school had a fantastic library – I even used to stay on there after class just to read. Oh dear, I sound very goody-goody, but it's true!

4 Presenter Did you like school?
D Not especially
Presenter Why?
D It was a boys' school and I got a bit fed up with just being with boys all the time.

5 Presenter Did you like school?
E It was all right – some bits were better than others, of course. The lessons I liked depended very much on the teacher – so for example physics and English were great, but chemistry and history were terrible. I generally liked sport, except in the winter. I made some good friends at school, and I'm still in touch with a few of them 30 years later, so I suppose that's positive!

6 Presenter Did you like school?
F Actually, I used to really love school. Lessons were fine, and I always did well without having to work too hard. But the real reason I loved school was because I had a very good social life. I had lots of friends and we used to play football in the playground at lunchtime. I was one of the gang. I felt that I belonged there. I've never really felt like that since then.

5 11)))

And our last story on today's *News Hour* is about an incredible coincidence. Have you ever put your name into Google or Facebook to see what comes up? One evening last April, an American woman, Kelly Hildebrandt, did just that. She was feeling bored, so she put her name into Facebook. She has quite an unusual name, so she was amazed to discover that there was another person on Facebook with exactly the same name and surname as her – but with one big difference. The other Kelly Hildebrandt was a man, and he lived in Texas. Kelly sent him a message and they began to email each other. Later they started to phone each other every day, and finally they met in person. They discovered that they had more in common than just their name – they both love the beach, and they both really enjoy cooking. Soon they realised that they were in love. At first they were worried that they might be related, but they found out that there was no family connection at all, and in October Kelly asked Kelly to marry him. The two Kelly's call each other 'Kelly girl' and 'Kelly boy', and they say that having the same name often causes confusion – once when Kelly boy booked travel tickets for them the travel agent almost cancelled one ticket because he thought that booking two tickets with the same name was a mistake. But there is one thing that the two Kellys are very clear about – if they have children they definitely won't call them Kelly!

5 12)))

Jenny I can't believe it. Your month here is nearly over. It's gone so fast.
Rob I know. I've had a great time, Jenny.
Jenny Me too. It's been really special. But...
Rob But what?
Jenny It won't be the same when you're in London and I'm here.
Rob But we'll still be in touch. You can visit me in London and I can come back here to see you.
Jenny It still won't be the same.
Rob No. No, it won't.
Jenny Maybe… I could come back to London with you?
Rob You can't do that Jenny. You've just got this job.
Jenny That's true.
Rob Well, we still have some time together. We're going out for dinner tonight!
Jenny Yes, and I'm going to take you somewhere really nice.
Rob Look at the time. I have to go now; it's my last interview in New York. I don't want to be late.
Jenny OK. See you later then.
Rob Bye.
Barbara Jenny, is Rob here?
Jenny Oh, you just missed him, Barbara.
Barbara I really need to talk to him. I'll try him on his cell phone. Hello, Rob? It's Barbara. Can you give me a call? There's something I'd like to talk about.

5 15)))

Rob Jenny!
Jenny Rob! I have something to tell you.
Rob I have something to tell you too. You go first.
Jenny Well. I thought again about moving to London…
Rob But you don't need to move to London.
Jenny What?
Rob Barbara called me earlier.
Jenny What about?
Rob She offered me a job. Here, in New York!
Jenny What?! Oh, that's great news.
Rob You don't seem very pleased.
Jenny I am, I mean, it's great! It's just that…
Rob What?
Jenny I sent Barbara an email this morning.
Rob And?
Jenny I told her I was quitting, and moving to London.
Rob Don't worry. Maybe she hasn't read your email yet.
Jenny I'll call her.
Barbara Hello, Barbara Keaton.
Jenny Barbara? It's Jenny.
Barbara Oh, hi Jenny.
Jenny Um, have you read your emails recently? There's one from me.
Barbara Oh yes. I can see it. I haven't opened it yet.
Jenny Don't open it! Delete it! Please just delete it. I'll explain later.
Barbara OK. It's gone. Is everything alright, Jenny?
Jenny Yes, thanks. Never better.

5 19)))

And finally on *News Today* here's a funny story to cheer you up on a Monday morning.

On Saturday night Katie Parfitt, a nurse from Manchester, came home from work. As soon as she opened the door, she realised that her cat, Joey, was behaving rather strangely. Instead of being pleased to see her, he started attacking her, and then, when she sat down to have something to eat, Joey jumped onto the table and sat on her plate. Then he jumped down onto the floor and immediately went to sleep. He slept all night, snoring very loudly. Katie couldn't understand what the matter was with Joey – he had never behaved like this before. However, when she met her neighbour the next morning, the mystery was solved.

5 20)))

My neighbour told me that he was having a drink in our local pub on Saturday. Suddenly he saw my cat Joey walk in though the door – it was open because it was a hot day. And then one of the people spilled his glass of beer on the floor and Joey starting drinking it – he was probably thirsty. So of course when Joey got home he was completely drunk! I took him to the vet the next day, but luckily he's fine now.

5 21)))

Iris Hello Rosemary. How are you this morning?
Rosemary Hello Iris. I'm fine thanks, but you'll never guess what's happened. Jack and Emma have broken up!
Iris No! Jack and Emma from number 36? That can't be true. I saw them last week and they looked really happy.
Rosemary No, it's definitely true. I heard them shouting. They were having a terrible argument.
Iris No! When?
Rosemary Last night. After he came home from work.
Iris What did they say?
Rosemary Well, I wasn't really listening…
Iris Of course not.
Rosemary But I couldn't help hearing. She was talking so loudly and of course the walls are very thin.
Iris So what did they say?
Rosemary Well, she said she that was going to stay with her mum! She told him that she wouldn't come back.
Iris Ooh, how awful. What about the children?
Rosemary She said she'd taken them to her sister. I suppose she'll take them with her in the end. And anyway, then five minutes later I saw her leaving the house with a suitcase!
Iris No! Why do you think she's leaving him? Is he seeing another woman?
Rosemary I don't know. Ooh, here's my bus.
Iris I must go and tell Mrs Jones at number 14. She always thought there was something… something strange about him…

5 22)))

Jack Hi Emma. I'm back. Where are you?
Emma I'm upstairs in the bedroom. I'm packing.
Jack Why? Where are you going?
Emma I'm going to stay with my mum.
Jack What happened to her?
Emma She's had an accident. She fell over in the street yesterday and she's broken her leg.
Jack How awful. Poor thing. Shall I go and make you a cup of tea?
Emma That'd be lovely. Thanks darling.
Jack How long do you think you'll have to stay?
Emma I won't come back until the weekend I don't think. I'll have to make sure she's OK. I've taken the children to my sister's for the night and she'll take them school tomorrow morning. Can you pick them up after school?
Jack Of course I can darling. Now don't worry about anything. We'll be absolutely fine. Drink your tea and I'll go and get your suitcase.
Emma Thanks, darling. The taxi'll be here in five minutes.

7

7A uses of the infinitive with *to*

1 I need **to buy** some new clothes. (3) 24))
   Try **not to talk** about politics.
2 It'll be nice **to meet** your parents.
   It's important **not to be** late.
3 I don't know where **to go** or what **to do**.
4 **A** Why did you go to the party?
   B **To meet** new people.
   I went to the party **to meet** new people.

- The infinitive is the base form of the verb. It is often used with *to*. It can be positive (e.g. *to be*) or negative (e.g. *not to be*).
- Use the infinitive with *to*:
  1 after some verbs, e.g. *want, need, would like*, etc. See **Verb forms** *p.158*.
  2 after adjectives.
  3 after question words, e.g. *what, where, when*, etc.
  4 to say why you do something.
     I came to this school **to learn** *English*. **NOT** *for learn English*.

> 🔍 **Infinitive without *to***
> Remember that we use the infinitive <u>without</u> *to* after auxiliary verbs (*do / does / didn't*) and after most modal verbs (*can, could, will, would*, etc.), e.g. **Do** *you* **live** *near here?* **Can** *you* **help** *me?* *I* **won't forget**. *What* **would** *you* **do**?

7B uses of the gerund (verb + *-ing*)

1 **Eating** outside in the summer makes me feel good. (3) 28))
   My idea of happiness is **getting up** late and **not going** to work.
2 I love **reading** in bed.
   I hate **not getting** to the airport early.
3 I'm thinking of **buying** a new car.
   He left without **saying** goodbye.

- The gerund is the base form of the verb + *ing*. It can be positive (e.g. *going*) or negative (e.g. *not going*).
- Use the gerund:
  1 as the subject or object of a sentence.
  2 after some verbs, e.g. *like, love, hate, enjoy*, etc. See **Verb forms** p.158.
  3 after prepositions.
- Remember the spelling rules for the *-ing* form. See **1C** *p.126* in MultiPack A.

7C *have to, don't have to, must, mustn't*

have to, don't have to

[+] I **have to** get up at seven every day. (3) 34))
    She **has to** speak English at work.
[-] We **don't have to** wear a uniform at this school.
    He **doesn't have to** work on Saturdays.
[?] **Do** I **have to** buy a grammar book?
    What time **does** she **have to** get up in the morning?

- Use *have to* + verb (infinitive) to talk about rules and obligations.
- Use *don't have* to + verb (infinitive) to say that there is no obligation, or that something is not necessary.
- Use *do / does* to make questions and negatives. **Do** I have to go? **NOT** *Have I to go?*
- Don't contract *have* or *has*. *I* **have to** *go*. **NOT** *I've to go*.

must / mustn't

[+] You **must** do your homework tonight. (3) 35))
    She **must** tidy her room before she goes out.
[-] You **mustn't** leave your bags here.
    I **mustn't** forget to call her tonight.
    (*mustn't* = *must not*)
[?] **Must** I buy a grammar book?
    When **must** we register for the exam?

- Use *must* + verb (infinitive without *to*) to talk about rules and obligations.
- *must / mustn't* is the same for all persons.
- Use *mustn't* + verb (infinitive without *to*) to say something is prohibited.

> 🔍 **must and have to**
> *Must* and *have to* are <u>very similar</u>, but there is a small difference. We normally use *have to* for a **general** obligation (a rule at work / school or a law). We normally use *must* for a **personal** obligation (one that the speaker imposes), e.g. a teacher to students or a parent to a child. But often you can use either *must* or *have to*.
>
> **mustn't and don't have to**
> *Mustn't* and *don't have to* have completely different meanings. Compare:
> You **mustn't** go. = It's prohibited. Don't go.
> You **don't have to** go. = You can go if you want to, but it's not obligatory / necessary.
>
> **Impersonal you**
> We often use *have to* and *must* with impersonal *you* (*you* = people in general), e.g.
> You **have to** wear a seatbelt in a car. You **mustn't** take photos in the museum.

7A

a Match the sentence halves.

Be ready   B

1 Do we need   E
2 In some countries it's important   D
3 I know you're tired, but try   F
4 We were late, so Simon offered   A
5 It's difficult   C

A to give us a lift to the station.
B to show your passport at check-in.
C not to forget people's names in a big class.
D to dress correctly in public.
E to buy some dollars at the airport?
F not to fall asleep during the film!

b Complete the sentences with a positive or negative infinitive.

do   not drive   go   have   learn   look for   not make   meet

I'm planning *to have* a party next week.

1 **A** Hi, I'm Donatella.
  B I'm Renée. Nice _to meet_ you.
2 What do you want _to do_ tonight?
3 I need _to go_ to the shop. I don't have any bread or milk.
4 Try _not to make_ a noise. Your father's asleep.
5 I'd really like _to learn_ how to drive.
6 Be careful _not to drive_ too fast on the way home – the roads are icy.
7 He's decided _to look for_ a new job.

◀ p.53

7B

a Complete the sentences with a verb in the list in the -*ing* form.

be   do   practise   remember   study   swim   teach   text   travel

I really enjoy *doing* exercise. It makes me feel great!

1 One thing that always makes me happy is _swimming_ in the sea.
2 You can't learn to play a musical instrument well without _practising_ regularly.
3 My mother's very bad at _remembering_ names.
4 _Teaching_ teenagers is very hard work.
5 My sister spends hours on the phone _texting_ her friends.
6 I hate _being_ the first to arrive at parties.
7 _Travelling_ by train is usually cheaper than by plane.
8 I'll go on _studying_ for as long as I can – I love being a student!

b Put the verbs in the -*ing* form or infinitive.

I like *listening* to the radio in the mornings. (listen)

1 _Doing_ Pilates is good for your health. (do)
2 We've decided _not to have_ a holiday this year. (not have)
3 We won't take the car. It's impossible _to park_. (park)
4 I'm not very good at _reading_ maps. (read)
5 You can borrow the car if you promise _to drive_ slowly. (drive)
6 Has it stopped _raining_? (rain)
7 I don't mind _cooking_, but I don't like _doing_ the washing-up. (cook, do)
8 I hate _getting up_ early in the morning. (get up)

◀ p.54

7C

a Complete the sentences with the correct form of *have to*.

I *don't have to* go to school on Saturdays

1 Janice _____ study very hard – she has exams soon.
2 You _____ stop your car at a red light.
3 _____ your sister _____ go to London for her job interview?
4 You _____ wear a uniform if you are a policeman.
5 We _____ get up early tomorrow. Our flight leaves at 6.30.
6 Harry _____ work today – his shop is closed.
7 I _____ go now. It's very late.
8 _____ we _____ go to bed? It's only 10 o'clock!

b Circle the correct form, *have to | must*, *don't have to*, or *mustn't*. Tick ✓ if both forms are possible.

☐ We *don't have to* | mustn't go to work next week. It's a holiday.
1 ☐ You *don't have to* | mustn't touch the oven. It's hot.
2 ☐ Do you *have to* | must send a photo with your passport form?
3 ✓ The concert is free. You *don't have to* | mustn't pay.
4 ✓ I'm late for a meeting. I have to | *must* go now.
5 ☐ You *don't have to* | *mustn't* leave the door open – the dog will get out.
6 ✓ We have to | *must* try that new restaurant in town.
7 ✓ In Britain you *have to* | must drive on the left.
8 ✓ *Do you have to* | *Must you* be tall to be good at tennis?

◀ p.56

Do ≠ must.

8

8A should / shouldn't

You **should** wear a suit to the interview.
I think you **should** change your job.
I don't think you **should** speak to her.
He's very stressed. He **shouldn't** work so hard.
You **shouldn't** drink coffee in the evening. It'll keep you awake.

- Use *should | shouldn't* + verb (infinitive without *to*) to give somebody advice or say what you think is the right thing to do.
- *should | shouldn't* is the same for all persons.
- We often use *I think you should…* or *I don't think you should…* **NOT** ~~I think you shouldn't…~~

> 🔍 **ought to**
> You can also use *ought to / ought not to* instead of *should / shouldn't*, e.g.
> You **ought to** wear a suit. He **ought not to** work so hard.

8B first conditional: *if* + present, *will / won't*

1 If I **miss** the last bus, **I'll get** a taxi. (4 2))
   If you **tell** her the truth, she **won't believe** you.
   What **will** you **do** if he **doesn't call** you?
2 If you **don't go**, she **won't be** very pleased.
   She **won't be** very pleased if you **don't go**.
3 If you **miss** the last bus, **get** a taxi.
   If you **miss** the last bus, you **can get** a taxi.

1 Use *if* + present to talk about a possible situation and *will | won't* + verb to talk about the consequence.
2 The *if*-clause can come first or second. If the *if*-clause comes first, we usually put a comma before the next clause.
3 You can also use the imperative or *can* + infinitive instead of *will* + infinitive in the other clause.

If I miss the last bus, I'll get a taxi.

8C possessive pronouns

Whose coat is it? It's my coat. (4 12))
   It's **mine**.
Whose jacket is it? It's your jacket.
   It's **yours**.
Whose phone is it? It's his phone.
   It's **his**.
Whose bag is it? It's her bag. It's **hers**.
Whose dog is it? It's our dog. It's **ours**.
Whose house is it? It's their house.
   It's **theirs**.

- Use possessive pronouns to talk about possession. *Is it **yours**? Yes, it's **mine**.*
- Use *Whose* to <u>ask</u> about possession. **Whose** *book is it?* **Whose** *is that bag?*

- Don't use possessive pronouns with a noun. **NOT** ~~It's mine book.~~
- Don't use *the* with possessive pronouns, e.g. *Is this **yours**?* **NOT** ~~Is this the yours?~~

pronouns and possessive adjectives overview

subject pronouns		object pronouns		possessive adjectives			possessive pronouns	
I	can come.	She loves	me.	This is	my	seat.	It's	mine.
You			you		your			yours
He			him		his			his
She			her		her			hers
It			it		its			its
We			us		our			ours
They			them		their			theirs

GRAMMAR BANK

8A

a Complete with *should* or *shouldn't*.

You *should* stop smoking.
1 You *shouldn't* work really long hours every day.
2 You *should* lose a bit of weight.
3 You *should* eat more fruit and vegetables.
4 You *shouldn't* put so much sugar in your coffee.
5 You *should* start doing some exercise.
6 You *shouldn't* drink less alcohol.
7 You *should* drink more water.
8 You *shouldn't* go to bed so late.

b Complete the sentences with *should* or *shouldn't* + a verb in the list.

drive	have	go	~~leave~~	relax	spend	study	walk	wear

We *should leave* early. It's going to start snowing soon.
1 You *should wear* a scarf. It's really cold today.
2 I *should study* this afternoon. I have an exam tomorrow.
3 You *shouldn't walk* alone in that part of the city. Get a taxi.
4 She *should relax* more. She's very stressed.
5 You *shouldn't drive* so fast at night – the roads are dangerous.
6 You *should go* to bed. You look tired.
7 Parents *should spend* more time with their children.
8 We *shouldn't have* a break yet – we only started work at 10.00.

◄ p.61

8B

a Match the sentence halves.

If you leave now, [C]
1 The ticket will be cheaper [D]
2 If I don't see you this afternoon, [G]
3 You'll learn more quickly [E]
4 If you get that new job, [F]
5 You won't pass your driving test [A]
6 If I lend you this book, [B]

A if you don't have enough lessons.
B will you give it back to me soon?
C ~~you'll catch the 8.00 train.~~
D if you travel after 9.00.
E if you come to every class.
F will you earn more money?
G I'll call you this evening.

b Complete with the correct form of the verbs.

If we *start* walking, the bus *will come*. (start, come)
1 If you *tell* me your secret, I *won't tell* anybody else. (tell, not tell)
2 If I *don't write* it down, I *won't remember* it. (not write, not remember)
3 *Will* you *call* me if you *get* any news? (call, get)
4 She *will help* you if you *ask* her nicely. (help, ask)
5 I *will phone* you if I *hear* from Alex. (phone, hear)
6 You *will miss* your friends if you *move* to Paris. (miss, move)
7 If you *listen* carefully, you *'ll understand* everything. (listen, understand)
8 The boss *won't be* very pleased if you *are* late for work. (not be, be)
9 I *'ll drive* you home if you *give* me directions. (drive, give)

◄ p.62

8C

a Circle the correct form.

Whose car is that? It's her / **hers**.
1 This isn't **my** / mine pen, it's Susan's.
2 I think this book is your / **yours**.
3 This isn't your suitcase, it's **ours** / our.
4 Where's Mary? I think these are **her** / hers gloves.
5 These keys are **mine** / the mine.
6 They showed us all theirs / **their** holiday photographs.
7 These seats are **theirs** / their, not ours. We're over there.
8 Is this yours / **your** bag?
9 This isn't my jacket. It's her / **hers**.

b Complete the sentences with a pronoun or possessive adjective.

This isn't my coffee, it's yours. Where's *mine*?
1 A Is that her car?
  B No, it's her boyfriend's. *His* is a white Peugeot.
2 Maya has a new boyfriend, but I haven't met *him* yet.
3 Look. Here's a photo of Alex and Kim with *their* new baby.
4 We've finished paying for our house, so it's *ours* now.
5 These are our tickets. Can you give Maria and Marta *theirs*?
6 We're very lucky. Our parents bought this dog for *us*.
7 We both love gardening. Would you like to see *our* garden?
8 London is famous for *its* parks.

◄ p.65

iTutor 141

9

9A second conditional: *if* + past, *would* / *wouldn't*

1 If a bull **attacked** me, **I'd run** away. **4 16** 🔊
   If you **didn't go** to bed so late, you **wouldn't be** so tired in the morning.
   Would you **take** the manager's job **if** they **offered** it to you?
2 If I **had** more time **I'd do** more exercise.
   I'd do more exercise **if** I **had** more time.
3 If we **went** by car, we **could stop** at places on the way.

1 Use *if* + past to talk about an imaginary or hypothetical future situation
   and *would / wouldn't* + verb to talk about the consequence.
• *would / wouldn't* is the same for all persons.
• Contractions: *'d = would* (*I'd, you'd, he'd*, etc.); *wouldn't = would not*.
2 The *if*-clause can come first or second. If the *if*-clause comes first, we
   usually put a comma before the next clause.
3 You can also use *could* + infinitive instead of *would* + infinitive in the
   other clause.

> **be in second conditionals**
> With the verb *be* you can use *were* (instead of
> *was*) after *I* / *he* / *she* / *it*, e.g.
> If Jack **was** / **were** here, he'd know what to do.
>
> Use *were* (not *was*) in the expression *If I* **were**
> *you,…*
> We often use this expression for advice,
> e.g. **If I were you**, I wouldn't take that job.

first or second conditional?

Compare the first and second conditionals.

• Use the **first conditional** for **possible** future
   situations.
   *If I **don't have to** work tomorrow, I'**ll help** you.*
   (= It's a possibility. Maybe I will help you.)
• Use the **second conditional** for **imaginary** or
   hypothetical situations.
   *If I **didn't have to** work tomorrow, I'**d help** you.*
   (= It's a hypothetical situation. I have to work, so I
   can't help you.)

9B present perfect + *for* or *since*

A Where do you live now?   **4 21** 🔊
B In Manchester.
A **How long have you lived** there?
B **I've lived** there **for** twenty years.

A Where do you work?
B In a primary school.
A **How long have you worked** there?
B **I've worked** there **since** 2005.

• Use the present perfect + *for* or *since* to talk about actions and states which
   started in the past and are still true now.
   *I'**ve lived** in Manchester **for** twenty years.* = I came to live in Manchester twenty
   years ago and I live in Manchester now.
• Don't use the present simple in this type of sentence, e.g. **NOT** ~~I live in~~
   ~~Manchester for twenty years.~~
• Use *How long…?* to ask questions about the duration of an action or a state.

for or since?

• Use *for* + a period of time, e.g. **for** *two weeks*, **for** *ten years*, **for** *a long time*, etc.
   *I've had this car **for** three months.*
• Use *since* with the beginning of a period of time, e.g. **since** *1980*, **since** *last June*, etc.
   *I've been afraid of spiders **since** I was a child.*

9C present perfect or past simple? (2)

1 A How long **was** Bob Marley a musician?   **4 28** 🔊
   B He **was** a musician for twenty years.
   A How many Grammys **did** he **win**?
   B He **didn't win** any.
2 A How long **has** Ziggy Marley **been** a musician?
   B He'**s been** a musician since he was ten.
   A How many Grammys **has** he **won**?
   B He'**s won** four.

1 Use the **past simple** to talk about a <u>finished</u> period of time in
   the past.
2 Use the **present perfect** to talk about a period of time from
   the past until now.
• Compare the past simple and present perfect.
   *Jack **was** married for ten years.* = Jack is not married now. He's
   divorced or dead.
   *Jack **has been** married for ten years.* = Jack is married now.

(handwritten top margin) If + subject + past simple, + subject... If I had... I

GRAMMAR BANK

9A

a Match the sentence halves.

You'd feel much better [A]
1 I'd enjoy the weekend more [E]
2 If it's sunny tomorrow, [D]
3 Would you wear it [C]
4 If we learned Portuguese, [F]
5 I wouldn't work [G]
6 If I went to live in London, [B]

A if you did some exercise.
B would you come to visit me?
C if I bought it for you?
D we could go to the beach.
E if I didn't have to work on Saturday.
F we could go and work in Brazil.
G if I didn't need the money.

b Complete with the correct form of the verbs.

If I _found_ a good job, I _would move_ to the USA. (find, move)
1 We _would buy_ the house if it _had_ a garden. (buy, have)
2 If you _tried_ Indian food, I'm sure you _would like_ it. (try, like)
3 You _would learn_ more if you _worked_ harder. (learn, work)
4 If we _rented_ a car, we _could_ drive up to the mountains. (rent, can)
5 We _would see_ our son more often if he _lived_ nearer. (see, live)
6 I _wouldn't go_ to that restaurant if I _were_ you – it's very expensive. (not go, be)
7 I _would take_ you to the airport if my mum _didn't have_ the car. (take, not have)
8 I quite like cycling, but I _wouldn't cycle_ to work if I _had_ a car. (not cycle, have)
9 _Would_ you _leave_ your country if you _got_ a well-paid job abroad? (leave, get)
10 I love living here. I _wouldn't be_ happy if I _had to_ leave. (not be, have to)

◀ p.68

9B

a Write questions with *How long* and the present perfect.

you / be married   _How long have you been married?_
1 you / be frightened of clowns _How long have you..._?
2 your sister / have her car _How long has your sister had her car_?
3 you / live here _How long have you lived here_?
4 your dad / be a teacher _How long has your dad been a..._?
5 you / know your boyfriend _How long have you known your boyfriend_?
6 Britain / be in the EU _How long has Britain been in the EU_?
7 you / have your cat _How long have you had your cat_?
8 he / work for the same company _How long has he worked for the same company_?

b Answer the questions in **a**. Use the present perfect + *for* or *since*.

I've been married for 20 years.
1 I've been frightened of clowns _since_ I was a child.
2 She _has had her car for_ three years.
3 I've lived here _for_ a long time.
4 He _has been a teacher since_ 1990.
5 I've known _since_ May.
6 It _has been since_ 1973.
7 We've had _for_ about two years.
8 He _has worked since_ 2008. ◀ p.71

(handwritten) She's   He has = He's.

9C

a Circle the correct form.

She is / *She's been* single since last summer.
1 *He left* / He has left school two years ago.
2 *I lived* / I've lived in Cardiff for two years, but then I moved to Swansea.
3 She lives / *She's lived* in Florida since 2010.
4 *My sister had* / My sister has had her baby yesterday!
5 I work in an office. I work / *I've worked* there for 20 years.
6 The city changed / *The city has changed* a lot since I was a child.
7 They're divorced now. *They were* / They have been married for ten years.
8 *I met* / I've met Sandra when I *was* / have been at university.

b Complete with the present perfect or past simple.

1 A Where does Rob live now?
  B In Madrid.
  A How long _has he lived_ there? (he / live)
  B For three months. He _moved_ there in September. (move)
2 A When _did Picasso die_? (Picasso / die)
  B In 1977, in Paris I think.
  A How long _did he live_ in France? (he / live)
  B For a long time. He _left_ Spain when he was 25. (leave)
3 A My brother and his wife get on very well.
  B How long _have they been_ married? (they / be)
  A They've _been_ married since 1995. They _met_ at university. (be, meet)
  B Really? _Was_ that in Paris? (be)

◀ p.72

iTutor 143

10

10A passive: *be* + past participle

Present: *am | is | are* + past participle 4 38))
- [+] Kevlar **is used** to make bullet-proof vests.
- [-] Tippex **isn't used** very much today.
- [?] **Are** disposable nappies **used** all over the world?

Past: *was | were* + past participle
- [+] The dishwasher **was invented** by Josephine Cochrane.
- [-] Windscreen wipers **weren't invented** until 1903.
- [?] When **was** the washing machine **invented**?

- You can often say things in two ways, in the active or in the passive.
  *Josephine Cochrane **invented** the dishwasher.* (**active**)
  *The dishwasher **was invented** by Josephine Cochrane.* (**passive**)
- In the **active** sentence, the focus is more on **Josephine Cochrane**.
- In the **passive** sentence the focus is more on **the dishwasher**.
- You can also use the passive when it isn't known or isn't important who does or did the action.
  *My car **was stolen** last week.*
  *Volvo cars **are made** in Sweden.*
- Use *by* to say who did the action.
  *The Lord of the Rings **was written by** Tolkien.*

10B used to / didn't use to ~~Vsed to (Play) → Veb infinitive~~

- [+] When I was a child, I **used to** play in the street. 4 43))
  My brother **used to** have very long hair.
- [-] Children **didn't use to** watch much TV when my father was young.
  My daughter **didn't use to** like vegetables, but now she loves them.
- [?] **Did** you **use to** wear a uniform at school? Yes, I did.
  Did you **use to** like your teachers? No, I didn't.

- Use *used to | didn't use to* + verb to talk about things that happened repeatedly or were true for a long period of time in the past, but are usually <u>not</u> true now, e.g. things that happened when you were a child.
- *used to | didn't use to* is the same for all persons.
- Instead of *used to* you can use the past simple with an adverb of frequency.
  *When I was a child, I **often played** in the street.*

> **used to or usually?**
> *used to* only exists in the past.
> For habits in the present, use *usually* +
> present simple, **NOT** ~~*use to*~~
> *I **usually cook** in the evenings.*
> **NOT** ~~I use to cook in the evenings.~~

10C might / might not (possibility)

We **might** have a picnic tomorrow, but it depends on the weather. 4 50))
She **might** come with us, but she's not sure yet.
I **might not** go to the party. I haven't decided yet.
You **might not** see him today. He's coming home late.

- Use *might | might not* + verb (infinitive without *to*) to say that perhaps you will or won't do something.
  *We **might** have a picnic tomorrow.* = Perhaps we will have a picnic tomorrow.
- *might | might not* is the same for all persons.
- *might not* is not usually contracted.

> **may / may not**
> You can also use *may* instead of *might* for possibility, e.g.
> *We **may** have a picnic tomorrow.*
> *I **may not** go to the party.*

10A

a Complete with present or past passive.

The Eiffel Tower *was completed* in 1889. (complete)

1 Many of the things we use every day _____ by women. (invent)
2 In the UK most children _____ in state schools. (educate)
3 Australia _____ by Captain Cook in 1770. (discover)
4 This morning I _____ up by the neighbour's dog. (wake)
5 Cricket _____ in the summer in the UK. (play)
6 The songs on this album _____ last year. (record)
7 Nowadays a lot of toys _____ in China. (make)
8 Carols are songs which _____ at Christmas. (sing)
9 These birds _____ in northern Europe. (not usually see)
10 'Rome _____ in a day.' (not build)

b Rewrite the sentences in the passive, beginning with the highlighted words.

Shakespeare wrote Hamlet in 1603.
Hamlet was written by Shakespeare in 1603.

1 Jonathan Ive designed the iPod and the iPhone.
2 Most Mediterranean countries produce olive oil.
3 Herschel discovered Uranus in 1781.
4 Barry Sonnenfeld directed the *Men in Black* films.
5 David Hockney painted *Mr and Mrs Clark and Percy* in 1970–1971.
6 Elvis Presley didn't write *Blue Suede Shoes*.
7 JK Rowling wrote the Harry Potter books.
8 They make Daihatsu cars in Japan.

◀ p.76

10B

a Look at how John has changed. Write five sentences about how he was **IN THE PAST**.

IN THE PAST

NOW

He used to be slim.

1 He used to have _____ long hair.
2 He didn't use to wear _____ glasses.
3 He didn't use to have _____ a beard.
4 He used to play _____ football.
5 He didn't use to wear _____ a tie.

b Make sentences with *used to*, *didn't use to*, or *did … use to?*

[?] you / have long hair
Did you use to have long hair?

1 [+] my sister / hate maths, but she loves it now
2 [?] where / you / work
3 [–] I / like vegetables when I was a child
4 [?] what / you / do in the summer holidays when you were young
5 [–] The British / drink a lot of coffee
6 [+] this building / be a cinema
7 [?] your brother / teach here
8 [–] I / be a Manchester United fan
9 [?] Jeff / have a motorbike
10 [+] telegrams / be a way of sending important messages

◀ p.79

10C

a Match the sentences.

Take some sun cream. [D]
1 Let's buy a lottery ticket. [H]
2 Phone the restaurant. [G]
3 Don't stand on the wall. [A]
4 Let's take a map. [C]
5 Try the shirt on. [B]
6 Don't wait for me. [I]
7 Be careful with that knife! [P]
8 Ask how much it costs. [E]

A You might fall.
B It may not be your size.
C We might get lost.
D It might be really sunny.
E We may not have enough money.
F You might cut yourself.
G It may be closed on Sundays.
H We might win.
I I may be late.

b Complete the sentences with *might* + a verb phrase.

| be cold   be ill   be in a meeting   go to the cinema |
| not have time   not like it   have fish and chips |

I'm not sure what to do tonight. I *might go to the cinema.*

1 Kim wasn't at school today. She may be ill
2 His phone is turned off. He might be in a meeting
3 It's an unusual book. You may not like it
4 I don't know if I'll finish it. I might not have time
5 I'm not sure what to order. I might have fish and chips
6 Take a jacket. It might be cold.

◀ p.80

11

11A expressing movement

The man **went up** the steps and **into** the church.
He **drove out of** the garage and **along** the street.
I **ran over** the bridge and **across** the park.

- To express movement use a verb of movement, e.g. *go, come, run, walk*, etc. and a preposition (or adverb) of movement e.g. *up, down, away*, etc.

> 🔍 **in or into? out or out of?**
> Remember, use *into / out of* + noun, and *in / out* if there isn't a noun.
> Come **into** the living room. Come **in**.
> He went **out of** the house. He went **out**.
> See **Expressing movement** p.162.

verb + Preposition / Adverb

11B word order of phrasal verbs

1 What time do you **get up**?
  I don't usually **go out** during the week.
2 **Put on** your coat. **Put** your coat **on**. **Put** it **on**.
  Turn off the TV. **Turn** the TV **off**. **Turn** it **off**.
3 I'm **looking for** my glasses.
  Have you found your glasses? No, I'm still **looking for** them.

- A phrasal verb = verb + particle (preposition or adverb), e.g. *get up, turn on, look for*.
  1 Some phrasal verbs don't have an object, e.g. *get up, go out*.
  2 Some phrasal verbs have an object and are separable. With these phrasal verbs you can put the particle (*on, off*, etc.) before <u>or</u> after the object.
- When the object is a pronoun (*me, it, him*, etc.) it <u>always</u> goes between the verb and particle.
  Here's your coat. **Put it on.** NOT ~~Put on it.~~
  3 Some phrasal verbs have an object and are inseparable, e.g. *look for*. With these phrasal verbs the verb (e.g. *look*) and the particle (e.g. *for*) are never separated.
  I'm **looking for** *my glasses.* NOT ~~I'm looking my glasses for.~~
See **Phrasal verbs** p.163.

11C so, neither + auxiliaries

1 **A** I love classical music.
  B So do I.
  A I went to a classical concert last night.
  B So did I.
2 **A** I'm not married.
  B Neither am I.
  A I don't want to get married.
  B Neither do I.

present simple	I don't like classical music.	Neither **do** I.
present continuous	I'm having a great time	So **am** I.
can / can't	I can swim.	So **can** I.
past simple	I didn't like the film. I was very tired.	Neither **did** I. So **was** I.
would / wouldn't	I wouldn't like to go there.	Neither **would** I.
present perfect	I've been to Brazil.	So **have** I.

- Be careful with the word order.
  So do I. | Neither do I. NOT ~~So I do. | Neither I do.~~

- Use *So do I, Neither do I*, etc. to say that you have something in common with somebody.
  1 Use *So* + auxiliary + *I* to respond to positive sentences.
  2 Use *Neither* + auxiliary + *I* to respond to negative sentences.
- The auxiliary you use depends on the tense.

> 🔍 **neither and nor**
> You can also use *nor* instead of *neither*, e.g.
> **A** *I didn't like the film.*
> **B** **Nor / Neither** *did I.*
> *Neither* is usually pronounced /'naɪðə/, but can also be pronounced /'niːðə/.

11A

a (Circle) the correct preposition.

I lost my mobile phone signal when we went *across* /(*through*) a tunnel.

1 We ran *to* / *down* the sea, and jumped *into* / *out of* the water.
2 If you go *over* / *past* the bank, you'll see the supermarket on the right.
3 He walked *along* / *across* the street until he got to the park.
4 The plane flew *on* / *over* the town and then landed.
5 The dog ran *towards* / *to* me, but then it stopped.
6 We cycled *over* / *out of* the bridge and *in* / *into* the city centre.
7 The racing cars went *round* / *under* the track 12 times.
8 The little boy suddenly ran *across* / *through* the road.

b Complete the sentences with the correct preposition.

He jumped *into* his car and drove away.

1 As I cycled under the bridge, a train went ___over___ it.
2 Come ___in___. The door's open.
3 This is the 3rd floor. Go ___down___ those stairs and you'll come to the 2nd floor.
4 He walked ___into___ the bar and ordered a drink.
5 I like going ___out___ on a Saturday night.
6 He took his passport ___out of___ his bag.
7 I'm exhausted. I've just cycled ___over___ a huge hill. ◀ *p.85*

11B

a (Circle) the correct form. If both are correct, tick ✔ the box.

Turn off your mobile / *Turn your mobile off* before the film starts. ✔

1 Tonight I have to *look my sister after* / *look after my sister.* ☐
2 Let's *go out this evening* / *go this evening out.* ☑
3 *Turn down the radio* / *Turn the radio down.* It's too loud. ☑
4 My brother is *looking for a new job* / *looking a new job for.* ☐
5 You should *throw away those old jeans* / *throw those old jeans away.* ☑
6 I don't like shopping for clothes online – I prefer to *try them on* / *try on them* before I buy them. ☑
7 *Take off your shoes* / *Take your shoes off* before you come in. ☑
8 That's my sister – I think you'd really *get on with her* / *get on her with.* ☐
9 If it doesn't fit, you should *take back it* / *take it back* to the shop. ☐
10 What time do you *get up in the morning* / *get in the morning up*? ☐

b Complete the sentences with *it* or *them* and a word from the list.

back   in   on (x2)   up (x3)   down

I can't hear the radio. Turn *it up*.

1 Your clothes are all over the floor. Pick ___them up___.
2 Here's your coat. Put ___it on___.
3 'What does this word mean?' 'Look ___it up___.'
4 To get your passport there are three forms. Please fill ___them in___ now.
5 You remember that money I lent you? When can you give ___it back___?
6 Is there anything on TV? Let's turn ___it on___ and see.
7 You won't remember my address. Write ___it down___.

◀ *p.87*

11C

a Complete **B**'s answers with an auxiliary verb.

A I like chocolate.   B So *do* I.

1 A I'm really thirsty.   B So ___am___ I.
2 A I didn't go out last night.   B Neither ___did___ I.
3 A I was born in Rome.   B So ___was___ I.
4 A I don't eat meat.   B Neither ___do___ I.
5 A I've been to Moscow.   B So ___have___ I.
6 A I can't sing.   B Neither ___can___ I.
7 A I'd like to go to Bali.   B So ___would___ I.
8 A I saw a film last week.   B So ___did___ I.
9 A I wouldn't like to eat that.   B Neither ___would___ I.
10 A I can play chess.   B So ___can___ I.

b Respond to **A**. Say you are the same. Use *So…I* or *Neither…I*.

A I don't like cabbage.   *Neither do I.*

1 A I live near the supermarket.   ___So do I___
2 A I'm not afraid of snakes.   ___Neither am I___
3 A I went to bed late last night.   ___So did I___
4 A I haven't been to Canada.   ___Neither have I___
5 A I don't have any pets.   ___Neither do I___
6 A I can speak three languages.   ___So I can___
7 A I always drink coffee in the morning.   ___So do I___
8 A I'm waiting for the bus to the airport.   ___So am I___

◀ *p.88*

12

12A past perfect

+	When I woke up the garden was all white. (5 17))
	It **had snowed** during the night.
	I suddenly realised that I**'d left** my mobile in the taxi.
−	We got home just in time – the match **hadn't started**.
	When she got to class, she realized that she **hadn't brought** her book.
?	**A** I went to Paris last weekend. I really loved it.
	B **Had** you **been** there before?
	A No, I **hadn't**.

- Use the past perfect when you are already talking about the past and want to talk about an earlier past action.
  *When I woke up the garden was all white. It **had snowed** during the night.* = It snowed <u>before</u> I woke up.
- Make the past perfect with had | hadn't + past participle.
- The form of the past perfect is the same for all persons.
- *had* is sometimes contracted to *'d*.

> 🔍 **had** or **would?**
> Be careful: *'d* can be *had* or *would*.
> *I didn't know that you**'d** found a new job.* (*'d* = had)
> *If you went by taxi, you**'d** get there more quickly.*
> (*'d* = would)

12B reported (or indirect) speech

direct speech	**reported speech** (5 23))
'I love you.'	He said (that) **he loved me**.
'I've just arrived.'	She said (that) **she had just arrived**.
'We'll come at eight.'	He told me (that) **they would come** at eight.
'I don't want to go to the party.'	Jack told Anna (that) **he didn't want** to go to the party.

- Use reported speech to report (to tell somebody) what another person said.
- We often introduce reported speech with *said* or *told* (+ person)
- After *said* or *told* **that** is optional, e.g. *He said (**that**) he loved me.*
- Pronouns often change in reported speech, e.g. *I* changes to *he* or *she*.
  'I'm tired.' **She** told me (that) **she** was tired.

- Verb tenses change like this:

direct speech	reported speech
'I **can** help you.' (present simple)	He said (that) he **could** help me. (past simple)
'I**'m watching** TV.' (present continuous)	She said (that) she **was watching** TV. (past continuous)
'I**'ll** phone you.' (will)	He told me (that) he **would** phone me. (would)
'I **met** a girl.' (past simple)	John told me (that) he **had met** a girl. (past perfect)
'I**'ve broken** my leg.' (present perfect)	Sara said (that) she **had broken** her leg. (past perfect)

> 🔍 **say** or **tell?**
> You <u>can</u> use *said* or *told* in reported speech but they are used differently.
> You <u>can't</u> use *said* with an object or pronoun.
> *He **said** (that) he loved me.* **NOT** ~~He said me (that) he loved me.~~
> You <u>must</u> use *told* with an object.
> *He **told me** (that) he loved me.* **NOT** ~~He told (that) he loved me.~~

12C questions without auxiliaries

subject	verb	(5 27))
Who	painted	*Mr and Mrs Clark and Percy?*
Which singer	made	reggae popular all over the world?
How many people	live	near the school?
Who	wants	a cup of coffee?

- When the question word (*Who?*, *What?*, *Which?*, *How many?*, etc.) is the <u>subject</u> of the verb in the question, we <u>don't</u> use an auxiliary verb (*do* | *does* | *did*).
  Who painted *Mr and Mrs Clark and Percy?*
  NOT ~~Who did paint…?~~
- In most other questions in the present and past simple we use the auxiliary verb *do* | *does* | *did* + the infinitive.
  *What music **do** you like?* **NOT** ~~What music you like?~~
  See **1A** *p.126* in MultiPack A.

12A

a Match the sentence halves.

I couldn't get into my flat because [C]
1 When our friends arrived [G]
2 I took the jacket back because [D]
3 Jill didn't come with us because [A]
4 I turned on the TV news [F]
5 Johnny was nervous because [E]
6 When I got to the supermarket checkout [B]

A she'd made other plans.
B I realized that I'd left my wallet at home.
C I'd lost my keys.
D I had bought the wrong size.
E it was the first time he had flown.
F to see what had happened.
G we hadn't finished cooking the dinner.

b Complete the sentences. Put the verbs in the past simple and past perfect.

We _didn't get_ a table in the restaurant because we _hadn't booked_. (not get, not book)
1 I _didn't recognize_ Caroline because she'd _changed_ a lot. (not recognize, change)
2 My friend _phoned_ to tell me that I _'d left_ my wallet in his car. (phone, leave)
3 When I _turned on_ the radio, the news _had already finished_. (turn on, already finish)
4 She _didn't lend_ me the DVD because she _hadn't watched_ it yet. (not lend, not watch)
5 The bar _had closed_ by the time we _arrived_. (close, arrive)
6 When we _got_ home we saw that somebody _had broken_ the kitchen window. (get, break)
7 Luckily it _had stopped_ snowing when we _left_ work. (stop, leave)

◄ p.93

12B

a Write the sentences in reported speech.

'I love you.' He told her that he _loved her_.
1 'I'm hungry.' She said that she _was hungry_.
2 'I don't like sad films.' He told her he _didn't like / Disliked_.
3 'I'll call the doctor.' He said he _would call the doctor_.
4 'I've bought a new phone.' Paul told us that he _had bought a new phone_.
5 'I live in the city centre.' She said that she _lived in the city centre_.
6 'We can't do it!' They said that they _couldn't do it_.
7 'I saw Eclipse at the cinema.' Julie said that she _had seen eclipse at the cinema_.

b Write the sentences in direct speech.

He told her that he was a doctor. He said: '_I'm a doctor._'
1 She said that she was studying German. She said: '_I'm studying German._'
2 Tony told me that his car had broken down. Tony said: '_My car has broke down._'
3 Paul said that he would send me an email. Paul said: '_I will send you an email._'
4 Wanda and Jack said they were in a hurry. Wanda and Jack said: '_We are in a hurry._'
5 He said he hadn't finished his essay yet. He said: '_I haven't finished my essay yet._'
6 She told us that she wouldn't arrive on time. She said: '_I won't arrive on time._'
7 David said he had just arrived. David said: '_I have just arrived._' ◄ p.94

12C

a Circle the correct question form.

What _you did_ | (_did you do_) last night?
1 What _happened_ | _did happen_ to you?
2 What _means this word_ | _does this word mean_?
3 How many people _came_ | _did come_ to the meeting?
4 Which bus _goes_ | _does go_ to town?
5 Which film _won_ | _did win_ the Oscar this year?
6 What _said the teacher_ | _did the teacher say_?
7 Who _made_ | _did make_ this cake? It's fantastic!

→ auxiliar can't be next to the verb.

b Write the questions. Do you know the answers?

How many Formula 1 championships _did Michael Schumacher win_? (Michael Schumacher / win)
1 When _____ president of the USA? (Barack Obama / become)
2 Which US state _____ with the letter 'H'? (start)
3 Which books _____? (J.R.R. Tolkien / write)
4 Who _____ the football World Cup in 2010? (win)
5 Which sport _____ the lightest ball? (use)
6 Where _____? (the 2008 Olympics / take place)
7 Which company _____? (Steve Jobs / start)

◄ p.96

iTutor 149

Verb forms

1 VERBS + INFINITIVE

a Complete the **to + verb** column with *to* + a verb from the list.

be bring buy catch drive find get married
go (x2) help pay rain see turn off

			to + verb
1	**decide**	We've decided ▨ to France for our holiday.	*to go*
2	**forget**	Don't forget ▨ all the lights.	to turn off
3	**hope**	We hope ▨ you again soon.	to see
4	**learn**	I'm learning ▨. My test's next month.	to drive
5	**need**	I need ▨ to the supermarket. We don't have any milk.	to go
6	**offer**	He offered ▨ me with my CV.	to help
7	**plan**	They're planning ▨ soon.	to get married
8	**pretend**	He pretended ▨ ill, but he wasn't really.	to be
9	**promise**	He's promised ▨ me back when he gets a job.	to pay
10	**remember**	Remember ▨ your dictionaries to class tomorrow.	to bring
11	**start**	It was very cloudy and it started ▨.	to rain
12	**try**	I'm trying ▨ a job, but it's very hard.	to find
13	**want**	I want ▨ the six o'clock train.	to catch
14	**would like**	I'd like ▨ a new car next month.	to buy

b (3 25)) Listen and check.

c Cover the **to + verb** column. Say the sentences.

◄ p.53

2 VERBS + GERUND (VERB + -*ING*)

a Complete the **gerund** column with a verb from the list in the gerund.

be cook do have make rain read talk tidy wake up work

			gerund
1	**enjoy**	I enjoy ▨ in bed.	*reading*
2	**finish**	Have you finished ▨ your room?	tidying
3	**go on** (= continue)	I want to go on ▨ until I'm 60.	being
4	**hate**	I hate ▨ late when I'm meeting someone.	waking up
5	**like**	I like ▨ breakfast in a café.	having
6	**love**	I love ▨ on a sunny morning.	raining
7	**(don't) mind**	I don't mind ▨ the ironing. It's quite relaxing.	doing
8	**spend (time)**	She spends hours ▨ on the phone.	talking
9	**start★**	It started ▨ at 5.30 in the morning.	working
10	**stop**	Please stop ▨ such a noise. I can't think.	making
11	**feel like**	I don't feel like ▨ today. Let's go out for lunch.	cooking

★ *start can be used with a gerund or infinitive, e.g. It started raining. It started to rain.*

b (3 29)) Listen and check.

c Cover the **gerund** column. Say the sentences.

◄ p.55

get

> 🔍 **get**
> *get* is one of the most common verbs in English. It has several different meanings, e.g. *arrive*, *become*, and can also be used with many prepositions or adverbs with different meanings, e.g. *get up*, *get on with*.

a Match the phrases and the pictures.

get = become (+ adjective / past participle)

5 get angry
3 get divorced
6 get fit
4 get lost
2 get married
1 get nervous

get = become (+ comparative)

7 get better
9 get colder
8 get worse

get = buy / obtain

11 get a job
12 get a newspaper
10 get a ticket

get + preposition (phrasal verbs)

15 get on / off a bus
13 get on (well) with
14 get up

get (to) = arrive

16 get home
18 get to school
17 get to work

get = receive

19 get an email
21 get a present
20 get a (text) message

b (3 55)) Listen and check.

c Cover the phrases and look at the pictures. Test yourself or a partner.

◀ *p.61*

159

Confusing verbs

a Match the verbs and pictures.

2 **wear** /weə/
jewellery
clothes

carry /ˈkæri/
a bag
a baby

8 **win** /wɪn/
a medal
a prize
a match

earn /ɜːn/
a salary
money

5 **know** /nəʊ/
somebody well
something

meet /miːt/
somebody for the first time
at 11 o'clock

1 **hope** /həʊp/
that something
  good will happen
to do sth

wait /weɪt/
for a bus
for a long time

3 **watch** /wɒtʃ/
TV
a match

look at /lʊk æt/
a photo
your watch

11 **look** /lʊk/
happy
about 25 years old

look like /lʊk laɪk/
your mother
a model

4 **miss** /mɪs/
the bus
a class

lose /luːz/
a match
your glasses

9 **bring** /brɪŋ/
your dictionary
sth back from holiday

take /teɪk/
an umbrella
your children to school

6 **look for** /lʊk fɔː/
your glasses
a job

find /faɪnd/
your glasses
a job

10 **say** /seɪ/
sorry
hello
something **to** sb

tell /tel/
a joke
a lie
somebody something

7 **lend** /lend/
money **to** sb

borrow /ˈbɒrəʊ/
money **from** sb

b (4 5)) Listen and check.

c Work with a partner. **A** say a verb, **B** say a possible continuation.

A Wait... **B** for a bus

◀ p.63

Please let me pass!

3045.33
1534.27
T INS 18452.00
3642.12
PENSION
SALARY 38924.0

🔎 **hope and expect**

hope = to want sth to happen and think it will happen, always for positive things, e.g. *I hope I'll pass the exam.*

expect = to think sth will happen, usually for a reason (not necessarily a positive thing), e.g. *I expect I'll fail because I haven't worked very hard.*

look and look like

After *look* we use an adjective or an age.

After *look like* we use a noun.

Animals

a Match the words and pictures.

20 bee /biː/
14 butterfly /ˈbʌtəflaɪ/
27 fly /flaɪ/
8 mosquito /məˈskiːtəʊ/
29 spider /ˈspaɪdə/

1 bull /bʊl/
21 chicken /ˈtʃɪkɪn/
16 cow /kaʊ/
10 goat /gəʊt/
23 horse /hɔːs/
25 pig /pɪg/
7 sheep /ʃiːp/

2 bat /bæt/
19 bear /beə/
28 bird /bɜːd/
12 camel /ˈkæml/
13 crocodile /ˈkrɒkədaɪl/
15 dolphin /ˈdɒlfɪn/
4 elephant /ˈelɪfənt/
3 giraffe /dʒəˈrɑːf/
22 jellyfish /ˈdʒelifɪʃ/
30 kangaroo /kæŋgəˈruː/
9 lion /ˈlaɪən/
18 monkey /ˈmʌŋki/
24 mouse (plural mice) /maʊs/
6 rabbit /ˈræbɪt/
26 shark /ʃɑːk/
17 snake /sneɪk/
11 tiger /ˈtaɪgə/
5 whale /weɪl/

b (4 17)) Listen and check.

c Cover the words and look at the pictures. Test yourself or a partner.

◀ p.68

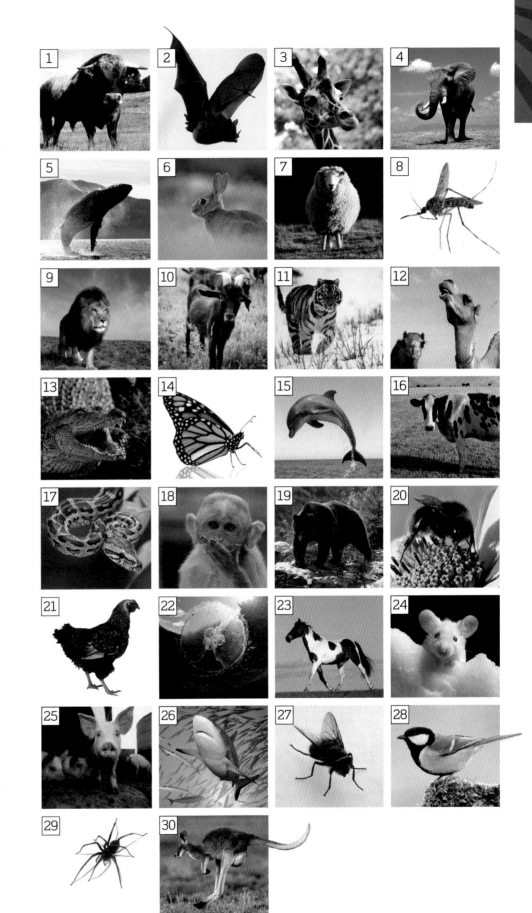

161

Expressing movement

a Match the words and pictures.

- 6 under (*the bridge*) /'ʌndə/
- 11 along (*the street*) /ə'lɒŋ/
- 10 round / around (*the lake*) /raʊnd/ /ə'raʊnd/
- 8 through (*the tunnel*) /θruː/
- 4 into (*the shop*) /'ɪntuː/
- 2 across (*the road*) /ə'krɒs/
- 3 over (*the bridge*) /'əʊvə/
- 12 up (*the steps*) /ʌp/
- 7 past (*the church*) /pɑːst/
- 9 towards (*the lake*) /tə'wɔːdz/
- 1 down (*the steps*) /daʊn/
- 5 out of (*the shop*) /'aʊt əv/

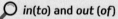

> 🔍 **in(to) and out (of)**
> After a verb of movement we use either
> *in / out* or *into / out of* + place, e.g.
> Come **in**. Come **into** my office.
> He ran **out**. He ran **out of** the room.

b (4 57))) Listen and check.

c Cover the words. Where did Snowy go?

> *He went down the steps...*

> 🔍 **away, off, and back**
> We use **away** to express movement to
> another place, e.g. **Go away**! *I don't want to
> speak to you. The man* **ran away** *when he saw
> the policeman.*

> We use **back** to express movement to the place
> where something or somebody was before,
> e.g. *After dinner we* **went back** *to our hotel.
> Their dog ran away and never* **came back**.

> We use **off** to express movement down or
> away, e.g. **Get off** *the bus at the railway
> station. The man* **ran off** *when he saw the
> policeman.*

◀ *p.84*

Phrasal verbs

a Match the sentences and the pictures.

9 The match will **be over** at about 5.30.

4 I need to **give up** smoking.

1 Don't **throw away** that letter!

10 **Turn down** the music! It's very loud.

5 **Turn up** the TV! I can't hear.

7 6 He **looked up** the words in a dictionary.

2 3 Could you **fill in** this form? fill in = fill out

12 I want to **find out** about hotels in Madrid.

8 It's bedtime – go and **put on** your pyjamas.

11 Could you **take off** your boots, please?

3 My sister's **looking after** Jimmy for me today.

6 I'm really **looking forward to** the holidays.

b (5 2)) Listen and check.

c Cover the sentences and look at the pictures. Remember the phrasal verbs.

d Look at these other phrasal verbs from Files 1–10. Can you remember what they mean?

get up
come on
go away (for the weekend)
go out (at night)
stand up
sit down

turn on (the TV)
turn off (the TV)
try on (clothes)
give back (something you've borrowed)
take back (something to a shop)
call back (later)
pay back (money you've borrowed)
switch off (the air conditioning)
write down (the words)
put away (e.g. clothes in a cupboard)
pick up (something on the floor)

carry on (doing something)
look for (something you've lost)
get on / off (a bus)
get on with (a person)

◀ p.87

🔍 **Type 1 = no object**
The verb and the particle (*on*, *up*, etc.) are **never separated**.
I get up at 7.30.

Type 2 = + object
The verb and the particle (*on*, *up*, etc.) **can be separated**.
Turn the TV on. OR *Turn on the TV.*

Type 3 = + object
The verb and the particle (*on*, *up*, etc.) are **never separated**.
Look for your keys. NOT ~~Look your keys for.~~

Irregular verbs

Present	Past simple	Past participle
be /biː/	was /wɒz/ were /wɜː/	been /biːn/
become /bɪˈkʌm/	became /bɪˈkeɪm/	become
begin /bɪˈgɪn/	began /bɪˈgæn/	begun /bɪˈgʌn/
break /breɪk/	broke /brəʊk/	broken /ˈbrəʊkən/
bring /brɪŋ/	brought /brɔːt/	brought
build /bɪld/	built /bɪlt/	built
buy /baɪ/	bought /bɔːt/	bought
can /kæn/	could /kʊd/	–
catch /kætʃ/	caught /kɔːt/	caught
choose /tʃuːz/	chose /tʃəʊz/	chosen /ˈtʃəʊzn/
come /kʌm/	came /keɪm/	come
cost /kɒst/	cost	cost
cut /kʌt/	cut	cut
do /duː/	did /dɪd/	done /dʌn/
drink /drɪŋk/	drank /dræŋk/	drunk /drʌŋk/
drive /draɪv/	drove /drəʊv/	driven /ˈdrɪvn/
eat /iːt/	ate /eɪt/	eaten /ˈiːtn/
fall /fɔːl/	fell /fel/	fallen /ˈfɔːlən/
feel /fiːl/	felt /felt/	felt
find /faɪnd/	found /faʊnd/	found
fly /flaɪ/	flew /fluː/	flown /fləʊn/
forget /fəˈget/	forgot /fəˈgɒt/	forgotten /fəˈgɒtn/
get /get/	got /gɒt/	got
give /gɪv/	gave /geɪv/	given /ˈgɪvn/
go /gəʊ/	went /went/	gone /gɒn/
grow /grəʊ/	grew /gruː/	grown /grəʊn/
have /hæv/	had /hæd/	had
hear /hɪə/	heard /hɜːd/	heard
hit /hɪt/	hit	hit
keep /kiːp/	kept /kept/	kept
know /nəʊ/	knew /njuː/	known /nəʊn/

Present	Past simple	Past participle
learn /lɜːn/	learnt /lɜːnt/	learnt
leave /liːv/	left /left/	left
lend /lend/	lent /lent/	lent
let /let/	let	let
lose /luːz/	lost /lɒst/	lost
make /meɪk/	made /meɪd/	made
meet /miːt/	met /met/	met
pay /peɪ/	paid /peɪd/	paid
put /pʊt/	put	put
read /riːd/	read /red/	read /red/
ring /rɪŋ/	rang /ræŋ/	rung /rʌŋ/
run /rʌn/	ran /ræn/	run
say /seɪ/	said /sed/	said
see /siː/	saw /sɔː/	seen /siːn/
sell /sel/	sold /səʊld/	sold
send /send/	sent /sent/	sent
shut /ʃʌt/	shut	shut
sing /sɪŋ/	sang /sæŋ/	sung /sʌŋ/
sit /sɪt/	sat /sæt/	sat
sleep /sliːp/	slept /slept/	slept
speak /spiːk/	spoke /spəʊk/	spoken /ˈspəʊkən/
spend /spend/	spent /spent/	spent
stand /stænd/	stood /stʊd/	stood
steal /stiːl/	stole /stəʊl/	stolen /ˈstəʊlən/
swim /swɪm/	swam /swæm/	swum /swʌm/
take /teɪk/	took /tʊk/	taken /ˈteɪkən/
teach /tiːtʃ/	taught /tɔːt/	taught
tell /tel/	told /təʊld/	told
think /θɪŋk/	thought /θɔːt/	thought
throw /θrəʊ/	threw /θruː/	thrown /θrəʊn/
understand /ʌndəˈstænd/	understood /ʌndəˈstʊd/	understood
wake /weɪk/	woke /wəʊk/	woken /ˈwəʊkən/
wear /weə/	wore /wɔː/	worn /wɔːn/
win /wɪn/	won /wʌn/	won
write /raɪt/	wrote /rəʊt/	written /ˈrɪtn/

Appendix

have got

I've got a brother and two sisters. **③ 45))**
I haven't got any pets.
She's got a beautiful house.
He hasn't got many friends.
Have they got any children? No, they haven't.
Has the hotel got a swimming pool? Yes, it has.

full form	contraction	negative	
I have got	I've got	I haven't got	
You have got	You've got	You haven't got	
He / She / It has got	He / She / It's got	He / She / It hasn't got	a car.
We have got	We've got	We haven't got	
You have got	You've got	You haven't got	
They have got	They've got	They haven't got	

?		✓		✗	
Have I got		I have.		I haven't.	
Have you got		you have.		you haven't.	
Has he / he / it got	a car? Yes,	he / she / it has.	No,	he / she / it hasn't.	
Have we got		we have.		we haven't.	
Have you got		you have.		you haven't.	
Have they got		they have.		they haven't.	

- You can use *have got* instead of *have* for possession in the present.
  ***I've got** a bike.* = **I have** a bike.
  ***Have you got** a car?* = **Do you have** a car?
- We also use *have got* to talk about family and illnesses, and to describe people.
  ***I've got** two sisters. **He's got** a cold.*
  ***She's got** long brown hair.*
- *have got* is not used in the past. For past possession use *had.*
  *I **had** a pet cat when I was a child.*
  ***Did you have** a pet?*
- *I've got… | Have you got…?* is common in the UK especially in conversation, but *I have… | Do you have…?* is also common.

a Write ⊞, ⊟, and ? sentences with the correct form of *have got.*

> they / big house ⊞ *They've got a big house.*
1 she / any brothers ⊟
2 you / big flat ?
3 we / a lot of work today ⊟
4 your sister / a boyfriend ?
5 Roger and Val / a beautiful garden ⊞
6 I / a really good teacher ⊞
7 My brother / a job at the moment ⊟
8 they / the same colour eyes ⊞
9 we / a meeting today ?
10 he / many friends at work ⊟

b Complete the sentences with the right form of *have got.*

> They love animals. They*'ve got* two dogs and five cats.
1 I hope it doesn't rain – I _____ my umbrella today.
2 _____ your phone _____ a good camera?
3 I _____ a new iPad. Do you want to see it ?
4 Sorry kids, I _____ enough money to buy sweets.
5 Jane _____ 50 pairs of shoes – can you believe it?
6 I can't call him now – I _____ a signal on my phone.
7 _____ you _____ your keys? I can't find mine.
8 Maria's so lucky – she _____ lovely curly hair.
9 One more question, Mr Jones. _____ you _____ any qualifications?
10 We might have problems getting there because we _____ satnav in our car.

Vowel sounds

	usual spelling	! but also
fish	**i** thin slim history kiss if since	English women busy decide repeat gym
tree	**ee** feel sheep **ea** teach mean **e** she we	people machine key niece receipt
cat	**a** cap hat back catch carry match	
car	**ar** far large scarf **a** fast pass after	aunt laugh heart
clock	**o** top lost socks wrong hot box	what wash want because
horse	**or** boring north **al** walk ball **aw** awful saw	water auction bought thought abroad warm
bull	**u** pull push **oo** football book look good	would should woman
boot	**oo** school choose **u★** use polluted **ew** few knew	do suit juice shoe lose through
computer	Many different spellings. /ə/ is always unstressed. <u>cle</u>ver <u>ner</u>vous <u>a</u>rrive po<u>lice</u> in<u>ven</u>tor <u>a</u>gree	
bird	**er** person verb **ir** dirty shirt **ur** curly turn	earn <u>work</u> world worse
egg	**e** spell lend west send very red	friendly weather sweater any said

	usual spelling	! but also
up	**u** sunny mustn't funny run lucky cut	come does someone enough young touch
train	**a★** change wake **ai** trainers fail **ay** away pay	break steak great overweight they grey
phone	**o★** open hope won't so **oa** coat goal	snow throw although
bike	**i★** quiet item **y** shy why **igh** might sights	buy eyes height
owl	**ou** trousers round account blouse **ow** crowded down	
boy	**oi** coin noisy point **oy** toy enjoy	
ear	**eer** beer engineer **ere** here we're **ear** beard earrings	really idea
chair	**air** airport stairs pair hair **are** square careful	their there wear bear
tourist	A very unusual sound. Europe furious sure plural	
/i/	A sound between /ɪ/ and /iː/. Consonant + *y* at the end of words is pronounced /i/. happy angry thirsty	
/u/	An unusual sound. education usually situation	

★ especially before consonant + *e*

○ short vowels   ● long vowels   ○ diphthongs

Consonant sounds

	usual spelling		! but also
parrot	**p** **pp**	promise possible copy flip-flops opposite appearance	
bag	**b** **bb**	belt body probably job cab rabbit rubbish	
key	**c** **k** **ck**	camping across skirt kind checkout pick	chemist's stomach mosquito account
girl	**g** **gg**	grow goat forget begin foggy leggings	
flower	**f** **ph** **ff**	find afraid safe elephant nephew off different	enough laugh
vase	**v**	video visit lovely invent over river	of
tie	**t** **tt**	try tell start late better sitting	walked dressed
dog	**d** **dd**	did dead hard told address middle	loved tired
snake	**s** **ss** **ci/ce**	stops faster miss message place circle	science
zebra	**z** **s**	zoo lazy freezing reason lose has toes	
shower	**sh** **ti** (+ **vowel**) **ci+a**	shut shoes washing finish patient information special musician	sugar sure machine moustache
television	An unusual sound. revision decision confusion		usually garage

	usual spelling		! but also
thumb	**th**	thing throw healthy south maths both	
mother	**th**	neither the clothes sunbathe that with	
chess	**ch** **tch** **t** (+**ure**)	chicken child beach catch match picture future	
jazz	**j** **dge**	jacket just journey enjoy bridge judge	generous teenager giraffe age
leg	**l** **ll**	little less plan incredible will trolley	
right	**r** **rr**	really rest practice try borrow married	written wrong
witch	**w** **wh**	website twins worried win why which whale	one once
yacht	**y** before **u**	yet year young yoga useful uniform	
monkey	**m** **mm**	mountain modern remember email summer swimming	
nose	**n** **nn**	need necklace none any funny dinner	know knock
singer	**ng**	angry ring along thing bring going	think thank
house	**h**	hat hate ahead perhaps hire helpful	who whose whole

⬤ voiced   ◯ unvoiced

This page was intentionally left blank.

Christina Latham-Koenig
Clive Oxenden
Paul Seligson

with Jane Hudson

ENGLISH FILE

Pre-Intermediate   Workbook B with key

OXFORD
UNIVERSITY PRESS

Paul Seligson and Clive Oxenden are the original co-authors of
English File 1 and *English File 2*

Contents

STUDY LINK iChecker

Audio: When you see this symbol iChecker, go to the iChecker disc in the back of this Workbook. Load the disc in your computer.

1

Type your name and press 'ENTER'.

2

Choose 'AUDIO BANK'.

3

Click on the exercise for the File. Then use the media player to listen.

You can transfer the audio to a mobile device, e.g. your iPod, from the 'audio' folder on the disc.

File test: At the end of every File, there is a test. To do the test, load the iChecker and select 'Tests'. Select the test for the File you have just finished.

There is also more practice available online at the English File website: www.oup.com/elt/englishfile

No copying or file sharing

This digital resource is protected by international copyright laws. You must not modify, adapt, copy, store, transfer or circulate the contents of this resource under any other branding or as part of any other product. You may not print out material for any commercial purpose or resale.

I love your daughter, Jack. I love her more than anything.
But frankly sir, I'm a little terrified of being your son-in-law.

Greg in the film Meet the Parents, *2000*

7A How to...

1 GRAMMAR uses of the infinitive with *to*

a Complete the sentences with the infinitive (with *to*) of a verb from the list.

not do   find   not finish   rent   see   not tell   ~~wash up~~

1 John's very polite. He offered __*to wash up*__ after the meal.
2 Thanks for coming. We hope _____ you again soon.
3 She wasn't enjoying the lasagne, so she decided _____ it.
4 My boyfriend is unemployed. He needs _____ a job.
5 I'll tell you what she said, but please promise _____ anybody.
6 I'm sorry I shouted at you. I'll try _____ it again.
7 They want to live together. They're planning _____ a flat.

b Write sentences using the adjective and the correct form of the verb.

1 **nice / meet**
Hello! How __*nice to meet*__ you.
2 **difficult / talk**
Do you find it _____ to my mum?
3 **easy / buy**
It's _____ presents for my girlfriend.
4 **important / not say**
It's _____ the wrong thing.
5 **great / hear**
Thanks for calling. It was _____ from you.
6 **fun / be**
It's _____ with your family.
7 **kind / invite**
Her parents were very _____ him.

c Complete the sentences with *to* and a verb.

1 He gave them some chocolates __*to say*__ thank you.
2 They're going to evening classes _____ Chinese.
3 We called the restaurant _____ a table.
4 He told us a joke _____ us laugh.
5 I went to a cash machine _____ some money.
6 Do you use your phone _____ photos?

d Complete the sentences with a question word from the list, and *to* + the verb in brackets.

~~how~~   how many   how much   what   when   where

1 She gave me her address, but I don't know __*how to get*__ there. (get)
2 My brother is always busy so I don't know _____ him. (call)
3 My mum asked me to get some eggs, but she didn't say _____. (buy)
4 We'd like to travel around the world, but we don't know _____ first. (go)
5 She wants to go to university, but she doesn't know _____. (study)
6 Who's going to be here for lunch? I have pasta, but I need to know _____. (make)

2 VOCABULARY verbs + infinitive

Complete the text with a verb from the list in the past tense.

forget   try   not want   promise   pretend   learn
offer   plan   ~~start~~   need   not remember

Charlie wasn't happy at his work so he [1] __*started*__ to apply for a new job. Soon, one company called him and [2] _____ to give him an interview. Charlie [3] _____ to tell his boss, so he [4] _____ to be ill. He told his boss that he had a stomach ache, and he [5] _____ to go to the doctor's. His boss [6] _____ to call him later to ask him how he was. Charlie was really hoping to get the job, so he was a bit nervous. He [7] _____ to drive to the interview, but there was a lot of traffic. In the end, he took the underground and was very late, and he [8] _____ to turn his mobile phone off. Unfortunately, it rang while he was in the interview, but Charlie didn't answer it. However when his boss called later he [9] _____ to act ill. The next morning, his boss said, 'I'd like to see you in my office.' Charlie [10] _____ to apologize, but his boss was very angry and Charlie nearly lost his job. But he [11] _____ an important lesson: not to lie to his boss again.

3 PRONUNCIATION linking, weak form of *to*

a Practise saying the sentences.

1 We want to know.

2 They hoped to win.

3 He promised to call.

4 I don't know what to do.

5 She forgot to go.

6 It's important to remember.

7 I learned to swim.

8 He started to cry.

b **iChecker** Listen and check. Then listen again and repeat the sentences.

4 READING

a Read the article. Is the writer generally positive or negative about mothers-in-law?

The truth about mothers-in-law

Although it's men who tell jokes about them, mothers-in-law are usually less popular with their daughters-in-law than with their sons-in-law. A recent study of 49 married couples found that two thirds of wives interviewed said that their mothers-in-law caused them 'unhappiness and stress', compared with 15% of the husbands.

There are a number of reasons for this. First of all, there is the question of experience. A mother-in-law has already brought up a family of her own, so she feels that she has a lot of knowledge to pass on. In this situation, it is very difficult for her to keep quiet. However, when a daughter-in-law is a new mother, she usually wants to find her own way of doing things. She often interprets her mother-in-law's advice as criticism, which can cause a conflict.

Secondly, there is the case of the husband. Both women care for him, although each of them loves him in a different way. On the one hand, he is the mother-in-law's son and she obviously wants the best for him. On the other hand, he is the wife's partner, and she wants him to support her. Both women can get very upset if they see the man taking sides, and this can cause an argument.

However, mothers-in-law actually have a lot to offer, despite their reputation for causing trouble. They are generally excellent babysitters, and they don't mind helping with the housework. As long as they have their own independent lives and help out only when needed, mothers-in-law can play a very useful role in any family. The important thing is that they should not get too involved in their sons' and daughters' relationship so that nobody feels bad.

b Read the article again and choose the best answer.

1 What did the study find out about mothers-in-law?
   a More men than women have problems with them.
   b More men than women tell jokes about them.
   ⓒ More women than men have problems with them.

2 What advice do mothers-in-law try to give their daughters-in-law?
   a How to look after their husband.
   b How to bring up children.
   c How to do housework.

3 According to the article, which situation makes daughters-in-law angry?
   a When their husband agrees with his mother.
   b When their husband talks to his mother.
   c When their husband argues with his mother.

4 Which women make the best mothers-in-law?
   a Those who are really close to their son.
   b Those who don't have a life of their own.
   c Those who know when to offer help.

c Underline five words you don't know. Use your dictionary to look up their meaning and pronunciation.

5 LISTENING

a **iChecker** Listen to a conversation between two people about a ban on mother-in-law jokes. Do they agree in the end? _____

b Listen again and complete the sentences with D (Dave) or J (Jane).

1 *D* thinks the ban is ridiculous.

2 ___ thinks that the jokes are offensive.

3 ___ thinks that it's important to have a sense of humour.

4 ___ makes a joke.

5 ___ thinks that the jokes don't show respect for parents.

6 ___ mentions a historical fact about mothers-in-law.

7 ___ quotes a historical joke.

8 ___ says that the jokes are sexist.

USEFUL WORDS AND PHRASES

Learn these words and phrases.

advice /əd'vaɪs/

tactic /'tæktɪk/

greet /griːt/

survive /sə'vaɪv/

honest /'ɒnɪst/

absolutely delicious /æbsəluːtli dɪ'lɪʃəs/

be punctual /bi 'pʌŋktʃuəl/

make conversation /meɪk kɒnvə'seɪʃn/

shake (sbd's) hand /ʃeɪk 'hænd/

(make) the right impression /ðə 'raɪt ɪmpreʃn/

Happiness is when what you think, what you say, and what you do are all in harmony.

Mahatma Gandhi, Indian political leader

7B Being happy

1 GRAMMAR uses of the gerund (verb + *-ing*)

a Complete the sentences with the *-ing* form of the verbs in brackets.

1 I hate ___*being*___ (be) cold. I find it really depressing.
2 You spend too long _____ (play) video games.
3 We stopped _____ (study) French because we didn't like the classes.
4 He's celebrating because he's finished _____ (write) his book.
5 It started _____ (snow) during the night while we were asleep.
6 I'm bored. I feel like _____ (go) for a walk.
7 My parents have bought a house by a beach, because they love _____ (swim).
8 I don't mind _____ (get) up early in the morning.
9 Kathy really enjoys _____ (listen) to her iPod.
10 The best thing about _____ (use) the bus is _____ (not drive) in busy traffic.

b Match the sentence beginnings and endings.

1 Do you ever dream of | c |
2 Are you interested in | |
3 Please don't leave without | |
4 She isn't very good at | |
5 We ended the evening by | |
6 I'm really looking forward to | |

a doing some part-time work?
b seeing you tonight.
c ~~stopping work and retiring?~~
d thanking everybody for coming.
e saying goodbye to me.
f parking her boyfriend's car.

c Complete the text with the *-ing* form of these verbs.

drive   exercise   get up   go   have   imagine   leave   listen   read   ~~send~~   stay   take   turn   ~~write~~

What makes you feel good?

Here are some more texts from our readers.

1   [1] ___*Writing*___ and then [2] ___*sending*___ a funny email or text message to my friends. And of course, [3] _____ their faces when they read it.

2   I really like [4] _____ at night when there's no traffic, [5] _____ to my favourite music. I feel completely free.

3   [6] _____ in bed on Sunday morning and [7] _____ the newspaper. Then [8] _____ very late and [9] _____ my dog for a long walk.

4   I enjoy [10] _____ to the gym and really [11] _____ hard, then [12] _____ a long hot shower followed by a nice cold drink. There's nothing better.

5   [13] _____ off my computer at the end of the day and [14] _____ work! It's the best moment of the day. I love it!

d Complete the text with the correct form of the verbs in brackets (-ing form or infinitive).

Reading the digital way

Many of us who love [1] _reading_ (read) are changing our habits. Today, a lot of us have decided [2] _____ (use) e-readers, and so we've stopped [3] _____ (buy) traditional books.

E-readers have a number of advantages. They are very easy [4] _____ (carry), so they are ideal for people who like [5] _____ (travel). If you're abroad, and you don't have anything [6] _____ (read), you don't need [7] _____ (look for) a bookshop that has books in your language – you can download it as a digital book. In addition to this, e-readers are very private, so you don't need [8] _____ (show) people what you are reading. Finally, when you finish [9] _____ (read) a book, you no longer have to find room for it on a bookshelf.

However, there are some disadvantages. Some people say their eyes hurt if they spend a long time [10] _____ (look) at the screen. Also, you have to be careful [11] _____ (not lose) your e-reader or you'll lose all your books. As well as this, if a friend would like [12] _____ (borrow) a book you've read, you can't offer [13] _____ (lend) it to them. With an e-reader, you can only go on [14] _____ (read) as long as the battery lasts, so you have to remember [15] _____ (take) your charger with you and you mustn't forget [16] _____ (charge) the battery.

2 VOCABULARY verbs + gerund

Match the sentences 1–6 with definitions a–f.

1 He hates doing the housework. | _c_ |
2 He feels like going for a run. | ☐ |
3 He doesn't mind cooking all the meals. | ☐ |
4 He's stopped playing football. | ☐ |
5 He spends hours chatting online. | ☐ |
6 He loves being with his friends. | ☐ |

a He doesn't do it any more.
b It's OK for him to do it.
c ~~He really doesn't like it.~~
d He does it a lot.
e He wants to do it now.
f He really likes it.

3 PRONUNCIATION the letter *i*

a Circle the word with a different sound.

fish	1	miss (mind) skin with
bike	2	promise hire kind size
fish	3	practise finish service surprise
bike	4	arrive engine invite online

b **iChecker** Listen and check. Then listen again and repeat the words.

4 LISTENING

a **iChecker** Listen to five speakers talking about when and where they sing. How many of the speakers don't enjoy singing?

b Listen again and match the speakers with sentences A–E.

Speaker 1   _C_
Speaker 2   __
Speaker 3   __
Speaker 4   __
Speaker 5   __

A He / She does a lot of singing at work.
B He / She doesn't mind singing badly in front of other people.
C ~~He / She enjoys singing at home.~~
D He / She likes singing when he/she is travelling.
E He / She was in a choir at school.

USEFUL WORDS AND PHRASES

Learn these words and phrases.

soup /suːp/
leftovers /ˈleftəʊvəz/
a feel-good film /ə ˈfiːlɡʊd fɪlm/
as soon as /əz ˈsuːn əz/
scales /skeɪlz/
breathe /briːð/
choir /ˈkwaɪə/
high notes /haɪ nəʊts/
magical /ˈmædʒɪkl/
bargain /ˈbɑːɡən/

7C Learn a language in a month!

1 GRAMMAR *have to, don't have to, must, mustn't*

a Look at the pictures. Complete the sentences with the correct form of *have to*.

1 **A** _Do_ teachers in your country _have to_ look smart?
B Not very smart. They ~~don't have to~~ wear formal clothes, but they ~~must to~~ look tidy.

2 **A** _Does_ British taxi drivers _have to_ go to university? Someone told me that.
B No. We _have to_ pass a special test, but we _don't have to_ go to university.

3 **A** _Do_ I _have to_ cook meals?
B No. You _don't have to_ do the cooking, but you _have to_ help the children to eat.

4 **A** _Does_ your husband _have to_ travel abroad in his job?
B No, he _doesn't have to_ travel abroad, but he _has to_ speak foreign languages.

b What do these signs mean? Write sentences with *must* or *mustn't*.

1 _You must_ pay in cash.
2 _You must_ turn left here.
3 _You mustn't_ make a noise.
4 _You mustn't_ use your mobile phone.
5 _You must_ stop here.
6 _You mustn't_ play football here.

c Complete the sentences with *mustn't* or *don't have to*.

1 The museum is free. You _don't have to_ pay.
2 You have to wear smart clothes. You _mustn't_ wear jeans.
3 The speed limit is 120 km/h. You _mustn't_ drive faster.
4 Your hours will be 9–5 Monday to Friday. You _don't have to_ work at weekends.
5 That river is dangerous. You _mustn't_ swim in it.
6 It's a very small flat. You _don't have to_ clean it every day.

2 VOCABULARY modifiers: *a bit, really*, etc.

Order the words to make sentences.

1 translation / useful / Online / aren't / sites / very
  Online translation sites aren't very useful.

2 to / quite / films / understand / It's / American / difficult
  It's _____.

3 new / fast / speaks / Our / very / teacher
  Our _____.

4 of / bit / those / unfriendly / a / students / Some / are
  Some _____.

5 is / English / idea / books / a / really / Reading / good
  Reading _____.

6 hard / incredibly / Chinese / to / It's / learn
  It's _____.

3 PRONUNCIATION *must, mustn't*

iChecker Listen and repeat. <u>Copy</u> the <u>rhy</u>thm

1 You **mustn't** take **photos**.
2 They **must make** the **exam easier**.
3 She **mustn't drive** a **car**.
4 He **must** be **early**.
5 We **mustn't talk** in the **library**.
6 You **must** take **one** pill **every day**.

4 READING

a Read the opinions about learning languages. Which do you think are the three best ideas?

What's the best way to…? Learn a language

This week we ask students from all over the world for their ideas.

Josef, Czech Republic

I think it's really hard to learn a language if you don't have anyone to talk to. I've joined a social networking site where I can chat in English to lots of other people like me. I'm more interested in using English to communicate than anything else, so I don't mind if my grammar isn't perfect.

Paolo, Portugal

I don't have time to go to an English class, but there's a great site on the internet which has classes in the form of podcasts. Every week, I download a few of these onto my phone, so that I can listen to the class when I'm going to and from work. I find the words and phrases that I have to listen to and repeat incredibly useful.

Marit, Norway

I'm a big fan of English pop music, so I spend a lot of time listening to different songs at home on my iPad. I've downloaded a new app that puts the lyrics on the screen and translates the song for you at the same time. I really enjoy learning English like this, and it's very good for my pronunciation, too.

Kiko, Japan

I can't afford to pay for one-to-one English classes, but I've found a great course online. I have to watch a short video, and then learn the grammar and vocabulary in it. If I have any questions, I can contact my online tutor who's very friendly. I'm really enjoying the course, and I've learned a lot from it.

Luis, Spain

I love books, and in my opinion, you can learn a lot of new words by reading in English. My journey to university is quite long, so I usually read books on my e-reader. You can click on difficult words and get a translation, which is very helpful.

Gloria, Brazil

My favourite way to learn a language is to go to a language school and join a class. There are classes for many levels of English, whether you're a beginner or you've been learning for a long time. It's great when you have other students in the class and you can learn and practise together, and of course having a teacher to help you is really important. It's good to do your homework too!

b Complete the sentences with the people's names.

1 _Marit_ thinks that listening to songs helps her pronunciation.

2 _____ says that reading can improve your vocabulary.

3 _____ has contact with an online teacher.

4 _____ thinks that speaking is more important than grammar.

5 _____ likes meeting and practising with other students.

6 _____ practises English mostly by listening.

5 LISTENING

a **iChecker** Listen to a radio programme about the Cherokee language. On what gadgets can the Cherokee people use their language today?

_____

b Listen again and answer the questions.

1 How many languages exist in the world today?
   Nearly 6,000

2 By 2100, how many will disappear?

3 How many members of the Cherokee tribe could speak Cherokee when the plan started?

4 How many Cherokees were there?

5 When did Apple release iOS 4.1 with Cherokee as an official language?

USEFUL WORDS AND PHRASES

Learn these words and phrases.

experiment /ɪkˈsperɪmənt/
fees /fiːz/
voicemail /ˈvɔɪsmeɪl/
permitted /pəˈmɪtɪd/
obligatory /əˈblɪɡətri/
complete beginner /kəmˈpliːt bɪˈɡɪnə/
entrance fee /ˈentrəns ˈfiː/
intensive course /ɪnˈtensɪv kɔːs/
against the rules /əˈɡeɪnst ðə ruːlz/

 **iChecker** **TESTS** FILE 7

Practical English At the pharmacy

1 VOCABULARY feeling ill

Complete the sentences.

1 Dan feels terrible. He thinks he has __flu__ (ULF).
2 I need to buy some tissues. I have a _____ (LCDO).
3 That fish wasn't very nice. Now I have a _____
  _____ (DBA OCHMSTA).
4 You feel very hot. I think you have a _____
  (EMRETUPETRA).
5 Please turn that music down. I have a _____
  (CHAEHEDA).
6 Kate smokes too much. She has a _____ (OGUHC).

2 GOING TO A PHARMACY

Complete the dialogue with these words.

allergic better every have ~~help~~ much often
symptoms take well

A Good afternoon. How can I ^{1} __help__?
B I'm not feeling very ^{2} _____.
A What are your ^{3} _____?
B I have a bad cough.
A Do you ^{4} _____ a temperature?
B No, I don't.
A Are you ^{5} _____ to any drugs?
B No, I don't think so.
A Take this cough medicine. It'll make you feel ^{6} _____.
B How much do I have to ^{7} _____?
A Ten ml ^{8} _____ six hours.
B Sorry? How ^{9} _____?
A Every six hours.
B OK, thanks. How ^{10} _____ is that?
A That's $4.50, please.

3 SOCIAL ENGLISH

Complete the sentences.

1 A That was a l_____ meal.
   B I'm gl_____ you enjoyed it.
2 A C_____ I have some more coffee, please?
   B There isn't any more. Anyway, drinking too much coffee isn't
      good f_____ you.
3 A I think I sh_____ go now.
   B Shall I take you home?
   A No, I'll walk. I'm s_____ I'll be fine.

4 READING

Match the signs 1–9 with their meaning A–I.

1 | E |

2 | |

3 | |

4 | | 5 | | 6 | |

7 | |

8 | |
9 | |
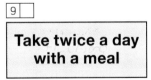

A You must keep this medicine where children can't
   find it.
B You must not give this medicine to small children.
C You mustn't drink this water.
D You must take this medicine at breakfast and dinner.
E ~~You should be careful not to take too much of this medicine.~~
F You should be careful if you feel ill after taking this
   medicine.
G You mustn't smoke here.
H You should be careful or you might fall over.
I   You have to turn your mobile off.

Advice is what you ask for when you already know the answer but wish you didn't.

Erica Jong, American writer

8A I don't know what to do!

1 GRAMMAR *should*

a Match the sentences with the pictures. Complete them with *should* or *shouldn't*.

1 She ___should___ eat her vegetables. `B`
2 She __should__ wear a coat. `F`
3 'You _shouldn't_ eat so much salt.' `E`
4 He _shouldn't_ drive to work. `A`
5 'You _should_ get some glasses.' `C`
6 She _shouldn't_ carry heavy bags. `D`

b Complete the advice with *should / shouldn't* and a verb from the box.

~~buy~~ call drink give go see tell

1 You ___shouldn't buy___ it because it won't fit you.
2 You _shouldn't drink_ coffee all day.
3 You _should go_ to bed earlier.
4 You _should see_ a doctor immediately.
5 You _should tell_ her how you feel.
6 You _shouldn't give_ them any sweets.
7 You _should call_ her and invite her to dinner.

c Read the problems A–G. Match them with the advice in **b**.

A I find it really difficult to get up in the morning, and I'm often late for work. My boss has noticed and she's quite angry with me. What should I do? `3`

B Yesterday, I hurt my foot while I was playing football. It didn't seem very serious at the time, but now my foot has gone black. What is your advice? `4`

C I've seen the perfect suit on sale in my favourite shop and it's exactly what I'm looking for. The only problem is it's an M and I'm an L. What do you think I should do? `1`

D I really like one of my colleagues at work, and I think she likes me, too. I'd really like to go out with her, but I don't know how to ask her. Any advice? `7`

E I have three children and they all have terrible problems with their teeth. We're always at the dentist's and each visit costs a lot of money. Any advice? `6`

F I've always been very nervous, but now it's getting worse. I don't have time to eat at work, so I have five or six coffee breaks during the day. What should I do? `2`

G I've had an argument with my girlfriend, and I don't know what to do. I feel very stupid and I really want to see her again. What do you think I should do? `5`

2 VOCABULARY *get*

Complete the sentences with the correct form of *get* and one of these words.

~~divorced~~ fit home lost text message on school
tickets worse up

1 Her parents aren't happy together, so they're going
to _get_ _divorced_ .
2 Are your children in bed when your husband
gets _home_ from work?
3 Our satnav wasn't working and we _get_
lost on the way to our friends' house.
4 I'm going to the gym because I want to _get_
fit .
5 The pain in my neck was _getting_ _worse_ ,
so I went to the doctor.
6 This morning I _got_ _tickets_ for the
concert online. They're very good ones at the front!
7 How well do you _get_ _on_ with your
brothers and sisters?
8 I've just _got_ a _text message_ from my boyfriend
saying he's going to be late.
9 I don't feel like _getting_ _up_ today. I'm
going to stay in bed.
10 I often _get_ to _school_ late, although it's
very near where I live.

After like, must be "INGy"

3 PRONUNCIATION /ʊ/ and /uː/

a (Circle) the word in each group which has a different sound.

ʊ bull	1	pull	(food)	would
uː boot	2	could	you	soon
ʊ bull	3	woman	wouldn't	soup
uː boot	4	book	do	two

b iChecker Listen and check. Then listen again and repeat the words.

4 LISTENING

a iChecker Listen to five speakers talk about a person they discuss their problems with. How many of them talk to members of their family?

b Listen again and match the speakers with the sentences A–E.

Speaker 1 _C_
Speaker 2 __
Speaker 3 __
Speaker 4 __
Speaker 5 __

A has had some similar experiences to this person.
B also gives advice to this person.
~~C is in a relationship with someone he/she met through this person.~~
D doesn't always agree with this person.
E first met this person when he/she was very young.

USEFUL WORDS AND PHRASES

Learn these words and phrases.

attend (a conference) /əˈtend/
risk (verb) /rɪsk/
macho /ˈmætʃəʊ/
instead /ɪnˈsted/
avoid somebody /əˈvɔɪd sʌmbədi/
be worth (doing) /bi wɜːθ/
change your mind /tʃeɪndʒ jɔː maɪnd/
go for (sth) /ɡəʊ fɔː/
keep in touch (with sbd) /kiːp ɪn tʌtʃ/

If everything seems to be going well, you have obviously overlooked something.

Murphy's Law

8B If something can go wrong...

1 GRAMMAR *if* + present, + *will* + infinitive (first conditional)

a Match the sentence halves.

Here are six more examples of Murphy's Law:

1 If you lose something,   `c`
2 If you arrive early at a party,   `e`
3 If you make an appointment with the doctor, `a`
4 If you don't do your homework,   `f`
5 If you buy a new carpet,   `b`
6 If you get into a hot bath,   `d`

a you'll feel better before you see him.
b you'll drop something on it the first day.
c you'll find it in the last place you look.
d the phone will ring.
e everyone else will be late.
f your teacher will ask you for it.

b Circle the correct form.

1 If the plane arrives late tonight, I **will miss** / miss the last bus.
2 If you **see** / **will see** an accident, call the police!
3 They won't get lost, if they **use** / **will use** their satnav.
4 We **don't get** / **won't get** to the cinema in time if we don't leave now.
5 If you **don't take** / **won't take** an umbrella, it'll definitely rain!
6 If my phone **doesn't work** / **won't work** here, can I use yours?
7 Kathy **is** / **will be** disappointed if she doesn't get the job.
8 If there **isn't** / **won't be** much traffic when we leave, it won't take long to get there.

c Complete the texts with the correct form of the verb in brackets. Then read and match the texts with the correct pictures, A–G.

Traditions and Superstitions

1 Giving a knife D
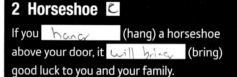
If a friend _gives_ (give) you a knife as a present and you _give_ (give) your friend a coin in return, your friendship _will last_ (last) forever.

2 Horseshoe C
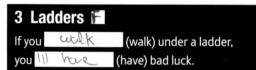
If you _hang_ (hang) a horseshoe above your door, it _will bring_ (bring) good luck to you and your family.

3 Ladders F
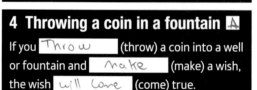
If you _walk_ (walk) under a ladder, you _will have_ (have) bad luck.

4 Throwing a coin in a fountain A
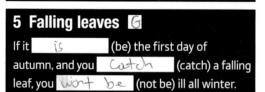
If you _Throw_ (throw) a coin into a well or fountain and _make_ (make) a wish, the wish _will come_ (come) true.

5 Falling leaves G

If it _is_ (be) the first day of autumn, and you _catch_ (catch) a falling leaf, you _won't be_ (not be) ill all winter.

6 Mirrors B
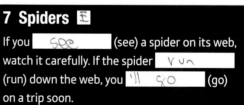
If you _break_ (break) a mirror, you _'ll have_ (have) seven years bad luck.

7 Spiders E
If you _see_ (see) a spider on its web, watch it carefully. If the spider _run_ (run) down the web, you _'ll go_ (go) on a trip soon.

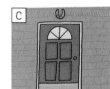

2 VOCABULARY confusing verbs

Complete the sentences with the correct verbs in the correct tense.

1 **look**, **look like**

You _look_ very smart in that suit. In fact, you _look like_ a businessman!

2 **lose**, **miss**

I _lose_ my ticket, so I _miss_ the train and I was late for work.

3 **say**, **tell**

My son doesn't often _tell_ lies, but if he does, he always _say_ sorry.

4 **hope**, **wait**

I'm _wait_ for the bus. I _hope_ it'll come soon because it's raining.

5 **look at**, **watch**

Our friends enjoyed _watch_ the video of our wedding, but they didn't want to _look at_ the photos of our honeymoon.

6 **know**, **meet**

She's _know_ him since the summer. She _meet_ him on a safari.

7 **borrow**, **lend**

If you need to _borrow_ some money, I can _lend_ you 50 euros.

8 **find**, **look for**

We were _find_ a cheap apartment on the internet and we _look for_ the perfect place.

9 **carry**, **wear**

He was _wear_ a big coat and _carry_ a heavy suitcase.

10 **bring**, **take**

I'll _take_ you to the airport if you _bring_ me back a souvenir.

3 PRONUNCIATION linking

a **iChecker** Listen to how the words are linked in each sentence.

1 If I walk, I'll arrive late.
2 It'll be hot if you go in August.
3 If it rains, I'll get a taxi.
4 She'll get angry if we don't invite her.
5 If we get up early, we can go to the market.
6 If I don't understand the menu, I'll ask the waiter.

b Listen again. Practise saying the sentences.

4 LISTENING

a **iChecker** Listen to a radio programme about natural disasters. How many tips does the expert give?

b Listen again and answer the questions.

1 Can you avoid natural disasters?   _No, you can't._
2 At what time of year should you not go to the Caribbean? _____
3 What will travel insurance probably pay for? _____
4 Why is it important not to panic? _____
5 Who should you contact as soon as possible? _____
6 What should you ask your airline when you book your flight? _____

USEFUL WORDS AND PHRASES

Learn these words and phrases.

blizzard /ˈblɪzəd/
cyclone /ˈsaɪkləʊn/
earthquake /ˈɜːθkweɪk/
flood /flʌd/
forest fire /ˈfɒrɪst faɪə/
monsoon /mɒnˈsuːn/
tsunami /tsuːˈnɑːmi/
spill (coffee) /spɪl/
parking space /ˈpɑːkɪŋ speɪs/
natural disaster /ˈnætʃrəl dɪˈzɑːstə/

8C You must be mine

1 GRAMMAR possessive pronouns

a Complete the questions and answers in the chart.

Whose...?	Possessive adjective	Possessive pronoun
1 *Whose bag is that?*	It's my bag.	It's *mine* _____.
2 *Whose books are those?*	They're your books.	They're _____.
3 _____	It's his laptop.	It's _____.
4 _____	They're her keys.	They're _____.
5 _____	It's our car.	It's _____.
6 _____	They're your coats.	They're _____.
7 _____	It's their house.	It's _____.

b Complete the sentences with a possessive adjective (*my, your*, etc.) or pronoun (*mine, yours*, etc.)..

1   **A** Are those __*my*__ glasses?
    B No, they're __*his*__. __*Yours*__ are in your pocket!

2   **A** Whose coats are these? Are they _____?
    B Yes, they're _____. Thanks a lot.

3   **A** Is that your boyfriend's car? It looks like _____.
    B No, it isn't. _____ car is bigger than that.

4   **A** Whose cat is that? It isn't _____.
    B I've seen it in the neighbours' garden. I think it's _____.

5   **A** Is that a new phone? _____ old one was black.
    B No, it's my sister's. _____ is broken, so I'm borrowing _____.

2 VOCABULARY
adverbs of manner

Make adverbs from the adjectives in the box and complete the sentences.

calm   dream   lazy   quiet   serious   ~~slow~~

1 Please walk more __*slowly*__. You're going too fast!
2 Sorry? I can't hear you. You're speaking very _____.
3 Mary hardly ever laughs. She takes things really _____.
4 'I don't feel like doing anything today,' he said _____.
5 'I'd love to retire early and live on a tropical island,' Mark said _____.
6 Although all the passengers were worried, the flight attendant spoke _____ and explained the problem.

3 PRONUNCIATION
word stress

a Under<u>line</u> the stressed syllable.

1 de|tec|tive
2 dis|tance
3 do|llar
4 ad|van|tage
5 en|joy
6 com|plete|ly
7 re|mem|ber
8 pro|mise
9 sus|pi|cious

b **iChecker** Listen and check. Then listen again and repeat the words.

4 READING

a Read the article about five famous British chefs. Do you recognize any of them?

Heston Blumenthal is an English chef who is famous for preparing food scientifically. After finishing secondary school, Heston went to France and taught himself to cook. He now owns the Fat Duck Restaurant in Bray, Berkshire, UK, which has three Michelin stars and has twice been voted Best Restaurant in the UK. He has had a number of TV shows and has also published several books.

Delia Smith is one of Britain's oldest cooks and she's the UK's best-selling cookery author. She started her career as a hairdresser at 16, but changed to cooking when she was 21. For 12 years, she wrote about cooking and famous chefs around the world before her first television appearance. She eventually had her own programme, where she explained carefully to viewers how to make basic dishes for the whole family.

Jamie Oliver is one of Britain's best-loved television chefs. His programmes have been broadcast internationally in countries like the USA, South Africa, Australia, Brazil, Japan, and Iceland, and his books have been translated into thirty languages. Jamie is most famous for his campaigns to encourage British and American schoolchildren to eat healthily. He's married with four children.

Nigella Lawson is a popular food writer and journalist who started work as a book reviewer and restaurant critic. She has always been interested in food and cookery, but she has never trained as a cook. Despite this, she has successfully hosted her own cooking shows on TV, especially in the USA, where she had almost two million viewers. She also has her own range of products called *Living Kitchen*.

Gordon Ramsay is one of Britain's top chefs and he has won sixteen Michelin stars in total. He owns restaurants all over the world, but he also helps other restaurant owners who are having problems with their business. Gordon is probably most famous as the host of the TV reality show *Hell's Kitchen*, where he often shouted angrily at the participants when they made a mistake.

b Read the article again and answer the questions. Write H, D, J, N, or G.

Who...?

1 ate in restaurants and read books in his / her first job   <u>N</u>
2 isn't very patient with people who are learning to cook   __
3 had a completely different job when he / she left school   __
4 uses chemistry in his / her cooking   __
5 thinks young people should eat better   __

c <u>Underline</u> five words you don't know. Use your dictionary to look up their meaning and pronunciation.

5 LISTENING

a **iChecker** Listen to a conversation about an experiment on a TV programme. Which question did the experiment hope to answer? Was it successful?

b Listen again. Mark the sentences T (true) or F (false).

1 The programme was on in the evening.   <u>T</u>
2 There were three cooks.   __
3 The rules for each course were that they had to use the same ingredients.   __
4 There were two judges.   __
5 The cooks were professional restaurant critics.   __
6 Ewan only remembers two dishes because the judges found it very difficult to decide who made them.   __

USEFUL WORDS AND PHRASES

Learn these words and phrases.

advantage /əd'vɑːntɪdʒ/
expenses /ɪk'spensɪz/
exclaim /ɪk'skleɪm/
trust /trʌst/
suspicious /sə'spɪʃəs/
calmly /'kɑːmli/
dreamily /'driːmɪli/
masterfully /'mɑːstəfəli/
the suburbs /ðə 'sʌbɜːbz/
somebody else /'sʌmbədi els/

iChecker **TESTS** FILE 8

All animals are equal – but some animals
are more equal than others.
From Animal Farm *by George Orwell, British writer*

9A What would you do?

1 GRAMMAR *if* + past, *would* + infinitive (second conditional)

a Match the sentence beginnings and endings.

1 If my sister were older,   [f]   a if he could swim.
2 My parents would buy a bigger house [e]   b you'd be really scared.
3 He'd go sailing   [a]   c if they couldn't watch TV?
4 What would people do   [c]   d if it wasn't raining.
5 If you saw that horror film,   [b]   e if they had more money.
6 I'd go for a walk   [d]   f ~~she could go to the party with me.~~

b Order the words to complete the sentences and questions.

1 car / would/ I / it / to / work / drive / a / had
  If I *had a car, I would drive it to work* .
2 you / found / do / a / you / million / would / if / euros
  What would you do if you found a million euros ?
3 if / he / could / a / afford / one / phone
  He'd buy a phone if he could afford one .
4 caviar / it / I / eat / gave / me / wouldn't
  If someone gave me caviar I wouldn't eat it .
5 say / could / talk / if / to / you / the / would / president / you
  What would you say if you could talk to the pres?dont ?
6 job / for / you / a / I / new / if / look / were
  I'd look for a new job if I were you .

c Complete the second conditional sentences with the correct form of the verbs in brackets.

1 If a bee *flew* (fly) into my bedroom, I *would open*
  (open) the window.
2 If my sister saw (see) a mouse in the kitchen,
  she would scream (scream).
3 We wouldn't have (not have) a dog if we didn't have
  (not have) a garden.
4 If my brother wasn't (not be) allergic to animals,
  he would get (get) a cat.
5 If I lived (live) in the country, I would learn
  (learn) to ride a horse.
6 What would you do (do) if a dangerous
  dog attacked (attack) you?

2 VOCABULARY animals

Complete the crossword.

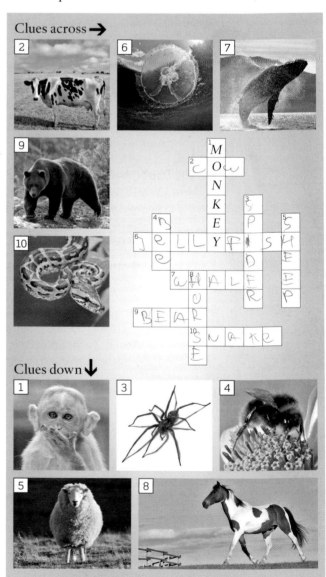

Clues across ➜

Clues down ↓

3 PRONUNCIATION word stress

a Underline the stressed syllables.

1 bu|tter|fly	5 dol|phin	9 li|on	13 spi|der
2 ca|mel	6 el|e|phant	10 mon|key	14 ti|ger
3 chi|cken	7 gi|raffe	11 mos|qui|to	
4 cro|co|dile	8 je|lly|fish	12 ra|bbit	

b iChecker Listen and check. Then listen again and repeat the words.

4 READING

a Read the first part of the text and tick (✓) the things you would do.

CROCODILE ATTACK!

If you were swimming at the edge of the water in Southern Florida, USA, and you saw a crocodile coming towards you, what would you do?

'I'd run away fast.'	☐	'I'd pretend to be dead.'	☐
'I'd try to open its mouth.'	☐	'I'd put my fingers into its eyes.'	☐
'I'd make a loud noise.'	☐	'I'd try to fight it.'	☐

b Now read the rest of the article. Which sentence is the best summary?

1 There's nothing you can do if a crocodile attacks you.
2 There are lots of things you can do if a crocodile attacks you.
3 There's only one thing to do if a crocodile attacks you.

Well, most of these are possible – the best thing to do depends on where the crocodile is at the time. If it comes towards you on land, experts say you should turn around and run away as fast as possible. Crocodiles can run faster than humans over a short distance, but they soon get tired. If they miss their first chance to catch their victim, they usually start looking for something else.

If you're in the water, then splash around to make a noise so that the animal gets confused. If this doesn't work, push your thumb or fingers into the crocodile's eye. This is the most sensitive area of the crocodile's body and it is the place where you can cause the animal the most pain . It will also be very surprised by your attack and it's quite possible that it will decide to leave you alone. Don't try and open the crocodile's mouth because the muscles are so strong that this is nearly impossible.

However, if the crocodile is in a bad mood , it's possible that it will carry on fighting. Your final opportunity is to pretend to be dead. If the crocodile thinks that its victim is dead, it opens its mouth for a few seconds to move the body into its throat . This can give you your last chance to escape, but it's a very dangerous plan.

Our final advice? It's much better to avoid crocodiles than to do any of the things above...

c Look at the highlighted words or phrases. Check their meaning and pronunciation with your dictionary.

5 LISTENING

a iChecker Listen to a news story about a shark attack. How did the man survive?

b Listen again and answer the questions.

1 Where is Eric Nerhus from?

2 What was he doing when the shark attacked?

3 Which parts of his body were in the shark's mouth?

4 What was Eric's vest made of?

5 Who rescued Eric?

6 How did Eric get to hospital?

7 What injuries did he have?

8 How big was the shark?

USEFUL WORDS AND PHRASES

Learn these words and phrases.

pockets /ˈpɒkɪts/
backwards /ˈbækwədz/
bite /baɪt/
float /fləʊt/
shout /ʃaʊt/
sting /stɪŋ/
suck /sʌk/
tie /taɪ/
wave /weɪv/
keep still /kiːp ˈstɪl/

I am not afraid of death, I just don't
want to be there when it happens.

Woody Allen, American film director

9B I've been afraid of it for years

1 VOCABULARY phobias and words related to fear

a Complete the phobias with the missing vowels.
Then match them with the definitions.

1 *agoraphobia* | b | a fear of spiders
2 cl_ _str_ph_b_ _ | ☐ | b ~~fear of open spaces~~
3 _r_chn_ph_b_ _ | ☐ | c fear of heights
4 gl_ss_ph_b_ _ | ☐ | d fear of closed spaces
5 _cr_ph_b_ _ | ☐ | e fear of public speaking

b Complete the sentences with a suitable word.

1 Are you fr*ightened* of snakes? A lot of people are.
2 I'm quite sc_____ of spiders. I don't like them much.
3 If you suffer from a f_____ of flying, you can't travel by plane.
4 My sister is te_____ of big dogs. She always crosses the road if she sees one.
5 My children don't like swimming. They're a_____ of water.
6 Olga has a ph_____ of insects. She never goes to the country.

2 GRAMMAR present perfect + *for* and *since*

a Circle the correct word, *for* or *since*, to complete each sentence.

1 Jess hasn't flown on a plane **for** / **since** many years.
2 I haven't seen my parents **for** / **since** my birthday.
3 He hasn't ridden a horse **for** / **since** he fell off one when he was twelve.
4 We've had our rabbit **for** / **since** six months.
5 My gran has agoraphobia. She hasn't left the house **for** / **since** two years.
6 I've been afraid of dogs **for** / **since** I was very young.
7 Oliver is ill. He hasn't eaten **for** / **since** two days.
8 We haven't been back there **for** / **since** the accident happened.

b Complete the text with *for* and *since*.

A celebrity's life
Kristen Stewart, actress

Kristen Stewart has been a famous actress [1] *for* about five years now. She has been an actress [2] _____ she was eight years old, when her agent saw her performing at school. Her first role was in a film where she didn't speak, but [3] _____ then she has been in many films. She is probably best known for playing Bella Swan in *The Twilight Saga*, a part which she has played [4] _____ four years.

Kristen has lived in Los Angeles [5] _____ she was born. Because she was acting at a young age, she couldn't go to school, so she studied online. [6] _____ then, she has completed high school. She is now one of the best-paid actresses in Hollywood.

Something many people don't know about Kristen is that she has equinophobia, or a fear of horses. She has had this problem [7] _____ most of her life, but her fans have only known about it [8] _____ 2012, when she was filming with horses. Kristen explained that she has been scared of them [9] _____ she was nine years old, when she had a terrible fall during a horse-riding accident.

c Complete the questions about Kristen Stewart.
Use *How long* or *When* and the verb in brackets.

1 _When did_ Kristen Stewart _start_ acting? (start)
  When she was eight.
2 _____ she _____ the part of Bella Swan?
  (play)
  For four years.
3 _____ Kristen _____ in Los Angeles? (live)
  Since she was born.
4 _____ Kristen _____ equinophobia? (have)
  For most of her life.
5 _____ fans _____ about her phobia? (hear)
  In 2012.

d Right (✓) or wrong (✗)? Correct the mistakes in the **bold**
phrases.

1 **Gill hates flying** since she was a child.
  Gill has hated flying   .
2 **How long time** has your brother been an actor?
  _____?
3 **We've been married** since 2000.
  _____.
4 He's been in the USA **for February**.
  _____.
5 How long **do you have** your dog?
  _____?
6 He's had this job **since eight years**.
  _____.
7 I've had four cars **since I learned to drive**.
  _____.
8 **She's known Sally** since they were at school.
  _____.

3 PRONUNCIATION sentence stress

iChecker Listen and repeat the sentences. <u>Copy</u> the
<u>rhy</u>thm.

1 **How long** have you **worked here**?
2 **How long** have they **been** <u>**married**</u>?
3 **How long** has she **known** him?
4 **We've lived** here for **six months**.
5 I've **studied** <u>**English**</u> for **three years**.
6 He's had a **phobia since** he was a **child**.

4 LISTENING

a **iChecker** Listen to a radio call-in programme
about phobias. What is cynophobia?

b Listen again and choose the correct answers.

1 The caller is worried about…
  a her pet.
  b someone in her family.
  c her phobia.
2 The dog bit…
  a the neighbour.
  b the caller.
  c the caller's son.
3 The caller wants some
  advice about…
  a preventing a phobia.
  b keeping dogs.
  c treating a phobia.
4 The psychologist tells the caller…
  a to keep her son away from dogs.
  b to talk about her son's experience with him.
  c to let her son play with a friend's dog.

USEFUL WORDS AND PHRASES

Learn these words and phrases.

cure /ˈkjʊə/
drug /drʌg/
heights /haɪts/
overcome (a fear) /əʊvəˈkʌm/
panic /ˈpænɪk/
afraid /əˈfreɪd/
frightened /ˈfraɪtnd/
rational (opp *irrational*) /ˈræʃənəl/
scared /skeəd/
terrified /ˈterɪfaɪd/
affect sbd / sth (verb) /əˈfekt/
have an effect on sbd/sth /hæv ən ɪˈfekt ɒn/

9C Born to sing

1 VOCABULARY biographies

Complete the phrases.

1 My grandad was ☐ c   a on his 65th birthday.
2 He went ☐ f   b in love with my gran at school.
3 He fell ☐ b   c born in 1945.
4 He left ☐   d to school when he was five.
5 He started ☐   e work when he was 17.
6 They got ☐   f school in 1960.
7 They had ☐   g three children.
8 He retired ☐   h married in 1968.

2 GRAMMAR present perfect or past simple (2)?

a (Circle) the correct verb forms.

My mum was born in Plymouth in 1948. When ¹(she left) / she's
left school, she started work in an office in Plymouth. Later, the
company ²sent / has sent her to a different office in Bristol,
where ³she met / she's met my dad. ⁴They fell / They've fallen
in love, and ⁵they got / they've got married in 1970. ⁶They had /
They've had three children – I'm the youngest.

⁷They moved / They've moved back to Plymouth again when
my dad retired. They bought a very nice house and ⁸they lived /
they've lived there for two years now. My dad ⁹just put /
has just put a greenhouse in the garden for growing vegetables –
¹⁰he was / he's been a keen gardener all his life. My parents
¹¹made / have made a lot of new friends and they're very
happy in their new home.

b Write the verbs in the past simple or present perfect. Use
contractions where necessary.

1 A How long *have* you *studied*   English? (study)
  B Since I was little. I *started*   learning it at school.
    (start)

2 A Are Tom and Gill married?
  B Yes, they are.
  A When _____ they _____ married? (get)
  B Last year. But they _____ together for about
    ten years now. (be)

3 A Is that man the new accountant?
  B Yes, he is.
  A How long _____ he _____ here? (work)
  B Only for two months. He _____ university in June.
    (finish)

4 A How long _____ you _____ your car?
    (have)
  B A long time! I _____ it in 2005, I think. (buy)

5 A When _____ Sandra _____ her
    boyfriend? (meet)
  B When she was at university. She _____ him for
    three years now. (know).

6 A How long _____ you _____ in London?
    (live)
  B Not long. I _____ six months ago. (arrive)

3 PRONUNCIATION word stress

a Write the words in the correct group.

~~award~~ ~~children~~ divorced married musician primary
retire secondary separate (verb) successful

1 Stress on 1st syllable	2 Stress on 2nd syllable
children	*award*

b **iChecker** Listen and check. Then listen again and
  repeat the words.

60

4 READING

a Read the text about John Lennon. Order the paragraphs 1–7.

John Lennon and his sons

A ☐ On 8 December, 1980, one of John Lennon's fans shot him outside his apartment. Since then, both of his sons have become musicians. Julian Lennon has made six albums and Sean Lennon has sung and played bass guitar with a number of different bands. So far, however, neither of them have been as successful as their father.

B ☐ John Lennon was born in Liverpool on 9 October, 1940. His parents separated when he was five, so he went to live with an aunt and uncle. However, he stayed in contact with his mother, who played him Elvis Presley records and taught him how to play the banjo.

C ☐ Before The Beatles broke up in 1970, John met the Japanese artist, Yoko Ono, and he divorced his first wife. He left the band and continued making music both on his own and with Yoko. Their son, Sean, was born on 9 October, 1975 and John stayed at home to look after him.

D ☐ When John was 15, his mother bought him his first guitar. He formed his first band called The Quarrymen while he was still at school. When he left school, he started a course at Art College, but the band took up a lot of his time, so he didn't finish the course.

E ☐ The band released their first single 'Love Me Do' in October, 1962. They started touring the country. John married his first wife, Cynthia, in secret, and his first son, Julian, was born while they were away. Fans went mad wherever The Beatles played and all of their albums reached the number one spot in the charts.

F ☐ 1 The singer-songwriter and guitarist John Lennon is one of the greatest musicians of all time. Songs like *Give peace a chance* and *Imagine* made him famous all over the world.

G ☐ John met Paul McCartney at the second performance of The Quarrymen and he soon joined the band. Later, George Harrison joined them as lead guitarist. In 1960, they became The Beatles and they started looking for a drummer. Ringo Starr replaced their original drummer, Pete Best, in 1962.

b Circle the correct verb form in the questions.

1 When **was** / **has been** John Lennon born?
2 What **did his mother buy** / **has his mother bought** for him?
3 How long **were** / **have been** The Beatles together?
4 How **did John Lennon die** / **has John Lennon died**?
5 How many albums **did Julian Lennon make** / **has Julian Lennon made**?
6 Which instrument **did Sean Lennon play** / **has Sean Lennon played** with different bands?

c Underline five words you don't know. Use your dictionary to check their meaning and pronunciation.

5 LISTENING

a iChecker Listen to a radio programme about the American actress and singer Judy Garland and her daughter, Liza Minnelli. How old were they when they first performed on stage?

b Listen again and mark the sentences T (true) or F (false).

Both women…

1	were born in the USA.	*T*
2	changed their names.	—
3	started performing when they were very young.	—
4	won Oscars.	—
5	sang together at the London Palladium.	—
6	had problems.	—
7	got married more than once.	—
8	had three children.	—

USEFUL WORDS AND PHRASES

Learn these words and phrases.

award /əˈwɔːd/	talented /ˈtæləntɪd/
captain /ˈkæptɪn/	be influenced by
funeral /ˈfjuːnərəl/	/bi ˈɪnfluənst baɪ/
injure /ˈɪndʒə/	(follow in sb's) footsteps
eldest /ˈeldɪst/	/ˈfʊtsteps/
respected /rɪˈspektɪd/	form a band /fɔːm ə bænd/

iChecker TESTS FILE 9

Practical English Getting around

1 VOCABULARY directions

Complete the directions.

To get to the hotel you need to ¹turn_ left and go ²str_____ on until you get to the roundabout. Go ³r_____ the roundabout and take the third ⁴e_____.
Then turn right at the traffic ⁵l_____ and ⁶t_____ the second turning on the ⁷l_____. The hotel is called The King's Head and it's on the ⁸r_____.

2 ASKING HOW TO GET THERE

Complete the dialogue with the missing sentences.

How do I get to SoHo on the subway?   OK. Thanks. See you later.
OK. And then?   How many stops is that?
Could you say that again?   Where is it?

A ¹ _How do I get to SoHo on the subway?_
B Go to the subway station at Grand Central – 42nd Street. Take line 6 towards Brooklyn Bridge – City Hall. Get off at Spring Street.
A ² _____
B OK. Take line 6 from Grand Central – 42nd Street to Spring Street.
A ³ _____
B Seven.
A ⁴ _____
B Then you can walk to the restaurant.
A ⁵ _____
B Come out of the subway on Spring Street. Go straight on for about 80 yards and the restaurant is on the right. It's called _Balthazar_.
A ⁶ _____
B And don't get lost.

3 SOCIAL ENGLISH

Complete the dialogue with the words in the box.

don't feel long said so stay think

A I'm ¹ _so_ sorry I'm late. I missed the bus.
B But you're always late.
A I ² _____ I'm sorry.
B Why don't you leave home earlier?
A Look, why ³ _____ we order? I'm really hungry.
B No. I don't want to ⁴ _____ here any more.
A OK. Why don't we go for a walk? I can get a burger or something.
B I don't ⁵ _____ like a walk. It's been a ⁶ _____ day and I'm tired.
A Listen. I'll take you home now. And tomorrow I'll make dinner for you at my house. What do you ⁷ _____?
B OK. I suppose that way you can't be late!

4 READING

a Read the article and answer these questions.

1 How far is it from the airport to Manhattan?   _15 miles_
2 How long does it take to drive there outside the rush hour?   _____
3 How much does AirTrain JFK cost for two people one way?   _____
4 How much does a taxi cost for four people?   _____
5 How much do taxis charge per suitcase?   _____
6 What time is the earliest bus to Manhattan?   _____
7 How much is the fare for an adult and a small child?   _____

JFK (John F Kennedy) International Airport is the largest of the three airports serving New York City. It is located in Southeast Queens, about 15 miles (24km) from Manhattan. Travel time to Manhattan by car during rush hour can be over an hour; at other times it's about thirty to forty minutes.

Getting into town from the airport

Although **AIRTRAIN JFK** does not travel directly to Manhattan, it connects passengers to New York's subway and bus networks. The journey costs $7 and takes about an hour, depending on your destination. If you don't mind carrying your own luggage, this is probably your best option.

TAXIS are available outside every terminal in the airport and there's a $45 flat fee to any location in Manhattan. Taxis will take up to four passengers and there is no additional charge for luggage.

NEW YORK AIRPORT SERVICE EXPRESS BUSES run every 15 to 30 minutes from 6.30 a.m. to 11.10 p.m. from each of the airport terminals. The fare is $13, but you can save money by buying round trip tickets online. One free child under 12 is included in the fare. You can choose to get off at Grand Central, Port Authority, or Penn Station and the ride takes about an hour.

b Underline five words or phrases you don't know. Use your dictionary to look up their meaning and pronunciation.

10A The mothers of invention

1 VOCABULARY verbs: *invent, discover*, etc.

Complete the sentences with the past participle of these verbs.

base call design discover give invent
open play show use

1 The London Olympic Stadium was ___designed___ by the architectural company, Populous.

2 The Statue of Liberty was ___gived___ to the people of the USA as a present from the French people.

3 Gold was first ___discovered___ in California in 1848.

4 Lemons and sugar are ___used___ to make lemonade.

5 The game of rugby was first ___played___ at Rugby School in the UK.

6 The first public movie was ___showed___ to an invited audience in Indiana in 1894.

7 The river that flows through Washington D.C. in the USA is ___called___ the Potomac.

8 The first games console was ___invented___ by Ralph H. Baer.

9 Heathrow airport's Terminal 5 was ___opened___ by the Queen in 2008.

10 Many characters in Somerset Maugham's books are ___based___ on real people.

2 GRAMMAR passive

a Order the words to make sentences.

1 discovered / were / Galileo / Saturn's rings / by /
   Saturn's rings were discovered by Galileo .

2 is / on / of / life / the film *The Iron Lady* / the / based / Margaret Thatcher
   The film the Iron Lady is based
   on of the Margaret Thatcher life .

3 Apple / invented / mobile phones / by / weren't
   mobile phones weren't invented
   by Apple .

4 isn't / petrol / lead / in / used / nowadays
   Lead isn't used in petrol
   nowadays .

5 sold / low-cost flights / online / are
   Low-cost flights are sold
   online .

6 an / were / architect / by / Petronus Towers / designed / the / Argentinian
   the Petronus Tower were
   designed by an Argentinian
   architect .

7 wasn't / Steven Spielberg / *Avatar* / by / directed
   Avatar wasn't directed by
   Steve Spielberg .

8 company / by / made / Minis / British / aren't / a / any more
   Minis aren't made by a British
   company anymore.

b Write sentences in the present or past passive.

1 what / your new baby / call
What is your new baby called ?

2 contact lenses / invent / a Czech chemist
Contact leses was invented by a Czech chemist

3 where / olives / grow
Where are olives growed ?

4 the VW Beetle / design / in the 1930s
the VW beetle was designed in the 1930

5 diamonds / find / in many different colours
diamands are finded in many different colous

6 when / vitamins / discover
When was vitamins discovered ?

7 Spanish / speak / in Spain and many parts of South America
in Spain and many parts of South america are speaded Spanish

8 where / the *Lord of the Rings* films / make
Where was matted the lord of the ? Rings

c Rewrite the sentences in the passive.

1 A factory in China makes these toys.
These toys *are made by a factory in China* .

2 People of all ages wear jeans.
Jeans are worn by people of all ages

3 Microsoft didn't invent laptop computers.
Laptop computers wasn't invented by Microsoft

4 Does a computer control the heating?
Is Computer ?

5 Stieg Larsson wrote *The Millennium Trilogy*.
The Millennium Trilogy was written by Stieg Larsson

6 People don't use cassette recorders very much today.
Cassette recorders weren't used much today by people.

7 Picasso didn't paint *The Scream*.
The Scream wasn't painted by Picasso .

8 Did the same person direct all the Harry Potter films?
Were all Harry Potter films direded by the same person ?

3 PRONUNCIATION -ed

a **iChecker** Listen and (circle) the past participle with a different -ed sound.

1 **d** dog	2 /ɪd/	3 **d** dog	4 /ɪd/	5 **t** tie
called	checked	opened	rained	decided
discovered	invented	wanted	started	produced
(painted)	pretended	designed	directed	based

b Listen again. Practise saying the words.

4 LISTENING

a **iChecker** Listen to a radio programme about things that have been invented by accident. Match the inventions 1–3 with the inventors a–c.

1 The microwave oven [b]   a George Crum
2 The X-ray   [ ]   b ~~Percy Spencer~~
3 Crisps   [ ]   c Wilhelm Roentgen

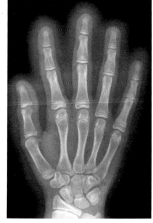

b Listen again and correct the sentences.

1 The discovery that microwaves heated food was made in ~~1954~~. *1945*
2 The microwaves melted a bar of chocolate on the table.
3 The man who discovered the X-ray machine was American.
4 He discovered that electrical rays could pass through water and air.
5 The image on the first X-ray is of the man's hand.
6 Thin fried potatoes are called crisps by Americans.
7 Their inventor was a waiter.
8 The crisps were first called 'Saratoga potatoes'.

The beautiful thing about learning is that
no one can take it away from you.

B B King, American musician

10B Could do better

1 VOCABULARY school subjects

a Match the school subjects and the questions.

1 Foreign languages — `c`
2 Geography — `h`
3 History — `e`
4 Literature — `b`
5 Maths — `a`
6 Physical Education — `f`
7 Science — `i`
8 Information Technology — `d`
9 Art — `g`

a What's 15 times 99?
b Who wrote *Macbeth*?
c How do you say 'Thank you' in German?
d How do you select a program?
e When did Queen Victoria die?
f How many metres is one lap of an athletics track?
g Who painted *Three Musicians*?
h What's the capital of Sweden?
i What's the chemical symbol for water?

b Match the questions in **a** with the answers.

1 Stockholm — `h`
2 Pablo Picasso — `g`
3 *Danke schön* — `c`
4 1,485 — `a`
5 William Shakespeare — `b`
6 H_2O — `i`
7 400 metres — `f`
8 Click on the icon. — `d`
9 1901 — `e`

2 GRAMMAR used to

a Complete the sentences with the correct form of *used to* and the verb phrase.

1 [?] *Did you use to be* (you / be) a good student?
2 [-] I *didn't use to behave* (behave) very well.
3 [+] We *used to wear* (wear) a uniform at school.
4 [?] *Did Alex use to have* (Alex / have) a nickname at school?
5 [-] Pupils *didn't use to study* (not study) IT when I went to school.
6 [+] Her school *used to be* (be) a same-sex school, but now it's mixed.
7 [-] We *didn't use to play* (not play) basketball in PE.
8 [?] *Did your teachers use to give* (your teachers / give) you a lot of homework?

b Correct the mistakes in the highlighted phrases.

1 I use to sit at the back of the class. — *I used to*
2 He used go to school on Saturday mornings. — *he used to go*
3 We didn't used to understand our German teacher. — *use to*
4 Did you used to go to school by bus? — *use to*
5 School use to start at 9.00 but now it starts at 8.30. — *used to*
6 Did your friends use help you with your homework? — *use to*

3 PRONUNCIATION used to / didn't use to

iChecker Listen and repeat the sentences. Copy the rhythm.

1 I **used** to be **good** at **maths**.
2 **We used** to **hate** the **teacher**.
3 She **didn't use** to **like school**.
4 They **didn't use** to **wear** a **uniform**.
5 **Did** you **use** to play **football** in **PE**?
6 Did **your school** use to **open** in the **holidays**?

4 READING

a Read the interview. Write the questions in the correct place.

~~Did you have a favourite teacher?~~

~~Where did you go to school?~~

~~Did you ever behave badly?~~

What's the most important lesson you learned at school?

~~What did you want to do when you left school?~~

What subjects were you good at?

My schooldays

DAVID SUCHET, actor, played Hercule Poirot in the TV series of Agatha Christie murder mysteries.
Interview by Tim Oglethorpe

1 *Where did you go to school?*

Grenham House, a boarding school in Kent, and Wellington School, a private school in Somerset.

2 What's the most important lesson ...

One thing my schooldays did teach me was the importance of teamwork. At boarding school, I was an outsider and I was really, truly unhappy there. When I started playing sport at Grenham House, I became a member of a team, and I felt a lot better about myself. Like sport, acting is also nearly always a team event and you rely just as much on other people as they do on you.

3 Did you ever behave badly?

Yes, I did. My brother and I both went to the same school and sometimes, we used to break the rules. In private schools at that time, a common punishment used to be 'the cane': a long stick which the head teacher used for hitting naughty boys. Both of us were caned on several occasions.

4 What subjects were you good at?

Well, I wasn't very academic at all, really, and I was very bad at maths. Luckily for me, I was really good at sport and that's the only reason they accepted me at Wellington. I was in the school rugby team, and I also played tennis. I played at Wimbledon once, in the junior tournament, and I got through to the second round.

5 What did you want to do when

Although I was good at sport, I never really considered taking it up professionally. Once I left Wellington, I wanted to become an actor and I didn't play nearly as much sport when I left school.

6 Did you have a favourite teacher?

Yes, my favourite teacher was Mr Storr, head of the school tennis team, and also my English teacher. One day, when I was 14 or 15, I had to read in class. After the class, he said to me, 'The way you read suggests you might enjoy acting. Would you consider playing Macbeth in the school play?' That was the beginning of my acting career, and I've never looked back since.

b Read the interview again. Mark the sentences T (true) or F (false).

1 He thinks it's important to work together with others. _T_

2 David didn't always enjoy his first school.

3 David wanted to be a tennis player when he left school.

4 He and his brother used to behave well.

5 In the past, the headmaster could hit pupils with a stick.

6 David didn't use to be a very good student.

7 He only got into Wellington because he was good at sport.

8 Mr Storr taught maths and coached the tennis team.

c Look at the highlighted words. Use your dictionary to look up their meaning and pronunciation.

5 LISTENING

a iChecker Listen to two people talking about language learning in schools. Were Tony and Amy good at languages when they were at school?

b Listen again and circle the correct answer.

1 Amy studied **German** / **French** the longest.

2 Amy can remember one language more than the others because she **practised it on holiday** / **studied it at university**.

3 Adults remember **some numbers** / **some adjectives** from their language classes.

4 According to the article, some people are **too busy** / **too uncomfortable** to speak a foreign language.

5 **German** / **Italian** is more popular than Spanish.

6 In the future, schools will **offer more European languages** / **make younger pupils learn languages**.

USEFUL WORDS AND PHRASES

Learn these words and phrases.

behaviour /bɪˈheɪvjə/

marks /mɑːks/

nickname /ˈnɪkneɪm/

disorganized /dɪsˈɔːgənaɪzd/

emotional /ɪˈməʊʃənl/

primary school /ˈpraɪməri skuːl/

secondary school /ˈsekəndri skuːl/

express yourself /ɪkˈspres jɔːˈself/

be good (bad) at /bi ˈɡʊd æt/

The first step to getting what you want out of life is this: Decide what you want.

Ben Stein, American writer

10C Mr Indecisive

1 GRAMMAR *might* (possibility)

a Max and Sam are telling a colleague about their plans for next weekend. Complete the text with *might* and a verb from the box.

~~be~~ eat go have invite make rain take

'We feel like doing something special next weekend, but we haven't decided what to do yet. It [1] *might be* sunny, so we [2] _might go_ for a walk in the country on Saturday. We [3] _might have_ lunch in a restaurant, or we [4] _might take_ some sandwiches with us.

On the other hand, it [5] _might rain_, so we won't be able to go out. In that case, we [6] _might invite_ some friends for dinner on Saturday. We [7] _might make_ dinner ourselves, or we [8] _might eat_ out, we're not sure.

Everything depends on the weather, really.'

b Complete the sentences with *might* or *might not* and a verb from the box.

be come fail get go ~~go out~~ have miss

1 I'm really tired so I _might not go out_ tonight.
2 Miguel doesn't speak English, so he _might not get_ the job with the American company.
3 If you have a temperature, you _might have_ flu.
4 My parents _might not come_ to our party – they're thinking of going on holiday then.
5 I haven't seen Johnny with Vanessa for a long time. They _might not be_ together any more.
6 If the taxi doesn't come soon, we _might miss_ the train.
7 We love skiing, so we _might go_ to the Alps for our next holiday.
8 Sue hasn't practised much so she _might fail_ her driving test.

2 VOCABULARY word building: noun formation

a Complete the chart with the correct noun or verb.

Verb	Noun
[1] *choose*	choice
confuse	[2] *confusion*
decide	[3] _decition_
[4] _die_	death
educate	[5] _education_
[6] _elect_	election
imagine	[7] _imagination_
[8] _Inform_	information
invite	[9] _invitation_
[10] _live_	life
opt	[11] _option_
[12] _Organize_	organization
[13] _succeed_	success

b Complete the sentences with verbs or nouns from **a**.

1 After the _death_ of my grandfather, my grandmother came to live with us.
2 I made the right _choice_ to continue studying when I left school. I loved university.
3 They're going to _invite_ all their friends to their party.
4 _Success_ at school depends on how hard you work.
5 We're sorry to _inform_ passengers that the 14.30 train to Birmingham is delayed.
6 He _decide_ to study history instead of geography at school.
7 Can you _imagine_ a world without electricity?
8 The documentary was about the _life_ of the author, Charles Dickens.

3 PRONUNCIATION diphthongs

a Tick (✓) the pairs of words which have the same sound and cross (✗) the pairs that don't.

1	m**igh**t	sc**ien**ce	✓
2	m**ay**	f**ai**l	__
3	kn**ow**	n**ow**	__
4	wh**ere**	w**ere**	__
5	h**ere**	th**ere**	__
6	t**ou**rist	**Eu**rope	__
7	sh**ow**	c**ow**	__
8	n**oi**sy	b**oy**	__

b **iChecker** Listen and check. Then listen again and repeat.

4 READING

a Read the text. What was the aim of the experiment?

b Read the text again and circle the correct answer.

1 The participants in the experiment were all **at university** / **at work**.

2 The two groups were shown the card game **in different places** / **at different times**.

3 The participants had to go back **some time later** / **the next day**.

4 **Some** / **All** of the participants went to bed between the two visits.

5 There were **two** / **four** packs of cards in the card game.

6 The cards in the packs were **the same** / **different**.

7 The group who were taught in the morning **won** / **lost** more often than the other group.

8 The experiment helped researchers find a connection between **being creative** / **REM sleep** and making decisions.

c Highlight five words you don't know. Use your dictionary to look up their meaning and pronunciation.

Let me sleep on it

For many years, people have said that a good night's sleep often helps when you have to make an important decision. Research done recently by an American University has shown that this idea is actually true.

The researchers used a card game for their experiment and 54 students between the ages of 18 and 23 took part. The scientists divided the participants into two groups. Both groups were given a short lesson in how to play the card game, either in the morning or in the evening. The lesson was very short, not long enough for either group to learn exactly how the card game worked. All of the students were asked to come back 12 hours later. The 28 students who had the class in the afternoon went home to a normal evening and their usual night of sleep, while the 26 who received the class in the morning came back after a day of normal activities without having a sleep.

On their second visit, the students played the game for long enough to learn that taking cards from the four different packs gave different results. Two of the packs had cards which helped players win more often while the other two packs had cards which made them lose. The object was to avoid losing the game.

In the experiment, the students who had had a normal night's sleep chose cards from the winning packs four times more than those who had spent the 12-hour break awake. The students who had slept also understood better how to play the game.

These results show that sleep helps a person make better decisions. The researchers think that this has something to do with rapid-eye-movement or REM sleep, which is the creative period of our sleep cycle. The experiment shows that there is a connection between REM sleep and decision making, but researchers do not yet know what the connection is.

5 LISTENING

a **iChecker** Listen to five speakers talking about decisions they have made. How many of them made good decisions?

b Listen again and match the speakers with the sentences.

Speaker 1 _C_ A He / She thought time was more important than money.
Speaker 2 __ B He / She didn't get a prize.
Speaker 3 __ C He / She didn't arrive on time.
Speaker 4 __ D He / She didn't enjoy a special occasion.
Speaker 5 __ E He / She didn't accept an invitation.

USEFUL WORDS AND PHRASES

Learn these words and phrases.

products /ˈprɒdʌkts/	make a decision /ˈmeɪk ə dɪˈsɪʒn/
dissatisfied /dɪsˈsætɪsfaɪd/	miss an opportunity /ˈmɪs ən ɒpəˈtjuːnəti/
indecisive /ɪndɪˈsaɪsɪv/	pick somebody up (= in a car) /ˈpɪk sʌmbədi ʌp/
electrical gadgets	pick sth /ˈpɪk/
/ɪlektrɪkl ˈɡædʒɪts/	take sth seriously /teɪk ˈsɪəriəsli/
be able to /bi ˈeɪbl tə/	

11A Bad losers

1 VOCABULARY sports, expressing movement

a Complete the sentences.

1 The player took two shots to hit the golf ball into the h_ole_ .
2 In athletics, the runners run round a tr_ack_ .
3 It was m_atch_ p_oint_ , and everyone was very tense, but his first s_erve_ went into the net.
4 The golf player had to try and hit the ball out of the b_unker_ .
5 The athletes were running fast towards the finishing line because they were on the last l_ap_ .
6 When you take a p_enalty_ , you have to kick the ball past the goalkeeper.
7 The player who took the c_orner_ kicked the ball to a team mate, who headed it into the goal.

b Underline the prepositions of movement in **a**.

c Complete the crossword.

Clues across ➡

2 GRAMMAR expressing movement

a Look at the pictures. Complete the sentences with the past simple of the verbs and the correct preposition.

cycle go hit kick run throw
across into over through under up

1 They ___cycled___ __up__ the hill.
2 The boy _kicked the_ ball _under_ the car.
3 The train _go_ _through_ the tunnel.
4 He _threw_ the ball _into_ the goal.
5 The children _run_ _across_ the road.
6 She _hit_ the ball _over_ the net.

Clues down ⬇

b Look at the picture, read the story, and complete it with the prepositions.

across   into   out of   past   ~~round~~   through   to
towards   under   along (x 2)

Last day at school for boy with dirty shoes!

Last Wednesday started as normal for 15-year-old Michael Brewster at Hove Park School.

At 10.30 a.m., Michael's class were jogging
[1] *round* the gym. But when Charles Duff,
the sports teacher, told Michael to clean his
dirty trainers, he got really angry. He ran
[2] _____ the gym, and back to the
changing rooms where he found Mr Duff's keys.
From there, he went [3] _____ the car
park, got [4] _____ Mr Duff's Ford
Mondeo, and started the car. Then he drove
[5] _____ the road, [6] _____
the bridge, [7] _____ the security guard,
and [8] _____ the school gates. Then
he turned left and drove [9] _____ the
road for about 100 metres [10] _____ the
maths teacher's house. That was when he lost
control. He tried to stop, but instead went
[11] _____ a field and crashed into
a tree. Michael has now left Hove Park School.

3 PRONUNCIATION sports

a Look at the phonetics and write the sport.

1 /ˈfʊtbɔːl/   *football*
2 /ˈvɒlibɔːl/   _____
3 /ˈməʊtə ˈreɪsɪŋ/   _____
4 /ˈskiːɪŋ/   _____
5 /ˈwɪndsɜːfɪŋ/   _____
6 /ˈsaɪklɪŋ/   _____
7 /ˈbɑːskɪtbɔːl/   _____
8 /ˈrʌgbi/   _____
9 /æθˈletɪks/   _____

b **iChecker** Listen and check. Then listen again and repeat the words.

4 LISTENING

a **iChecker** Listen to five people talking about bad losers. Which games or sports do they mention?

_____

b Listen again. Who…?

1 lost a friend after playing sport with him / her   *Speaker 2*
2 is in a team with someone who's a bad loser   _____
3 has a parent who is a bad loser   _____
4 used to let one of their children win   _____
5 has a colleague who is a fanatical sports fan   _____

USEFUL WORDS AND PHRASES

Learn these words and phrases.

coach   /kəʊtʃ/
corner   /ˈkɔːnə/
hole   /həʊl/
lap   /læp/
penalty   /ˈpenəlti/
beat   /biːt/
crash   /kræʃ/
race   /reɪs/
referee   /refəˈriː/
score a goal   /ˈskɔː(r) ə gəʊl/

11B Are you a morning person?

1 VOCABULARY phrasal verbs

a Complete what the people are saying in each picture.

1 Turn _down_ the radio! It's very loud!
2 Don't worry! The match will be _over_ soon.
3 We need someone who can look _after_ our dog while we're on holiday.
4 Take _off_ your shoes before you come in!
5 Can you fill _in_ this form, please?
6 Put _on_ a different jacket! That one looks awful!

b Complete the sentences with these verbs.

find-out get on with give up go out look forward to look up
take back throw away try on turn up

1 Chris called the station to _find out_ the times of the trains.
2 I never _throw away_ empty jam jars. I wash them and then re-use them.
3 It's very cold in here. Can you _turn up_ the heating?
4 The teacher told us to _look up_ the words we didn't understand.
5 We love travelling, so we always _look forward to_ our holidays.
6 I don't really like my sister's new boyfriend. I don't _get on with_ him at all.
7 They only _go out_ on Friday or Saturday nights because they start work early during the week.
8 It's best to _try on_ clothes before you buy them.
9 We're going to _take back_ our new coffee machine because it doesn't work properly.
10 Anna's going to _give up_ sweets and chocolate for a month to try to lose weight.

2 GRAMMAR word order of phrasal verbs

a Circle the correct phrases. If both are possible, tick (✓) the sentence.

1 Please **turn off the lights** / **turn the lights off** before you go to bed. ✓
2 Thanks for the money. I'll **pay it back** / **pay back it** tomorrow. ✗
3 I can't find my keys. Can you help me **look for them** / **look them for**? ✗
4 Why don't you **try on that dress** / **try that dress on**? I think it'll suit you. ✓
5 My mum usually **looks after my kids** / **looks my kids after** when we go out. ✗
6 If you've finished playing, please **put the toys away** / **put away the toys**. ✓

b Rewrite the sentences with a pronoun. Change the word order if necessary.

1 Can you write down **your email address**?
   Can you write it down?
2 She'll give back **the exams** on Friday.
   She'll give them back on friday,
3 Are you looking forward to **your party**?
   Are you looking forward to it ?
4 I called back **my mother** when I got home.
   I called back her when I got home
5 We don't get on with **our new neighbours**.
   We don't get on with them.
6 Shall we turn on **the TV**?
   Shall we turn on it ?

3 PRONUNCIATION linking

iChecker Listen and repeat the sentences. Try to link the words.

1 Throw it away!
2 Turn it up!
3 Write it down!
4 Put it away!
5 Give it back!
6 Fill it in!

4 READING

a Read the article. Complete the gaps with these phrasal verbs.

find out   get up   give up   go out   put on   take off
turn on   write down

b Read the article again. Tick (✓) the people with good habits and cross (✗) the bad ones.

1 I go to bed every night at 11 o'clock. ✓
2 I sleep for six hours during the week and ten hours at the weekend. ✗
3 I always have lunch at my desk to save time. ✗
4 I always wear sunglasses. ✗
5 My bedroom is sometimes too cold. ✗
6 I sometimes watch a film to help me to go to sleep. ✗
7 I usually have dinner at 7.30 p.m. ✓
8 I often have a cup of coffee before I go to bed. ✗
9 I keep a notebook by the side of my bed. ✓
10 I sometimes meditate if I can't sleep. ✓

c Look at the highlighted words or phrases and guess their meaning. Use your dictionary to look up their meaning and pronunciation.

5 LISTENING

a (iChecker) Listen to an interview with Graham, a taxi driver who usually works at night. Is he positive or negative about his job?

b Listen again. Mark the sentences T (true) or F (false).

1 Graham goes to sleep immediately after getting home from work. _F_
2 The first meal he has when he gets up is lunch. ___
3 His children wake him up in the afternoon. ___
4 He never feels tired when he wakes up. ___
5 He eats three times a day. ___
6 He doesn't mind his working hours. ___

USEFUL WORDS AND PHRASES

Learn these words and phrases.

buzz /bʌz/
energetic /enəˈdʒetɪk/
live (adjective) /laɪv/
sleepy /ˈsliːpi/
wild (night) /waɪld/
bowl (of cereal) /ˈbəʊl/
any time /ˈeni taɪm/
social life /ˈsəʊʃl laɪf/
set (your alarm clock) /set/
stay in bed /ˈsteɪ ɪn bed/

Still tired in the morning?

Five tips for getting a better night's sleep

Sleep at the same times

1 _Find out_ how much sleep you need and make sure that you get it. Go to bed and 2 _get up_ at the same time each day and you will have more energy than if you sleep the same number of hours at different times.

Make sure you are exposed to light during the day

Your body needs natural light to produce the hormone melatonin, which regulates your sleeping and waking cycle. Don't stay inside all day – 3 _go out_ in your lunch break, for example for a short walk. On a sunny day 4 _take off_ your sunglasses for at least half an hour to let light onto your face.

Create a relaxing routine before going to bed

Have a hot bath. Then 5 _put on_ your pyjamas and make sure your bedroom is at the right temperature. Don't watch TV in bed, as it will stimulate rather than relax you.

Avoid stimulants

Don't eat big meals or drink coffee late at night. Avoid drinking alcohol before you go to bed and 6 _give up_ smoking! Cigarettes can cause a number of sleep problems.

Getting back to sleep

If you wake up in the middle of the night and can't get back to sleep, try a relaxation technique like meditation. If that doesn't work, 7 _turn on_ the light and read a book. If you're worried about something, 8 _write down_ your problem on a piece of paper so that you can deal with it in the morning.

If the tips above don't help, you might need to see a sleep doctor.

11C What a coincidence!

1 GRAMMAR *so*, *neither* + auxiliaries

a Complete the conversation with the phrases from the box.

> ~~Neither did I~~   Neither have I   ~~Neither was I~~
> So am I   So do I   So would I

A Hi, Tom. Do you ever watch *Who do you think you are?* You know, that TV series about celebrities who find out about their families?
B Yes, I do. But I didn't see it last night.
A ¹ _Neither did I_ . I wasn't at home.
B ² _Neither was I_ . But I usually watch it every week.
A ³ _So do I_ . I think it's really interesting. I'd love to find out about my family.
B ⁴ _So would I_ . I'm thinking about looking for some information on the internet.
A ⁵ _So am I_ . But I haven't done anything about it yet.
B ⁶ _Neither have I_

b Respond to the statements with *So* or *Neither*, to say that you are the same.

1 I'm going out tonight.
   _So am I_ .
2 I enjoyed the party.
   So did I .
3 I haven't done the homework.
   Neither had I .
4 I was late today.
   So was I .
5 I'm not hungry.
   Neither am I .
6 I can't drive.
   Neither can I .
7 I'd love to travel round the world.
   So would I .
8 I don't have any pets.
   Neither do I .

2 VOCABULARY similarities

Complete the text with words from the box.

> ~~as~~   ~~both~~   ~~identical~~   ~~like~~   ~~neither~~
> ~~similar~~   ~~so~~

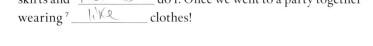

People think my best friend Sue and I are sisters, because we're very ¹ _similar_ . Sue's from the same town ² _as_ me, and we look very ³ _identical_ each other. We ⁴ _both_ like shopping, and we have the same taste in clothes. I usually wear trousers and tops, and ⁵ _so_ does Sue. She doesn't like short skirts and ⁶ _neither_ do I. Once we went to a party together wearing ⁷ _like_ clothes!

3 PRONUNCIATION sentence stress, word stress

a **iChecker** Listen to the sentences.

1 **So** did **I**.
2 **So** can **I**.
3 **So** have **I**.
4 **Neither** am **I**.
5 **Neither** do **I**.
6 **Neither** was **I**.

b Listen again and repeat the sentences. <u>Copy</u> the <u>rhy</u>thm.

c **iChecker** Listen and under<u>line</u> the stressed syllable. Then listen again and repeat the words.

1 i|den|ti|cal
2 si|mi|lar
3 co|in|ci|dence
4 a|ma|zing
5 dis|co|ver
6 e|very|where
7 per|son|a|li|ty
8 def|in|ite|ly

4 READING

a Read the article and choose the best title.

1 A town with a mystery
2 The problems of having twins
3 Why couples have twins

Today, there are two thousand families living in the village of Kodinhi in southern India. Among them, there are 220 sets of twins, which is six times the global average. What makes this even more unusual is that India has one of the lowest birth rates of twins in the world.

Nobody can explain the reason why the village has so many twins. Some people say the cause might be genetic, but local doctor, Dr Sribiju, doesn't think so. He says that there haven't always been twins in Kodinhi – parents suddenly started having them about sixty or seventy years ago. Neither does he believe that a new kind of pollution has caused the twins to be born. In that case, he argues, there would be more twins with malformations. Luckily, most of Kodinhi's twins are born healthy. Dr Sribiju thinks that the twins are born because of something the villagers eat and drink. He wants to discover just what that is, so that he can use it to help other couples who can't have children.

Having twins in this part of India can be a big problem for a family. It's expensive, and it can be dangerous for the mother's health. That's why the villagers of Kodinhi have started a support group. The group is called the Twins and Kin* Association, or TAKA for short. The president of the group is 50-year-old Pullani Bhaskaran, who has twin sons of his own. He wants all the twins in Kodinhi to join the group so that they can help each other. With the 220 pairs of twins in the village and the other people in their families, TAKA currently has 600 members.

Glossary
kin = family member

b Read the article and mark the sentences T (true) or F (false).

1 Parents don't usually have twins in India. _T_
2 A century ago, there used to be more twins in Kodinhi.
3 Dr Sribiju thinks that there are a lot of twins because of the pollution in Kodinhi.
4 Dr Sribiju thinks that couples who want children could learn from the villagers of Kodinhi.
5 It can be a health risk for women in Kodinhi to have twins.
6 The President of TAKA has a twin brother.

c Look at the highlighted words and phrases and guess their meaning. Use your dictionary to look up their meaning and pronunciation.

5 LISTENING

a (iChecker) Listen to a radio programme about famous twins. Match the twins (1–3) with the headings (a–c).

1 Romulus and Remus _c_   a criminal twins
2 The Kray Brothers _____   b celebrity twins
3 The Olsen Twins _____   c ~~historical twins~~

b Read the sentences. Listen again and write RR (Romulus and Remus), KB (the Kray Brothers) or OT (the Olsen Twins).

1 Their parents didn't want them. _R R_
2 They were British. _____
3 They're still alive. _____
4 They met some very famous people. _____
5 They had a serious argument. _____
6 They became famous very young. _____

USEFUL WORDS AND PHRASES

Learn these words and phrases.

tastes /teɪsts/
identical twins /aɪˈdentɪkl ˈtwɪnz/
security guard /sɪˈkjʊərəti gɑːd/

adopt (a child) /əˈdɒpt/
by coincidence /baɪ kəʊˈɪnsɪdəns/
great to meet you /greɪt tə ˈmiːt juː/
go to college (AmE) /gəʊ tə ˈkɒlɪdʒ/
look exactly like /lʊk ɪgˈzæktli laɪk/

(iChecker) (TESTS) FILE 11

Practical English Time to go home

1 ON THE PHONE

Complete the dialogues.

1 **A** Hello, can I s*peak* to Oliver, please?
  B T*his* is Oliver.
  A Hi Oliver, this is Mark. I'm r*eturning* your call.

2 **A** Hi Amy.
  B I'm s_____, you have the
     wr_____ number.

3 **A** Hello, this is reception. How can I help you?
  B Good morning. Mr Clarke, please.
  A I'm sorry, the l_____ is b_____.
  B OK, can I l_____ a m_____?
  A Yes, of course.
  B Can you tell him Fiona called? I'll c_____
     b_____ later.

4 **A** Good morning, London 24seven.
  B Hello, can I speak to Alison, please?
  A Just a second, I'll p_____ you through.

2 SOCIAL ENGLISH

Circle the correct word or phrase.

1 **A** Does your girlfriend know you're here?
  B No, I'll **call her** / **call to her** now.

2 **A** I've got a new job!
  B That's **great news** / **a great news**.

3 **A** I've got something to tell you.
  B Me, too. But you **do first** / **go first**.

4 **A** What are you doing here?
  B I'll explain **after** / **later**.

5 **A** Is everything alright?
  B **Never better** / **Ever better**.

3 READING

a Read the text. Which sentence is the best summary?

  1 British and American English are almost exactly the same.
  2 The most important difference between British and American English is the vocabulary.
  3 Travellers don't have problems understanding British and American English.

British and American English

If you've learnt British English and you're travelling in the States, or if you've learnt American English and you're travelling in Britain, you'll notice some differences. An obvious difference is the accent, but most travellers find that they don't have too many problems with this. There are some grammatical differences, but they shouldn't make it difficult to understand people, or to communicate. That leaves differences in vocabulary, which can cause misunderstandings. Sometimes the difference is only the spelling, for example, in British English *centre*, *colour*, and *travelled*, and in American English *center*, *color*, and *travelled*. But sometimes the word is completely different in British and American English, so it's a good idea to be prepared.

b Match the British English with the American English.

1	bill	c	a	cab
2	chips		b	cell phone
3	chemist's		c	~~check~~
4	ground floor		d	elevator
5	lift		e	first floor
6	mobile		f	fries
7	petrol		g	line
8	queue		h	the subway
9	toilet		i	pharmacy
10	shop		j	rest room
11	taxi		k	store
12	trainers		l	sneakers
13	the underground		m	gas

c Underline five words or phrases you don't know. Use your dictionary to look up their meaning and pronunciation. Make sure you can say them in British and American English.

12A Strange but true!

1 GRAMMAR past perfect

a Complete the sentences with the past perfect form of the verbs in brackets.

1 The streets were white because it __*had snowed*__ the night before. (snow)

2 I suddenly remembered that I _hadn't closed_ the windows before I left the house. (not close)

3 We got to the cinema ten minutes after the film _had started_ . (start)

4 Tina felt nervous because she _hadn't flown_ before. (not fly)

5 Paul lent me the book after he_'d read_ it. (read)

6 They missed the flight because they _hadn't heard_ the announcement. (not hear)

b Write questions in the past perfect.

1 **A** I drove my boyfriend's car this morning.
   B you / drive it / before
   Had you driven it before ?

2 **A** My friends ate sushi in Japan.
   B they / eat sushi / before
   Had they eaten sushi before?

3 **A** My brother won a gold medal.
   B he / win a medal / before
   Had he won a medal before?

4 **A** The children made a cake yesterday.
   B they / make a cake / before
   Had they made a cake before?

5 **A** My sister ran in the London marathon last weekend.
   B she / run a marathon / before
   Had she run a marathon before?

6 **A** We went to Brazil on holiday.
   B you / be there / before
   Had you been there before ?

c Make these two sentences into one. Use the past perfect and the past simple.

1 We bought some souvenirs. Then we went back to the hotel.
   After *we had bought some souvenirs, we went back to the hotel* .

2 Max did the ironing. Then he put the clothes away.
   After Max _had done the ironing, he put the clothes aw_

3 They watched the news. Then they turned off the TV.
   After _they had watched the news, they turned off th_

4 I read the book. Then I gave it back.
   When _I had read the book, I gave it back._

5 Ruth tried on the top. Then she went to the checkout.
   After Ruth _had tried on the top, she went to the check_

6 We had dinner. Then we did the washing up.
   After _We had had dinner, we did the washing up_

d Circle the correct verb.

Last week my neighbour was on holiday. One night I ¹ **(heard)** / **had heard** a strange noise in her house. I ² **(opened)** / **had opened** the door to have a look, and I found that someone ³ **broke** / **(had broken)** into the house.

Luckily, he (or she!) ⁴ **already left** / **(had already left)** when I got there, and they ⁵ **didn't steal** / **(hadn't stolen)** much as far as I could see – just the TV.

I was looking for my mobile yesterday morning, but I couldn't find it. I was sure I ⁶ **didn't lose** / **(hadn't lost)** it, because I ⁷ **saw** / **had (seen)** it twenty minutes before. Then I realized that I ⁸ **(left)** / **had left** it in my trouser pocket, and I ⁹ **put** / **(had put)** my trousers in the washing machine!

2 PRONUNCIATION contractions:
had / hadn't

a Write the sentences with contractions.

1 He had forgotten it. *He'd forgotten it.*
2 We had lost it. *We'd lost it*
3 You had seen her. *You'd seen her*
4 It had been a terrible day. *It'd been a terrible day*
5 I had not sent it. *I hadn't sent it*
6 She had not done it. *She hadn't done it*
7 They had not told me. *They hadn't told me*

b [iChecker] Now listen and check. Then listen and repeat the sentences. Copy the <u>rhy</u>thm.

3 VOCABULARY verb phrases

Complete the sentences with the past simple or past participle of the verbs from the box.

~~get on~~ ~~get out of~~ ~~free~~ realize put ~~go on~~
~~have~~ leave ~~be~~ ~~belong~~

1 He was re-arrested 24 hours after he had been ___*freed*___ from prison.
2 The check-in clerk ___*put*___ my suitcase on the belt and gave me my boarding pass.
3 This ring ___*belonged*___ to my mother when she was young.
4 She wasn't worried because she had ___*left*___ the baby with her mother.
5 My parents weren't at home because they had ___*gone on*___ holiday a few days before.
6 After we had ___*got out of*___ the pool, we sunbathed for a while.
7 We went to the beach and _____ a swim.
8 When I got to my class, I ___*realized*___ that I had forgotten my books.
9 He ___*was*___ in prison when his son was born.
10 The train left a few minutes after they had ___*got on*___ it.

4 LISTENING

a [iChecker] Listen to four true news stories. Number the pictures in the order you hear the stories.

b Listen again and correct the mistakes in the sentences.

1 Dennis Leighton was going to visit his ~~sister~~. *daughter*
2 He had been in his car for ~~13~~ hours. *30*
3 Erin Langworthy was on holiday in ~~Kenya~~. *Zambia*
4 She was taken to hospital after she had walked to safety. *swum*
5 Lena Paahlsson lost the ring while she was doing the washing up. *cooking*
6 Today the ring is too big for her. *small*
7 The crocodile had gone into Jo Dodd's kitchen. *living room*
8 Mrs Dodd called the Crocodile Management Centre. *Husband*

USEFUL WORDS AND PHRASES

Learn these words and phrases.

wave /weɪv/	close to (adj) /ˈkləʊs tə/
arrest /əˈrest/	outdoor /aʊtdɔː/
belong /bɪˈlɒŋ/	fortunately /ˈfɔːtʃənətli/
realize /ˈrɪəlaɪz/	net /ˈnet/
steal /stiːl/	rob (a bank) /rɒb/

12B Gossip is good for you

1 GRAMMAR reported speech

a Complete the reported speech.

Direct speech	Reported speech
1 'I want to leave him.'	She said that she *wanted to leave him*.
2 'I don't like her parents.'	He told me that he *didn't like her parents*.
3 'I'm getting divorced.'	She told me that she *was getting divorced*.
4 'I've been to the police station.'	He told me that he *had been to the police station*.
5 'I haven't met his girlfriend.'	She said that she *hadn't met his girlfriend*.
6 'I saw James with another woman.'	He said that he *he had seen James with another woman*.
7 'I can't cook.'	She told me that she *she couldn't cook*.
8 'I won't tell anyone.'	He said that he *wouldn't tell anyone*.
9 'I'll speak to her tomorrow.'	She said that she *would speak to her tomorrow*.
10 'I've got a lot of work to do.'	He told me that he *had got a lot of work to do*.

b Write the sentences in direct speech.

1 She said she was busy.
   She said: ' *I'm busy* .'

2 Jane said that she wanted a cup of coffee.
   She said: ' *I want a cup of coffee* .'

3 They told me that they hadn't seen the new
   neighbours yet.
   They said: ' *haven't seen the new neighbours yet* .'

4 Steve told me that he didn't want to go to
   the cinema.
   He said: ' *I don't want to go to the cinema* .'

5 Helen and Paul said they would go to the party.
   They said: ' *We'll go to the party* .'

6 He said that his computer had just broken.
   He said: ' *My computer has just broken* .'

7 She told me that the city was very old.
   She said: ' *the city is very old* .'

8 They said that they would visit me.
   They said: ' *We'll visit me* .'

2 VOCABULARY say or tell?

a Circle the correct words.

1 Her husband (said) / told that he was working late.
2 She said / told me that she wasn't happy.
3 They said / told us that they were getting married.
4 You said / told that she didn't like men with beards.
5 I said / told you that I had a new girlfriend.
6 We said / told that we were going to be late.
7 Anna said / told you that she didn't have a car.
8 I said / told her that John was busy.
9 He said / told that we had to do exercise five.
10 You said / told that she had called Mike this morning.

b Complete the sentences with *said* or *told*.

1 She _said_ that she had been to a friend's house.
2 We _____ our parents we wouldn't be home for lunch.
3 I _____ you that the man wasn't her brother.
4 They _____ that they were going on holiday.
5 He _____ me that he didn't have a girlfriend.
6 You _____ that you weren't going out tonight.
7 James _____ that he was busy tonight.
8 I _____ that the film started at eight o'clock.
9 We _____ them that his sister was on holiday.
10 Olivia _____ me that she had called Jack this morning.

3 PRONUNCIATION double consonants

a Look at the phonetics and write the words.

1 /ˈgɒsɪp/   _gossip_
2 /ˈmærɪd/   married
3 /ˈletə/   letter
4 /ˈmɪdl/   middle
5 /ˈhʌri/   hurry
6 /ˈdɪfrənt/   different
7 /ˈsɒri/   sorry
8 /ˈsʌmə/   summer
9 /ˈmesɪdʒ/   message
10 /ˈhæpi/   happy

b **iChecker** Listen and check. Then listen again. Practise saying the words.

4 LISTENING

a **iChecker** Listen to Alan and Jess discussing a survey. Do they both gossip at work? No

b Listen again and mark the sentences T (true) or F (false).

1 Jess and Alan think that woman gossip more than men.
   _T_

2 According to the results of the survey, Jess and Alan are right. men
   F

3 The survey was done by a newspaper.
   F   Telecomunicas company

4 Nobody was surprised by the results of the survey.
   F

5 Over 50 percent of the men in the survey said they gossiped at work.
   T

6 Less than 50 per cent of women said they gossiped.
   T

7 The men in the survey talked about topics related to work. female colleagues
   F   PK other.

8 The women talked about their male colleagues.
   F   T.V series
              Problems familie

USEFUL WORDS AND PHRASES

Learn these words and phrases.

genes /dʒiːnz/
gossip /ˈgɒsɪp/
share /ʃeə/
according to /əˈkɔːdɪŋ tə/
feel guilty /fiːl ˈgɪlti/
in general /ɪn ˈdʒenrəl/
pass on /ˈpɑːs ɒn/
social skill /ˈsəʊʃl skɪl/

How many roads must a man walk down
before you can call him a man?

Bob Dylan, US singer and songwriter

12C The *English File* quiz

1 GRAMMAR questions without auxiliaries

a Circle the correct question.

1 a Who did paint *The Kiss*?
  b **Who painted *The Kiss*?**

2 a Which instrument does Angus Young of AC / DC play?
  b Which instrument plays Angus Young of AC / DC?

3 a How many lives do cats have in the UK?
  b How many lives have cats in the UK?

4 a What did happen in Japan on 11th March 2011?
  b What happened in Japan on 11th March 2011?

5 a Which American singer did die on 25th June 2009?
  b Which American singer died on 25th June 2009?

6 a Who did Beyoncé marry in 2008?
  b Who Beyoncé married in 2008?

7 a What animal caught a train for 50 kms?
  b What animal did catch a train for 50 kms?

8 a What invented Peter Durand in 1810?
  b What did Peter Durand invent in 1810?

b Match the questions in **a** with these answers.

a Nine.   3
b An earthquake and a tsunami.   4
c Michael Jackson.   5
d Gustav Klimt.   1
e Jay-Z.   6
f Tinned food.   8
g The guitar.   2
h A dog.   7

c Complete the questions for the answers.

1 What *made Mark Zuckerberg* famous?
  Facebook made Mark Zuckerberg famous.

2 When *did Spain won* the football World Cup?
  Spain won the football World Cup in 2010.

3 How long *did REM stay* together?
  REM stayed together for 31 years.

4 Who *plays* *Jack Sparrow* in *Pirates of the Caribbean*?
  Johnny Depp plays *Jack Sparrow* in *Pirates of the Caribbean*.

5 How *did Amy Winehouse died*?
  Amy Winehouse died from alcohol poisoning.

6 Where *do polar bears live*?
  Polar bears live in the Arctic.

7 How many *roads join* at the Arc de Triomphe in Paris?
  Twelve roads join at the Arc de Triomphe in Paris.

8 Which country *produces the most bananas* in the world?
  India produces the most bananas in the world.

2 VOCABULARY revision

a Circle the word or phrase that is different. Say why it's different.

1 curly   long   (slim)   straight
  It's not used to describe hair.

2 friendly   generous   kind   (overweight)

3 bracelet   earrings   necklace   (tracksuit)

4 a course   exercise   (a phone call) housework   "do"

5 crowded   polluted   (dangerous)   (exciting)

6 market   shopping   (town hall)   department
              centre   store

7 decide   (finish)   forget   pretend "to"

8 (get up)   get old   get fit   get lost "Be.."

9 bee   butterfly   (bat)   mosquito

b Complete the sentences with **one** word.

1 Why don't you try *on* that dress?

2 She was born *on* March 24th, 1996.

3 I'll have to take my new top *back* to the shop. It has a hole.

4 Please don't throw *away* my old jeans. I still wear them.

5 You'll have to speak *to* the manager about your complaint.

6 I'm looking *forward* to going away at the weekend.

7 The children ran *across* the road without looking. Luckily, there wasn't much traffic.

8 They arrived *in* London at midnight.

9 We carried *on* working until it was time to go home.

10 Can you please pick *up* that rubbish from the floor?

c Complete the missing verbs.

1 *go* sightseeing
2 *stay* at a campsite
3 *fall* in love with somebody
4 *make* a mistake
5 *do* the shopping
6 *lend* money to somebody
7 *spend* hours doing something
8 *get* on well with somebody
9 *earn* a salary
10 *find* a job

3 PRONUNCIATION revision

a (Circle) the word with a different sound.

1	æ cat	cap hat (want)
2	ʊ bull	book push school
3	uː boot	lose hope suit
4	ʌ up	turn gloves sunny
5	eɪ train	lazy safe bald
6	əʊ phone	towel goat throw
7	aɪ bike	kind shy thin
8	aʊ owl	cow horse mouse
9	ɔː horse	boring awful word
10	ɪə ear	beard earrings wear
11	eə chair	hair scared fear
12	k key	crowded city across
13	tʃ chess	church beach chemist's
14	dʒ jazz	large forget giraffe

b iChecker Listen and check.

4 READING

a Read the article and match the questions to the answers.

Don't ask me!

A survey of 2,000 parents has discovered that two thirds of them are unable to answer their children's questions about science. See if you can match the ten most common questions with their answers below.

1 Why is the moon sometimes out in the day?   *E*
2 Why is the sky blue?   ___
3 Will we ever discover aliens?   ___
4 How much does the Earth weigh?   ___
5 How do aeroplanes stay in the air?   ___
6 Why is water wet?   ___
7 How do I do long multiplication?   ___
8 Where do birds and bees go in winter?   ___
9 What makes a rainbow?   ___
10 Why are there different times on Earth?   ___

A Bees stop flying and birds stay together in groups or migrate.
B People decided to have 'time zones' so that it would be light during the day everywhere on Earth. If there weren't time zones, some people would have midday in the middle of the night!
C The Earth weighs 6,000,000,000,000,000,000,000,000kg.
D Because of their chemistry, some liquids can be absorbed by solid things.
E The moon can be lit up by the sun, depending on where it is in the sky. If it reflects the sun's rays, we can see it, even during the day. It all depends on its angle towards the Earth.
F Multiply the single numbers and the tens separately, then add them together.
G Sunlight arrives on Earth in every colour, but it hits particles in our air that 'shine' blue.
H Planes have special wings which push air down. This pushing action is stronger than gravity, and so the plane goes up in the air.
I Sunlight going through water drops in the air 'separates' into all the colours.
J No one knows.

b Underline five words that you don't know. Use your dictionary to look up their meaning and pronunciation.

5 LISTENING

a iChecker Listen to five people talking about quiz shows. Complete the names of the shows.

1 *Master* _____
2 *A Question of* _____
3 _____ *my Bluff*
4 *Who wants to be a* _____?
5 _____ *Quiz*

b Listen again. Match some questions which could have been on these quiz shows with the speakers.

Speaker 1   *E*   A Who sang *Every breath you take*?
Speaker 2   ___   B Who painted *Sunflowers*?
                         A Picasso   B Van Gogh   C Cezanne   D Monet
Speaker 3   ___   C How many times has Brazil won the World Cup?
Speaker 4   ___   D What does 'willy nilly' mean?
Speaker 5   ___   ~~E When was Charles Dickens born?~~

This page was intentionally left blank.

Listening

7 A))

Dave Oh, that's ridiculous!

Jane What is?

Dave They've decided to ban jokes about mothers-in-law!

Jane Who has?

Dave The council, of all people. They've written a leaflet for workers who have to deal with the public, and it says that mother-in-law jokes are 'offensive'.

Jane Well, I suppose they are, really. I mean, there are a lot of mothers-in-law out there, and the jokes are about them.

Dave No, but it's just a bit of fun, isn't it? I mean, I think it's really important to have a sense of humour. It's good for you – it makes you feel better.

Jane That's easy for you to say, isn't it? You're a man, so you'll never be a mother-in-law. I will, one day.

Dave Yes, but you won't be my mother-in-law, will you? Sorry, I was only joking!

Jane Ha ha…Does it say anything else about the jokes?

Dave Yes. It says they show 'disrespect for parents'.

Jane OK. Well, maybe they do. Young people are healthy, fit, and attractive. It's easy for them to laugh at older people, don't you think?

Dave Oh, come on! These jokes about mothers-in-law have been around since Roman times.

Jane Where did you get that idea from?

Dave It says here that there's a Roman writer called – hang on a minute – called 'Juvenal' who said in the first century A.D. – wait, listen to this – 'it's impossible to be happy when one's mother-in-law is still alive'. Ha ha! That's classic!

Jane Um.

Dave And all the best comedians tell jokes about mothers-in-law, too. I think they're funny.

Jane Like I said, that's because you're a man. And the comedians you're talking about are also men. It's just another example of the sexist world we live in. I mean, there aren't many jokes about fathers-in-law, are there?

Dave Oh, for goodness' sake!

7 B))

Speaker 1 I like singing while I'm having a shower. The bathroom is a great place to sing because nobody can hear you – at least, I hope nobody can hear, because I sing really loudly! I usually sing very old classic songs, which I'd never sing in public!

Speaker 2 I always feel like singing when I'm alone in my car on a summer's day. I turn up the radio, open the window, and sing along to whatever comes on. I don't do this in the middle of town, of course; only if I'm driving through the country, but I must say I find it really relaxing.

Speaker 3 I've always really enjoyed singing with the kids I teach – I'm a primary school teacher. Young children love singing, and they like it even more if the songs have actions. It's amazing how much they learn from songs – there are alphabet songs, counting songs, and all sorts. We always have lots of fun when we're singing together.

Speaker 4 Actually, I can't sing very well at all, so I'm always really embarrassed if I have to sing in public. When I was at secondary school, I had to be in the school choir, but I never actually sang. I just mouthed the words and pretended to sing.

Speaker 5 When I'm out with my friends, we sometimes go to a karaoke in the centre of town. It's one of my favourite places, as we always have a good time. We spend most of the evening singing together and nobody seems to mind if we do it badly. In fact, it's better if we do sing badly as it makes everybody laugh.

7 C))

Presenter …And here's some good news for one of the world's endangered languages. There are nearly six thousand languages in the world today, and experts say that nearly half of them are dying out. That means that around three thousand languages will disappear in the next century or so. One language in danger of dying out is the Cherokee language, spoken by the Cherokee people of North America. Or at least it <u>was</u> in danger until the leaders of the tribe decided to do something about it. They got worried when they realized that only 8,000 of the 290,000 Cherokee people in the world today actually spoke the language and they came up with a plan. They got in touch with the electronics company, Apple, and asked them to include Cherokee on the official list of languages used on their products.

At first, it seemed impossible that Apple would take any notice of the Cherokee, as their products already had fifty languages on them. The big surprise came in September 2006, when the Apple iOS 4.1 operating system was released with Cherokee on the official list of languages. Since then, the Cherokee people have been able to use their language on all Mac computers, iPhones, the iPod touch, and the iPad. These devices were popular with the younger members of the tribe from the start, but now the older members are taking an interest, too – especially those who use mobile phones.

So, it looks as if the Cherokee language won't die out just yet after all. And if the language stays alive, the culture will stay alive, too, something that the leaders of the tribe will be very happy about.

8 A))

Speaker 1 I don't usually talk about my problems, but if something's going wrong, I sometimes mention it to Phil. He's on my basketball team, and we get along OK. In fact, he's the one who introduced me to the girl I'm dating at the moment.

Speaker 2 The person who I talk to most is my sister. We don't look like each other at all, but we both have very similar personalities. She's a really good listener, and she always gives me good advice. She sometimes tells me her problems too, and I try to help her.

Speaker 3 My friend Jenny is on my course at university, and I tell her absolutely everything. We're quite different, which means we often think in different ways. Sometimes we argue, but we're never angry with each other for long – just until one of us apologizes.

Speaker 4 The person who understands me most is my friend John, who lives next door. We've grown up together, so he knows me very well. My main problem at the moment is my job, which I hate. John thinks I should look for a new one, and he's probably right.

Speaker 5 My gran lives with us, and I spend a lot of time talking to her. Although she's older than me, she's always interested in what I have to say. We've got quite a lot in common, and some things that have happened to me also happened to her when she was young.

8 B))

Presenter Now, everyone loves travelling, and we all enjoy telling stories about the places we've been to. But what happens if there's an earthquake while you're away? Travel expert, Monica Fields, is here in the studio with us today to give us some tips on what to do in a natural disaster. First of all, Monica, is it possible to avoid them?

Monica Well, no, actually, it isn't. Nobody really knows exactly when a disaster like a forest fire or a blizzard will happen, so you can't really avoid them. What you can do, however, is be prepared.

Presenter How can you do that?

Monica Well, first of all, if you plan to visit a region where there are natural disasters at certain times of the year, try not to go at that time. For example, there are often bad storms, hurricanes, or cyclones in the Caribbean in May and June, so don't go there then.

Presenter That sounds sensible. What else can you do?

Monica It's really important to buy travel insurance before you go. This will pay for extra nights in a hotel, for example, if you can't fly home and have to stay in your resort longer than you had planned. I never understand why some people don't take out travel insurance.

Presenter Right. So, what should you do if a natural disaster actually happens while you're abroad?

Monica The first thing you should do is to stay calm and be patient.

Presenter That sounds easy, Monica, but natural disasters can be very frightening, can't they?

Monica Yes, of course, but if you panic, things will only get worse. Secondly, you need to contact your family and friends at home as soon as possible. If they hear about the disaster on the news, they'll be incredibly worried.

Presenter Yes, I can see that. What else should you do?

Monica Well, it's always a good idea to know what your airline will do if there's a natural disaster. If you are flying to a country where natural disasters are frequent, you should ask your airline when you book your ticket if they will change your ticket if you need to leave the country quickly, or if you have to stay longer because there is a natural disaster.

Presenter Thank you for joining us, Monica, and thanks for your useful advice.

8 C))

Ewan Did you watch TV last night, Helen?

Helen No, I didn't. What was on?

Ewan There was a really interesting cooking programme on after dinner.

Helen Was there? What made it so good?

Ewan Well, it was a sort of experiment, really. They were trying to answer the question: do men and women cook differently?

Helen Really? So what did they do to try to find the answer?

Ewan They invited a male cook and a female cook to prepare five different courses of a meal. Both cooks had to use the same main ingredient for each course, but they didn't have to make the same dish. Then, they served the dishes to a panel of judges, who tasted them, and decided if they were made by the man or the woman.

Helen Who were the judges?

Ewan Well, there were two men and two women. They were all food experts – either chefs themselves or restaurant critics.

Helen What about the cooks? Were they professionals, too?

Ewan Yes. They were from two of the best restaurants in the country.

Helen And what sort of things did they cook?

Ewan All kinds of things really, but the only ones I remember are a meat dish with garlic and a bright pink dessert.

Helen What was so special about those two dishes?

Ewan I remember them because the judges had real problems in deciding if they were made by the male chef or the female chef. In the end, they all got it wrong!

Helen So, did they manage to answer the question, then? Do men cook differently from women?

Ewan Not really. The only conclusion they came to was that it was impossible to tell if a particular dish was made by a man or a woman. That's all, really.

Helen So, it was a bit of a waste of time then, really.

Ewan No, it wasn't! I really enjoyed the programme, even if they didn't answer the question!

9 A

Newsreader And our final story on tonight's programme is about an Australian diver who has survived a shark attack. 46-year-old Eric Nerhus was fishing off the coast of Cape Howe, New South Wales, when a great white shark attacked him. He was under the water at the time, and he didn't see the animal swimming towards him. Mr Nerhus's head, shoulders, and one of his arms ended up in the shark's mouth, but, fortunately, he was wearing a heavy metal vest. When the shark tried to bite the man in half, its teeth hit the vest and not his body. Mr Nerhus knew he had to do something, so he felt for the shark's eye with the hand of his other arm. When he found it, he surprised the animal by pressing his fingers into its eye. The shark reacted by opening its mouth, giving Mr Nerhus a chance to escape. Despite his injuries, Eric managed to swim up to the surface of the water. His son pulled him onto his boat, and took him quickly to the shore. Meanwhile, another friend called the emergency services. Mr Nerhus was flown to hospital by helicopter. He had deep cuts all over his body and a broken nose, but he was very lucky to be alive. Attacks by great white sharks usually result in death because of their size and strength. The shark that attacked Mr Nerhus was over three metres long.

9 B

Presenter Hello, and welcome to the programme. Today, we've got psychologist, Dr Chris Hopper, in the studio with us to answer your questions about phobias. Hello, Chris.

Chris Good morning.

Presenter And our first caller is Cynthia Sharp from Dundee. What's your question, Cynthia?

Cynthia Um, hello, Dr Hopper. Um, my question is actually about our son, James. He's six years old, and he had a bad experience with a dog last night.

Chris I'm sorry to hear that, Cynthia. What exactly happened?

Cynthia Well, we were outside a neighbour's house, and, um, I was chatting with the mum when one of their dogs ran out. It was a big dog, um, and it came running out of the house barking. James panicked, and tried to hide behind me, but the dog jumped on him and bit him. It wasn't a serious injury, but we're very worried that he'll be afraid of dogs now. We don't want him to get a phobia. What should we do?

Chris Well, Cynthia, you're quite right to be worried about this incident because, cynophobia, that is, a fear of dogs, is often caused by a bad experience with a dog as a child. The best thing you can do is to give your son a positive experience with a different dog as soon as possible. If you have any friends who have a quiet and friendly dog, go and visit them. Let your son touch the dog if he wants to and don't remind him about his bad experience.

Presenter That sounds like good advice, Chris. And our next caller is Marion Williams from Cardiff. Marion?

9 C

Presenter Hello and welcome to those of you who just joined us. Continuing on our theme of celebrity families, the focus of today's programme is actress and singer, Judy Garland, and her daughter, Liza Minnelli. Now, Judy Garland's real name was Frances Ethel Gumm, and she was born on June 10th, 1922 in Grand Rapids, Minnesota. Her parents ran a theatre and Judy first appeared on stage singing a Christmas song with her two older sisters when she was two years old. When she was 13, Judy joined the film company

Metro Goldwyn Mayer and at the age of 16, she played Dorothy in *The Wizard of Oz*. The film was extremely successful, and she won a children's Oscar for her performance. Metro Goldwyn Mayer terminated her contract in 1950 because of her problems with alcohol and drugs. However, she continued to perform, and in 1964 she did a series of concerts at the London Palladium. In fact, it was in London where Judy Garland was found dead after she took a drug overdose in 1969. Judy got married five times and had three children. One of these children was Liza Minnelli who was 23 when her mother died.

Liza was born in Hollywood, California, on March 12th, 1946. She grew up in film studios, and, like her mother, made her first stage appearance at the age of two. She was only five when her parents got divorced. After performing successfully with her mother at the London Palladium in 1964, Liza became a professional nightclub singer. She made several albums, and later starred as a singer in the 1972 film, *Cabaret*, a role for which she won an Oscar. Despite her successful singing and acting career, Liza has had similar problems to her mother. She has been to rehab clinics several times because of her addiction to drugs and alcohol. She has also been married four times, but, unlike her mother, she never had children. Today, Liza Minnelli is in her sixties, but she still makes occasional television appearances.

10 A

Presenter Hello, and welcome to the programme. Today we have scientist, Doug McLeod, in the studio with us. He's going to tell us about some of the everyday things we know and love that were invented by accident. Doug?

Doug Hello, Janet. Well, I'm going to start with the microwave oven. In 1945, an engineer called Percy Spencer was testing some new radar equipment. He had a chocolate bar in his pocket, and while he was standing in front of the machine, it melted. After that, he also tried using the microwaves from the radar equipment to cook popcorn. Percy realized that microwaves could heat and cook food, and so the microwave oven was born.

Presenter How interesting! What else have you got for us, Doug?

Doug Next is something that is found in hospitals all over the world: the X-ray machine. In 1895, a German physicist called Wilhelm Roentgen was experimenting with electrical rays in a dark room. He was directing them through a glass tube covered with black paper. Suddenly, he saw a light on a screen on the wall and he realized that the rays could pass through the glass and the paper. After that, he experimented with his own hand, and found that he could see the bones. The first X-ray ever made was an image of Roentgen's wife's hand – you can even see her wedding ring!

Presenter That's fascinating, Doug. We've got time for one more.

Doug Many different kinds of food were discovered by accident, Janet, and I've chosen something that we call 'crisps', but Americans call 'potato chips'. These were invented by a chef called George Crum, who was working in a restaurant near Saratoga Springs, New York. A customer complained that the chips he was served were too thick. The chef was angry about this, so he fried some very thin potatoes and covered them with salt. The customer loved them, and after that 'Saratoga chips' became popular all over the USA. Eventually, they were produced for people to eat at home.

Presenter Thanks for joining us.

10 B

Tony Amy, did you study foreign languages at secondary school?

Amy Yes, I did. Actually, I used to be quite good at languages.

Tony Which ones did you study?

Amy Well, I did French for five years, then I did German for six years, and I studied Spanish for a year in my lunch break.

Tony And how much French can you remember?

Amy Not much! But I can remember my German, because I did it for my degree at Cambridge. Why all the questions, Tony?

Tony Well, I've just read this article about the state of language learning in schools in the UK, and it isn't looking good. It says that adults only remember about seven words from the languages they studied at school.

Amy Only seven words? That isn't very good, is it? What sort of words do they remember?

Tony Common words, like *Hello*, *Goodbye*, *Please*, *Thank you*, *beer*, *one*, *two*, and *three*, and the question *Do you speak English?*

Amy So, what happens when people are abroad? Do they practise the language?

Tony Not at all. In fact, the article suggests that people often choose not to go on holiday to countries where they have to worry about language problems.

Amy That's probably because they're too lazy to learn a language.

Tony No, it isn't that. The article says it's because they're too embarrassed to try and speak it.

Amy OK. So which languages do pupils study at school today?

Tony Hang on a minute, there's a list here somewhere… Here it is. It says 65% of pupils study French, 25% study German, 22 % Spanish, and 2% Italian. Polish is becoming more popular, too.

Amy And what are schools going to do about the problem?

Tony Well, first of all, they're going to introduce language classes for children in primary schools. And then they're going to start offering languages from outside Europe, for example Mandarin Chinese and Urdu.

Amy That sounds quite difficult. Anyway, Tony, which languages did you use to study at school?

Tony Only French. And I was terrible at it!

10 C

Speaker 1 I made a bad decision once when I was travelling home to Plymouth from university in Manchester, a journey of nearly 450 km. The choice was going by train or by bus, and I opted for the train as it was quicker. Unfortunately, the train broke down on the way, so in the end I took two hours longer than I expected.

Speaker 2 The worst decision I ever made was giving my son a skateboard for his tenth birthday. On the morning of his birthday, we went down to the park to try it out. Sadly, he fell off the board as soon as he got on it, and broke his arm. We had to cancel his birthday party, and we spent the whole day in hospital instead.

Speaker 3 I had two job interviews and both companies offered me a job. In the first job, they offered me more money, but it was a long way from where I live – an hour travelling every day. The second job was less money, but it was very near my house. In the end, I chose the second job instead, and I'm very happy I did, because last month the first company closed down.

Speaker 4 On one occasion, I had to decide between a good friend of mine and a boy I really liked. I was going to a concert with my friend, and then this boy asked me to go to the cinema with him on the same night. In the end, I said no to the boy, and went to the concert with my friend. I found out later that the boy already had a girlfriend, so I think I made the right decision.

Speaker 5 You won't believe what happened to me! I used to play the lottery with some colleagues at work. One day, I decided that I was fed up with never winning, so I stopped playing. My colleagues carried on without me, and just one week later, they had the winning numbers! They won a lot of money, and I didn't get any of it!

11 A)))

Speaker 1 The worst loser I know is my mum. We often used to play cards together when I was little, and if my mum was losing, it was safer to stop playing. She was always happy when she was winning, but when she was losing, you could see her getting angrier and angrier until she exploded. Sometimes, she used to go out of the room, because she was so upset!

Speaker 2 I once had a friend who was a bad loser at tennis. In fact, we stopped talking to each other because of a tennis match. We were about twenty at the time, and on this occasion we were arguing over a point. I said the ball was out and she said it was in. In the end, she just threw her racket into the net and left. We've never spoken since.

Speaker 3 I have to be very careful at work when we're talking about football. I have a colleague who gets really upset when his team loses, and he hates it if you make a joke about it. I tried it once, and he just stood up, walked out, and closed the door with a bang. He didn't speak to me for days after that, so I don't think I'll try it again.

Speaker 4 My son is a very bad loser, in fact he always has been. He's 12 now, but he still hates losing. We used to play board games together when he was little, but he always used to cry if he didn't win. I had to choose between letting him win all the time, or making him upset if I won. In the end, I stopped playing that kind of game with him.

Speaker 5 One of the guys who plays basketball with me gets incredibly upset during games, and he spends most of the time shouting at the other players. He's a really nervous person at the best of times, but when we're losing, it really is too much. The referee throws him off the court at least twice a month, and once our coach told him to go home.

11 B)))

Interviewer Can I ask you about your job, Graham?

Graham Yes, of course. Go ahead.

Interviewer What time do you go to bed?

Graham Well, I don't often get home before six o'clock in the morning, and it usually takes me a little while to relax. It's probably about seven by the time I go to sleep.

Interviewer And what time do you have to get up again?

Graham I usually get up at one o'clock, to have lunch with my family. After that, I go back to bed again for an hour or so, until about three o'clock.

Interviewer Do you need an alarm clock to wake up?

Graham No, I never use one. I wake up the first time when my children come home from school for lunch. The second time, my wife wakes me up. That's when I get up properly.

Interviewer How do you feel when you wake up?

Graham It depends on the day, really. If I've only worked for a day or two, I'm full of energy, but if it's after the fifth or sixth night in a row, I'm absolutely exhausted. That's when I find it really hard to get out of bed.

Interviewer What do you do about meals, Graham?

Graham Well, like I said, my first meal of the day is what you would call lunch. Then, I have dinner at about midnight with some other drivers in a café. When I get home in the morning, I have something light, like a ham sandwich or some toast before I go to bed.

Interviewer Would you like to change your working hours, Graham?

Graham If I changed my working hours, I wouldn't earn as much money! There's a lot more work at night, because people go out for dinner and to the theatre or clubs, and then it's late and they need to get home, and they don't want to drive because they've usually had a drink or two. I quite enjoy my job, really, because I meet lots of interesting people.

11 C)))

Presenter And to finish off today's programme, we're going to take a look at some famous twins. Let's start with probably the earliest set of twins in history:

Romulus and Remus. Now, the legend says that they were abandoned by their parents, because twins were thought to bring bad luck. Fortunately, they were found by a female wolf, who looked after them when they were babies. According to legend, the boys grew up, and later founded the city of Rome. After some time, they began to argue, and eventually Romulus killed Remus. As Romulus was the only brother alive, the city was called Rome after him.

Let's move on in history to the 1950s, when a set of twins called the Kray Brothers caused a lot of trouble in London's East End. Ronnie and Reggie Kray were both nightclub owners. They had expensive lifestyles, and through their nightclubs they met several American stars like Frank Sinatra and Judy Garland. However, they were also incredibly violent gangsters, and they became the leaders of organized crime in the city. They were involved in many robberies and murders, until they were eventually arrested in 1969. They were both sent to prison for life, and they both died when they were in their sixties.

On a happier note, the youngest twins ever to become famous are the Olsen twins. Mary Kate and Ashley Olsen were given the same role on the American TV series *Full House* when they were only six months old. They played the part of a little girl, and they played the same part for eight years. The producers used both sisters to play the same part, so that they didn't break the law on the number of hours a child could work. The show was very popular with American audiences. Today, the twins have grown up, and they have a fashion business.

And I'm afraid that's all we have time for. Join me, Roy Thompson, at 4 o'clock tomorrow afternoon for another two hours of *Thompson's Choice*. Bye for now.

12 A)))

Newsreader And now it's time for the news.

Police have found the 82-year-old man who went missing last Monday evening. Dennis Leighton was found in his car on the M25 motorway. He had left home on Monday morning to drive to his daughter's house, a distance of about 90 kilometres. However, Mr Leighton had got lost, and he had spent 30 hours driving round in circles trying to find the right exit. Mr Leighton had stopped at several service stations to sleep, but he then carried on driving. After being treated in hospital for hypothermia, he has finally been reunited with his family.

A tourist had a lucky escape yesterday while she was doing a bungee jump off the Victoria Falls in Zambia. Twenty-two-year-old Erin Langworthy fell into the river because her bungee rope had broken when she jumped. She landed in the water with her feet still tied to the broken rope, and then she swam to safety. Ms Langworthy was taken straight to hospital after the accident, but had no serious injuries.

A Swedish woman has found the white gold wedding ring that she lost over 16 years ago. Lena Paahlsson had taken off the ring while she was cooking with her daughters. When she went to put it back on again, it had disappeared. That is, until yesterday, when she was picking vegetables in her garden, and she found the ring around a carrot. The ring doesn't fit Mrs Paahlsson any more, but she is going to have it made bigger.

An Australian woman had a frightening experience last night, when she discovered an adult crocodile in her living room. Forty-two-year-old Jo Dodd got out of bed when she heard her dog barking. She opened the bedroom door, she saw a crocodile in the middle of the room. Mrs Dodd woke her husband, who called the local Crocodile Management Centre, and a crocodile catcher came to take the animal away. The crocodile had escaped from a nearby crocodile farm earlier in the week.

And that's all for now. I'll be back again at 9 o'clock for the next news bulletin.

12 B)))

Alan Who do you think gossips more, Jess? Men or women?

Jess Well, I gossip quite a lot with my female colleagues at work, so I suppose that women are the biggest gossips. What do you think?

Alan Yes, that's what I thought too, but it says here that it's actually men who are the biggest gossips. That's what the results of this survey say, anyway.

Jess What survey?

Alan This one here in the newspaper. It says the survey was carried out by a telecommunications company. They wanted to do research into gossiping for a new service they're offering. The aim of the survey was to find out what sort of people enjoy gossiping, and how much time they spend doing it.

Jess So what did they find out?

Alan Well, they had quite a big surprise. The study showed that a fifth of the men they interviewed said they spent at least three hours a day gossiping.

Jess Wow! That's a lot! And where do they usually gossip?

Alan Most of them said they usually gossiped at work. Hang on…I can give you the exact figures. Yes, here we go, …55 per cent of the men said they gossiped at work compared to 46 per cent of the women.

Jess Goodness! I didn't realize men had so much to say! Did they tell the researchers what they usually talked about?

Alan Yes. They said that their main topics of conversation were their women colleagues, and who in the company would get the next promotion.

Jess The bit about women colleagues doesn't surprise me in the least. So, what about the women in the survey? Did they say what they talked about?

Alan Yes, they did. They told the researchers that they talked about the problems they were having in their families. They also chatted about what was happening in their favourite TV series.

Jess OK. So what about you, Alan? Do you ever gossip at work?

Alan What? Me? No, never! I wouldn't dream of it!

12 C)))

Speaker 1 I used to watch a quiz show called *Mastermind*. It was a very serious show, and the quizmaster was Magnus Magnusson. Each of the four contestants had to answer two rounds of questions: firstly, on their specialist subject, for example, Dickens, or the Second World War, and then on general knowledge. The thing I remember most is the quizmaster's catch phrase, 'I've started, so I'll finish.'

Speaker 2 My favourite quiz show is *A Question of Sport*. It's been on TV for years – since 1968, in fact, and, although I don't watch it any more, it's still very popular. There are two teams with the same captain each time, and all of the guests are sportsmen and women. The teams have to answer questions about sport, and the show is quite amusing, actually.

Speaker 3 I used to watch *Call my Bluff*, a quiz show about words. There were always two teams made up of a captain and two celebrities. Each team was given a word, a very unusual word, and the three team members had to give a different definition – one was true and the other two were false. The other team had to guess the correct definition. It used to be quite funny.

Speaker 4 I've always enjoyed the quiz show, *Who wants to be a Millionaire?* It started in the UK in 1998, and it's still on TV today. In each show, one contestant is asked a series of questions, and they have to choose the right answer out of four possible options. It's quite exciting, really, as the contestant can win up to a million pounds if they're good.

Speaker 5 My favourite quiz show when I was a teenager was *Pop Quiz*. It wasn't on for long – only a couple of years – but I used to love it. There were two teams made up of a captain, who was the same person each time, and some guests, who were all pop stars. The teams had to answer different questions about pop music and musicians, and I used to watch it every week.

Answer key

7A

1 GRAMMAR

a 2 to see 3 not to finish 4 to find
   5 not to tell 6 not to do 7 to rent

b 2 difficult to talk 3 easy to buy
   4 important not to say 5 great to hear
   6 fun to be 7 kind to invite

c 2 to study / learn 3 to book 4 to make
   5 to get 6 to take

d 2 when to call 3 how many to buy
   4 where to go 5 what to study
   6 how much to make

2 VOCABULARY

2 offered 3 didn't want 4 pretended
5 needed 6 promised 7 planned
8 forgot / didn't remember 9 forgot /
didn't remember 10 tried 11 learned

4 READING

a The writer is generally positive about
  mothers-in-law.

b 2 b 3 a 4 c

5 LISTENING

a no

b 2 J 3 D 4 D 5 J 6 D 7 D 8 J

7B

1 GRAMMAR

a 2 playing 3 studying 4 writing
   5 snowing 6 going 7 swimming
   8 getting 9 listening 10 using, not driving

b 2 a 3 e 4 f 5 d 6 b

c 3 imagining 4 driving 5 listening
   6 Staying 7 reading 8 getting up
   9 taking 10 going 11 exercising
   12 having 13 Turning 14 leaving

d 2 to use 3 buying 4 to carry 5 travelling
   6 to read 7 to look for 8 to show
   9 reading 10 looking 11 not to lose
   12 to borrow 13 to lend 14 reading
   15 to take 16 to charge

2 VOCABULARY

2 e 3 b 4 a 5 d 6 f

3 PRONUNCIATION

a 2 promise 3 surprise 4 engine

4 LISTENING

a one

b Speaker 2 D Speaker 3 A Speaker 4 E
  Speaker 5 B

7C

1 GRAMMAR

a 1 don't have to, have to
   2 Do … have to, have to, don't have to
   3 Do … have to, don't have to, have to
   4 Does … have to, doesn't have to, has to

b 2 You must 3 You mustn't 4 You mustn't
   5 You must 6 You mustn't

c 2 mustn't 3 mustn't 4 don't have to
   5 mustn't 6 don't have to

2 VOCABULARY

2 quite difficult to understand
  American films
3 new teacher speaks very fast
4 of those students are a bit unfriendly
5 English books is a really good idea
6 incredibly hard to learn Chinese

4 READING

a Students' own answers.

b 2 Luis 3 Kiko 4 Josef 5 Gloria 6 Paolo

5 LISTENING

a On all Mac computers, iPhones, the iPod
  touch and the iPad.

b 2 around 3,000 3 8,000 4 290,000
   5 2006

1 VOCABULARY

2 cold 3 bad stomach 4 temperature
5 headache 6 cough

2 GOING TO A PHARMACY

2 well 3 symptoms 4 have 5 allergic
6 better 7 take 8 every 9 often 10 much

3 SOCIAL ENGLISH

1 lovely, glad 2 Can, for 3 should, sure

4 READING

2 C 3 A 4 I 5 H 6 G 7 F 8 B 9 D

8A

1 GRAMMAR

a 2 should, F 3 shouldn't, E 4 shouldn't, A
   5 should, C 6 shouldn't, D

b 2 shouldn't drink 3 should go
   4 should see 5 should tell
   6 shouldn't give 7 should call

c B 4 C 1 D 7 E 6 F 2 G 5

2 VOCABULARY

2 gets home 3 got lost 4 get fit
5 getting worse 6 got tickets 7 get on
8 got, text message 9 getting up
10 get, school

3 PRONUNCIATION

a 2 could 3 soup 4 book

4 LISTENING

a two

b Speaker 2 B Speaker 3 D Speaker 4 E
  Speaker 5 A

8B

1 GRAMMAR

a 2 e 3 a 4 f 5 b 6 d

b 2 see 3 use 4 won't get 5 don't take
   6 doesn't work 7 will be 8 isn't

c 2 hang, 'll bring, C
   3 walk, 'll have, F
   4 throw, make, will come, A
   5 's, catch, won't be, G
   6 break, 'll have, B
   7 see, runs, 'll go, E

2 VOCABULARY

a 2 lost, missed 3 tell, says
   4 waiting, hope 5 watching, look at
   6 known, met 7 borrow, lend
   8 looking for, found 9 wearing, carrying
   10 take, bring

4 LISTENING

a five

b 2 In May and June.
   3 Extra nights in a hotel if you can't fly home.
   4 Things will only get worse.
   5 Your family and friends at home.
   6 What they will do if there is a natural
     disaster.

8C

1 GRAMMAR
a 2 yours
  3 Whose laptop is that, his
  4 Whose keys are those, hers
  5 Whose car is that, ours
  6 Whose coats are those, yours
  7 Whose house is that, theirs

b 2 yours, ours 3 his, His 4 ours, theirs
  5 Your, Mine, hers

2 VOCABULARY
2 quietly 3 seriously 4 lazily
5 dreamily 6 calmly

3 PRONUNCIATION
a 2 distance 3 dollar 4 advantage
  5 enjoy 6 completely 7 remember
  8 promise 9 suspicious

4 READING
a Students' own answers.

b 2 G 3 D 4 H 5 J

5 LISTENING
a The experiment hoped to found out
  if men and women cook differently.
  It wasn't successful.

b 2 F 3 T 4 F 5 F 6 T

9A

1 GRAMMAR
a 2 e 3 a 4 c 5 b 6 d

b 2 would you do if you found a million euros
  3 a phone if he could afford one
  4 gave me caviar I wouldn't eat it
  5 would you say if you could talk to the
    president
  6 look for a new job if I were you

c 2 saw, would scream
  3 wouldn't have, didn't have
  4 wasn't, would get
  5 lived, would learn
  6 would … do, attacked

2 VOCABULARY
a Across: 2 cow 6 jellyfish 7 whale
  9 bear 10 snake
  Down: 3 spider 4 bee 5 sheep 8 horse

3 PRONUNCIATION
a 2 camel 3 chicken 4 crocodile 5 dolphin
  6 elephant 7 giraffe 8 jellyfish 9 lion
  10 monkey 11 mosquito 12 rabbit
  13 spider 14 tiger

4 READING
a Students' own answers.

b 2

5 LISTENING
a By pressing his fingers into the shark's eye.

b 1 Australia
  2 Fishing
  3 His head, shoulders, and one of his arms.
  4 Metal
  5 His son
  6 By helicopter
  7 He had deep cuts all over his body and a
    broken nose.
  8 Over three metres long

9B

1 VOCABULARY
a 2 claustrophobia d 3 arachnophobia a
  4 glossophobia e 5 acrophobia c

b 2 scared 3 fear 4 terrified 5 afraid
  6 phobia

2 GRAMMAR
a 2 since 3 since 4 for 5 for
  6 since 7 for 8 since

b 2 since 3 since 4 for 5 since 6 Since
  7 for 8 since 9 since

c 2 How long has … played
  3 How long has … lived
  4 How long has … had
  5 When did … hear

d 2 ✗ How long
  3 ✓
  4 ✗ since February
  5 ✗ have you had
  6 ✗ for eight years
  7 ✓
  8 ✓

4 LISTENING
a a fear of dogs

b 2 c 3 a 4 c

9C

1 VOCABULARY
2 d 3 b 4 f 5 e 6 h 7 g 8 a

2 GRAMMAR
a 2 sent 3 she met 4 They fell 5 they got
  6 They had 7 They moved 8 they've lived
  9 has just put 10 he's been 11 have made

b 2 did … get, 've been
  3 has … worked, finished
  4 have … had, bought
  5 did … meet, 's known
  6 have … lived, arrived

3 PRONUNCIATION
a 1 married, primary, secondary, separate
  2 divorced, musician, retire, successful

4 READING
a A 7 B 2 C 6 D 3 E 5 G 4

b 2 did his mother buy
  3 were
  4 did John Lennon die
  5 has Julian Lennon made
  6 has Sean Lennon played

5 LISTENING
a They were both two years old.

b 2 F 3 T 4 T 5 T 6 T 7 T 8 F

Practical English Getting around

1 VOCABULARY
2 straight 3 round 4 exit 5 lights
6 take 7 left 8 right

2 ASKING HOW TO GET THERE
2 Could you say that again?
3 How many stops is that?
4 OK. And then?
5 Where is it?
6 OK. Thanks. See you later.

3 SOCIAL ENGLISH
2 said 3 don't 4 stay 5 feel 6 long
7 think

4 READING
a 2 30–40 minutes 3 $14 4 $45
  5 nothing 6 6.30 a.m. 7 $13

10A

1 VOCABULARY
a 2 given 3 discovered 4 used 5 played
  6 shown 7 called 8 invented 9 opened
  10 based

2 GRAMMAR
a 2 The film *The Iron Lady* is based on the
    life of Margaret Thatcher
  3 Mobile phones weren't invented by Apple
  4 Lead isn't used in petrol nowadays
  5 Low-cost flights are sold online

6 The Petronus Towers were designed by an Argentinian architect
7 *Avatar* wasn't directed by Steven Spielberg
8 Minis aren't made by a British company any more

b 2 Contact lenses were invented by a Czech chemist
3 Where are olives grown
4 The VW Beetle was designed in the 1930s
5 Diamonds are found in many different colours
6 When were vitamins discovered
7 Spanish is spoken in Spain and many parts of South America
8 Where were the *Lord of the Rings* films made

c 2 are worn by people of all ages
3 weren't invented by Microsoft
4 the heating controlled by a computer
5 was written by Stieg Larsson
6 aren't used by people very much today
7 wasn't painted by Picasso
8 the Harry Potter films directed by the same person

3 PRONUNCIATION

a 2 checked   3 wanted   4 rained   5 decided

4 LISTENING

a 2 c   3 a

b 2 in Percy Spencer's pocket, not on the table.
3 German, not American
4 glass and paper, not water and air.
5 the man's wife's hand, not his hand
6 potato chips, not crisps
7 a chef, not a waiter
8 'Saratoga chips', not 'Saratoga potatoes'

1 VOCABULARY

a 2 h   3 e   4 b   5 a   6 f   7 i   8 d   9 g
b 2 g   3 c   4 a   5 b   6 i   7 f   8 d   9 e

2 GRAMMAR

a 2 didn't use to behave
3 used to wear
4 Did Alex use to have
5 didn't use to study
6 used to be
7 didn't use to play
8 Did your teachers use to give

b 2 He used to go
3 We didn't use to understand
4 Did you use to
5 School used to
6 Did your friends use to help

4 READING

a 2 What's the most important lesson you learned at school?
3 Did you ever behave badly?
4 What subjects were you good at?

---

5 What did you want to do when you left school?
6 Did you have a favourite teacher?

b 2 T   3 F   4 F   5 T   6 T   7 T   8 F

5 LISTENING

a Amy was good at languages at school, but Tony wasn't.

b 2 studied it at university
3 some numbers
4 too uncomfortable
5 German
6 make younger pupils learn languages

1 GRAMMAR

a 2 might go   3 might have   4 might take
5 might rain   6 might invite   7 might make
8 might eat

b 2 might not get   3 might have
4 might not come   5 might not be
6 might miss   7 might go   8 might fail

2 VOCABULARY

a 3 decision   4 die   5 education   6 elect
7 imagination   8 inform   9 invitation
10 live   11 option   12 organize   13 succeed

b 2 decision   3 invite   4 Success   5 inform
6 decided   7 imagine   8 life

3 PRONUNCIATION

a 2 ✓   3 ✗   4 ✗   5 ✗   6 ✓   7 ✗   8 ✓

4 READING

a To discover if a good night's sleep helps when you have to make an important decision.

b 2 at different times   3 some time later
4 Some   5 four   6 different   7 lost
8 REM sleep

5 LISTENING

a two

b Speaker 2 D   Speaker 3 A   Speaker 4 E
Speaker 5 B

1 VOCABULARY

a 2 track   3 match point, serve   4 bunker
5 lap   6 penalty   7 corner

b 1 into   2 round   3 into   4 out of
5 towards   6 past   7 to, into

c Across: 4 down   5 up   7 towards   8 across
Down: 1 out of   2 round   3 into   6 past
7 through   8 along

---

2 GRAMMAR

a 2 kicked, under   3 went through
4 threw, into   5 ran across   6 hit, over

b 2 out of   3 to   4 into   5 along   6 under
7 past   8 through   9 along   10 towards
11 across

3 PRONUNCIATION

a 2 volleyball   3 motor racing   4 skiing
5 windsurfing   6 cycling   7 basketball
8 rugby   9 athletics

4 LISTENING

a cards, tennis, football, board games, basketball

b 2 Speaker 5   3 Speaker 1   4 Speaker 4
5 Speaker 3

1 VOCABULARY

a 2 over   3 after   4 off   5 in   6 on

b 2 throw away   3 turn up   4 look up
5 look forward to   6 get on with   7 go out
8 try on   9 take back   10 give up

2 GRAMMAR

a 2 pay it back   3 look for them   4 ✓
5 looks after my kids   6 ✓

b 2 She'll give them back on Friday
3 Are you looking forward to it
4 I called her back when I got home
5 We don't get on with them
6 Shall we turn it on

4 READING

a 2 get up   3 go out   4 take off   5 put on
6 give up   7 turn on   8 write down

b 1 ✓   2 ✗   3 ✗   4 ✗   5 ✗   6 ✗   7 ✓   8 ✗
9 ✓   10 ✓

5 LISTENING

a positive

b 2 T   3 F   4 F   5 T   6 T

1 GRAMMAR

a 2 Neither was I   3 So do I   4 So would I
5 So am I   6 Neither have I

b 2 So did I   3 Neither have I   4 So was I
5 Neither am I   6 Neither can I
7 So would I   8 Neither do I

2 VOCABULARY

2 as   3 like   4 both   5 so   6 neither
7 identical

3 PRONUNCIATION

c 2 s<u>i</u>milar 3 co<u>i</u>ncidence 4 <u>a</u>mazing
5 disc<u>o</u>ver 6 <u>e</u>verywhere 7 person<u>a</u>lity
8 d<u>e</u>finitely

4 READING

a 1

b 2F 3F 4T 5T 6F

5 LISTENING

a 2a 3b

b 2KB 3OT 4KB 5RR 6OT

Practical English Time to go home

1 ON THE PHONE

a 2 sorry, wrong
  3 line, busy, leave, message, call, back
  4 put

2 SOCIAL ENGLISH

a 2 great news 3 go first 4 later
  5 Never better

3 READING

a 2

b 2f 3i 4e 5d 6b 7m 8g 9j
  10k 11a 12l 13h

12A

1 GRAMMAR

a 2 hadn't closed 3 had started
  4 hadn't flown 5 had read 6 hadn't heard

b 2 Had they eaten sushi before
  3 Had he won a medal before
  4 Had they made a cake before
  5 Had she run a marathon before
  6 Had you been there before

c 2 had done the ironing, he put the
     clothes away
  3 they had watched the news, they turned
     off the TV
  4 I had read the book, I gave it back
  5 had tried on the top, she went to the
     checkout
  6 we had had dinner, we did the washing up

d 2 opened 3 had broken 4 had already left
  5 hadn't stolen 6 hadn't lost 7 had seen
  8 had left 9 had put

2 PRONUNCIATION

a 2 We'd lost it. 3 You'd seen her.
  4 It'd been a terrible day. 5 I hadn't sent it.
  6 She hadn't done it. 7 They hadn't told me.

3 VOCABULARY

2 put 3 belonged 4 left 5 gone on
6 got out of 7 had 8 realized 9 was
10 got on

4 LISTENING

a A2 C4 D3

b 2 30 hours (not 13)
  3 Zambia (not Kenya)
  4 swum to safety (not walked)
  5 cooking (not washing up)
  6 too small (not big)
  7 living room (not kitchen).
  8 Mrs Dodd's husband (not Mrs Dodd)

12B

1 GRAMMAR

a 2 didn't like her parents
  3 was getting divorced
  4 'd been to the police station
  5 hadn't met his girlfriend
  6 'd seen James with another woman
  7 couldn't cook
  8 wouldn't tell anyone
  9 'd speak to her tomorrow / the next day
  10 'd got a lot of work to do

b 2 I want a cup of coffee
  3 We haven't seen the new neighbours yet
  4 I don't want to go to the cinema
  5 We'll go to the party
  6 My computer has just broken
  7 The city is very old
  8 We'll visit you

2 VOCABULARY

a 2 told 3 told 4 said 5 told 6 said 7 told
  8 told 9 said 10 said

b 2 told 3 told 4 said 5 told 6 said
  7 said 8 said 9 told 10 told

3 PRONUNCIATION

a 2 married 3 letter 4 middle 5 hurry
  6 different 7 sorry 8 summer
  9 message 10 happy

4 LISTENING

a Jess gossips, but Alan doesn't.

b 2F 3F 4F 5T 6T 7T 8F

12C

1 GRAMMAR

a 2a 3a 4b 5b 6a 7a 8b

b b4 c5 d1 e6 f8 g2 h7

c 2 did Spain win
  3 did REM stay
  4 plays
  5 did Amy Winehouse die
  6 do polar bears live
  7 roads join
  8 produces the most bananas

2 VOCABULARY

a 2 overweight – It isn't used to describe
     personality.
  3 tracksuit – It isn't an item of jewellery.
  4 a phone call – It doesn't use the verb 'do'.
  5 exciting – It isn't a negative word.
  6 town hall – It isn't somewhere you can
     do shopping.
  7 finish – It isn't a verb that can be followed
     by 'to'.
  8 get up – It isn't a use of 'get' which means
     'become'.
  9 bat – It isn't an insect.

b 2 on 3 back 4 out / away 5 to
  6 forward 7 into / across 8 in
  9 on 10 up

c 2 stay 3 fall 4 make 5 do 6 lend
  7 spend 8 get 9 earn 10 find

3 PRONUNCIATION

a 2 school 3 hope 4 turn 5 bald
  6 towel 7 thin 8 horse 9 word 10 wear
  11 fear 12 city 13 chemist's 14 forget

4 READING

a 2G 3J 4C 5H 6D 7F 8A
  9I 10B

5 LISTENING

a 1 mind 2 Sport 3 Call 4 Millionaire
  5 Pop

b Speaker 2 C Speaker 3 D Speaker 4 B
  Speaker 5 A

This page was intentionally left blank.

This page was intentionally left blank.

This page was intentionally left blank.

OXFORD
UNIVERSITY PRESS

Great Clarendon Street, Oxford, OX2 6DP, United Kingdom

Oxford University Press is a department of the University of Oxford.
It furthers the University's objective of excellence in research, scholarship,
and education by publishing worldwide. Oxford is a registered trade
mark of Oxford University Press in the UK and in certain other countries

© Oxford University Press 2013

The moral rights of the author have been asserted

First published in 2013

2017 2016 2015 2014

10 9 8 7 6 5 4 3 2

No unauthorized photocopying

ISBN: 978 0 19451798 0   MultiPack B
ISBN: 978 0 19451799 7   Student's Book / Workbook B
ISBN: 978 0 19459797 5   iTutor
ISBN: 978 0 19459812 5   iChecker
ISBN: 978 0 19477277 8   Access Code Card
ISBN: 978 0 19472039 7   Online Practice

Printed in China

This book is printed on paper from certified and well-managed sources

ACKNOWLEDGEMENTS

STUDENT'S BOOK ACKNOWLEDGEMENTS

*The authors would like to thank all the teachers and students round the world whose
feedback has helped us to shape* English File.

The authors would also like to thank: all those at Oxford University Press (both
in Oxford and around the world) and the design team who have contributed
their skills and ideas to producing this course.

*Finally very special thanks from Clive to Maria Angeles, Lucia, and Eric, and from
Christina to Cristina, for all their support and encouragement. Christina would also like
to thank her children Joaquin, Marco, and Krysia for their constant inspiration.*

*The publisher and authors would also like to thank the following for their invaluable
feedback on the materials*: Beatriz Martín, Brian Brennan, Elif Barbaros,
Gill Hamilton, Jane Hudson, Joanna Sosnowska, Wayne Rimmer, Urbán
Ágnes, Anne Parry, Belén Sáez Hernáez, Edelweis Fernández Elorz, Emilie
Řezníčková, Erika Feszl, Imogen Clare Dickens, Jonathan Clarke, Kieran
Donaghy, Kinga Belley, Laura Villiger Potts, Manuela Gazzola, Mariusz
Mirecki, Paolo Jacomelli, Pavlina Zoss, Rebecca Lennox, Robert Anderson,
Sandy Millin, Sophie Rogers, Washington Jorge Mukarzel Filho.

*The Publisher and Authors are very grateful to the following who have provided
information, personal stories, and/or photographs*: Sara Mohr-Pietsch,
p.86 (interview)

*The authors and publisher are grateful to those who have given permission to reproduce
the following extracts and adaptations of copyright material*: p.78 Extract from
Could Do Better, edited by Catherine Hurley © 1997 Simon & Schuster Inc.
Reproduced by permission; p.83 Extract from 'Dolphins save swimmers from
shark attack', *The Guardian*, 23 November 2004 © Copyright Guardian News &
Media Ltd 2004. Reproduced by permission; p.99 Extract from "Astonishing
coincidence: Couple meet 20 years after both having same heart operations…
in SAME hospital, on SAME day, by SAME surgeon', *Daily Mail*, 29 July 2010.
Reproduced by permission.

*The publishers would like to thank the following for their kind permission to reproduce
photographs*: Alamy pp.52–53 (Universal/Dreamworks/Phillip Caruso),
68 (Photoshot Holdings Ltd/jellyfish, Arco Images GmbH/bee), 73 (Pictorial
Press/Julio Iglesias), 76 (mediablitzimages (uk) Limited/hair dryer), 76 (Joe
Fox/policeman), 77 (Feng Yu/tin opener), 83 (Martin Strmiska), 86 (Realimage/
radio), 115 (Donald Nausbaum/painting), 158 (Eye Ubiquitous/Eiffel tower),
160 (PCN Photography/win medal, Commercial Megapress Collection/
woman in striped t-shirt); Catherine Blackie pp.160 (photo on phone, men
friends, woman with umbrella); Sarah Cardenas p.89; Caters News Agency
p.99 (family); Corbis Images pp.54 (Joseph Lindau/girl with fringe), 60 (Hans
Neleman), 69 (G.Baden/mouse), 161 (DPA/Wolfgang Kumm/bee); Thomas
S England pp.88, 89 (twins); FLPA Images p.69 (Imagebroker/dog); Getty
Images pp.54 (Brit Erlanson/woman wavy hair), 54 (Dimitri Veryitsiotis/man
in blue t-shirt, man in black t-shirt), 61 (B Blue), 68 (Frank Krahmer/bull,
Paul Sutherland/shark), 72 Redferns/Bob Marley), 73 (Fabrice Coffrini/Ziggy
Marley, Redferns/Enrique Iglesias), 76 (ML Harris/dishwasher, Davies and Starr/
zip, Grant Faint/windscreen wiper, Katherine Fawssett/washing machine),
77 (Arsenal/football), 78 (Tim Graham/Princess Diana, Winston Churchill,
79 (Redferns/John Lennon, AFP/Helen Fielding), 84 (tennis, high jump, Peter
Cade/ski, Ports Illustrated/basketball, cycling, AFP/handball/rugby), 85 (John
McEnroe), 94 (Getty Images/Rob Lang/men gossiping), 115 (Donald Nausbaum/
painting, Jetta Productions/golf), 116 (Jamie McCarthy), 158 (Victoria Blackie/
Man with L plate), 160 (Nicki Pardo/girl red hair, Stephen Lovekin/bracelets),
161 (Picavet/bull, Frank Kindersley/bat, WIN-Initiative/giraffe, Paul Souders/
whale, Ben Hall/rabbit, Danita Delimont/sheep, Stefan Sollfors/mosquito,
John Giustina/lion, Kieran Scott/goat, Mark Horn/camel, Jim Brandenburg/
crocodile, Mike Hill/dolphin, Peter Cade/cow, Visuals Unlimited,Inc, John
Abbott/snake, Suchitra prints/monkey, Paul Oomen/bear, Paul Souders/
jellyfish, Kelly Funk/horse, Tim Flach/mouse, Joel Sartore/pig, Jeff Hunter/
shark, James Cotier/fly, Tier Und Naturfotografie J&C Sohns/kangaroo);
Robert Harding Picture Library p.69 (Age footstock/snake); I&A Photolibrary
p.86 (BBC/Adrian Weinbrecht/Sara Mohr-Pietsh); Oxford University Press
Capture Web pp.54 (Getty Images/Hybrid Images/girl blonde hair, Corbis/
man with moustache), 55 (Alamy/Russell Underwood Images/man shower,
Andres Rodriguez/girl with microphone), 55 (Getty Images/David de Lossy/
girls singing in car), 71, 76 (Getty Images/Comstock/babies), 78 (Alamy/
Stephen Mulcahey/Head boy/Head girl, Bele Olmez/pencil), 85 (ball), 86 (Getty
Images/Creative Crop/cereal), 94 (Corbis Images/Image Source/three women,
Alamy/Johner Images/girls gossiping), 117 (Getty Images/Lazi& Mellenthin),
158 (Image Source/man reading), 160 (Getty Images/Digital Vision/man at bus
stop, Image Source/Cultura/watch TV, running for bus, Image Source/John
Rowley/shaking hands, Getty Images/Barbara Penoyar/man with flowers, Getty
Images/Image source/tell joke, Image Source/Fancy/mother and daughter),
161 (elephant, tiger, butterfly, chicken, spider); Photolibrary p.161 (bird); Press
Association pp.56–57, 85 (John Howard); Rex Features pp.77 (Bournemouth
News/monopoly board), 77 (Action Press/Ken Follet), 160 (Startracks Photo/
handbag, Sipa Press/football match); Stefan Svanström p.63.

Pronunciation chart artwork: by Ellis Nadler

Illustrations by: Peter Bull Studios pp.63, 74; Adria Fruitos/Good Illustration
pp.78, 79; Atsushi Hara/dutchuncle pp.58, 84, 87, 92, 93, 140, 141, 144, 145,
146, 149, 159, 163; Satoshi Hashimoto/dutchuncle agency p.162; Ob!/Private
View Agency p.62; Tim Marrs pp.54, 70, 74, 96; Jonathan Krause pp.64, 65

Commissioned photography by: Gareth Boden pp.56 (at bar), 76 (Tippex), 80, 81.
MMStudios pp.56 (signs), 77 (book), 160 (salary/bring your dictionary, look for/
find your glasses, lend/borrow money)

Practical English stills photography by: Rob Judges, Jacob Hutchings, and Richard
Hutchings pp.58, 59, 74, 75, 90, 91

WORKBOOK ACKNOWLEDGEMENTS

The authors would like to thank all the teachers and students round the world whose feedback has helped us shape English File.

The authors would also like to thank: all those at Oxford University Press (both in Oxford and around the world) and the design team who have contributed their skills and ideas to producing this course.

Finally very special thanks from Clive to Maria Angeles, Lucia, and Eric, and from Christina to Cristina, for all their support and encouragement. Christina would also like to thank her children Joaquin, Marco, and Krysia for their constant inspiration.

The authors and publishers are grateful to the following who have given permission to reproduce the following extracts and adaptations of copyright material: p.44 Extract from 'Mothers-in-law are lovely in their place. Their own place, that is' by Luisa Dillner, *The Independent*, 28 February 2010. Reproduced by permission; p.46 Extract from 'Apple Teams Up To Use iPhone To Save Cherokee Language' by Murray Evans. Reproduced by permission of Associated Press; p.66 Extract from 'David Suchet remembers his school sporting achievements and the teacher who inspired him to pursue acting' by Tim Oglethorpe, *The Daily Mail Weekend Magazine*, 24 October 2009. Reproduced by permission of Solo Syndication; p.66 Extract from 'Bonjour is about all we learn from 5 years of French' by Laura Clark, *The Daily Mail*, 02 August 2007. Reproduced by permission of Solo Syndication; p.68 Extract from 'No need to sleep on this one: A good night's rest really does help you make important decisions', *The Daily Mail*, 20 June 2011. Reproduced by permission of Solo Syndication.

Although every effort has been made to trace and contact copyright holders before publication, this has not been possible in some cases. We apologize for any apparent infringement of copyright and if notified, the publisher will be pleased to rectify any errors or omissions at the earliest opportunity.

The publishers would like to thank the following for their kind permission to reproduce photographs: Alamy Images p.48 (Scott Hortop/laptop); Barcroft Media p.74 (Niklas Hallen/India twins); Corbis pp.48 (Dirk Lindner/i-pod), 55 (TW Photo/Gordon Ramsay), 56 (Wolfgang Kumm/dpa/bee), 61 (Kevin Knight/Julian Lennon), 63 (Andy Rain/EPA/aeroplanes, Martyn Goddard/mini), 64 (Scott camazine/x-ray); Getty Images pp.53 (AFP/earthquake/fire/hurricane, Esch Collection/blizzard), 55 (Wireimage/Heston Blumenthal, Delia Smith, Nigella Lawson), 56 (Peter Cade/cow, Paul Souders/jellyfish/whale, Paul Oomen/bear, Visuals Unlimited, Inc, John Abbott/snake, Suchitra prints/monkey, Danita Delimont/sheep, Kelly Funk/horse), 58 (TBR), 59 (Nick Ridley), 60 (Andrew Bret Wallis), 61 (John Lennon, Sean Lennon, Judy Garland, Liza Minnelli), 62 (Walter Bibikow), 63 (ULTRA.F/Petronus Towers), 64 (Brian Hagiwara/crisps), 74 (LatitudeStock/Justin Williams/Romulus and Remus, Kray Brothers), 78 (Ulrik Tofte/girls whispering, Yellow Dog Productions/men chatting); The Kobal Collection p.63 (Film 4/*The Iron Lady*, Twentieth Century Fox/*Avatar*); Oxford University Press pp.44 (Alamy/MBI), 48 (Corbis/Ken Seet/class), 51 (Tom Grill/Tetra Images), 56 (spider), 63 (Saturn, phone, petrol pump), 64 (microwave), 68, 72 (Getty Images/Diane Diederich), 73 (Getty Images/Scott Markewitz), 75 (Union Jack flag, US flag), 78 (Corbis Premium/backview of women); Rex Features pp.46 (Geoff Moore), 48 (Alex Segre/kindle), 55 (Erik Pendzich/Jamie Oliver), 66 (ITV/David Suchet), 74 (Billy Farrell Agency/Olsen twins).

Illustrations by: Peter Bull pp.47, bottom 49; Atsushi Hara/Dutch Uncle Agency pp.50, 54; Satoshi Hashimoto/Dutch Uncle Agency p.69; Tim Marrs p.42; Jérôme Mireault/Colagene Illustrations p.70; Ellis Nadler pp.51, 81; Roger Penwill p.47 top; Kath Walker Illustration pp.45, 52, 69 top, 76, 77

Picture research and illustrations commissioned by: Catherine Blackie

Design by: Stephen Strong